Reminiscences

of

Vice Admiral Robert Burns Pirie

U. S. Navy (Ret.)

U. S. Naval Institute
Annapolis, Maryland
December, 1974

Preface

This volume incorporates the transcript of eight taped interviews with Vice Admiral Robert Burns Pirie, USN (Ret.). They were conducted by John T. Mason, Jr. for the Oral History program of the U. S. Naval Institute over a period dating from May, 1972 to May, 1974.

Admiral Pirie's naval career spans a period of great moment in the development of naval aviation. He has dealt with the subject with admirable perspective. Consequently the memoir should prove of much use to researchers in the field. A detailed index has been added as a useful tool.

The Admiral has read the transcript and has made some minor corrections. These corrections have been incorporated in a re-typed copy, but essentially the transcript is verbatim from the tapes.

VICE ADMIRAL ROBERT BURNS PIRIE, U. S. NAVY, RETIRED

Vice Admiral Pirie was graduated from the Naval Academy on June 3, 1926, Color Company Commander for the Class of 1926. He was designated Naval Aviator in June 1929, and subsequently served at sea in the carriers LEXINGTON and LANGLEY, as Aide and Flag Lieutenant to Rear Admiral Alfred W. Johnson, USN, Commander Aircraft, Scouting Fleet, and as Senior Aviator on board the cruiser RALEIGH; as a flight test officer at the Naval Air Station, Anacostia, D. C., and as an instructor in the aviation training squadron at the Naval Academy.

In June 1938 he assumed command of the seaplane tender TEAL, operating in Alaskan and Aleutian waters and in October 1939 became Executive Officer of Scouting Squadron 5-B, based on the carrier YORKTOWN. From late 1940 until the outbreak of World War II he was Superintendent of Training at the Naval Air Station, Miami, and when detached in September 1942 reported to the Staff of Vice Admiral Towers, USN, Commander Air Force, Pacific Fleet. He was awarded the Legion of Merit for outstanding service as Assistant Air Operations Officer on the Staff from October 1942 until March 1943.

He next served as Executive Officer in the carrier MISSION BAY from her commissioning in September 1943 until May 1944, in Hunter-Killer operations in Atlantic waters, and returned to the Pacific for duty from July 1944 until March 1945 as Chief of Staff and Aide to Rear Admiral G. F. Bogan, USN, Commander Carrier Division 25 and later Commander Carrier Division 4 in Admiral Mitcher's Task Force FIFTY-EIGHT. During this period he participated in the assault and capture of the Marianas (Saipan, Tinian, and Guam); the assault and capture of Palau; the initial raid on the Philippine Islands; Okinawa, and Formosa; the Battle of Leyte Gulf; and the South China Sea Raid, Jauary 1945. For services during this period he was awarded the Silver Star Medal; a second Legion of Merit and the Bronze Star Medal, both with Combat "V." He also is entitled to the Presidential Unit Citation, with stars for service in the carrier flagships FANSHAW BAY, LEXINGTON, ESSEX, and BUNKER HILL.

During the final months of the war he served as Air Operations on the Staff of Fleet Admiral E. J. King, USN, Commander in Chief, U. S. Fleet, Washington, D. C., and in January 1946 returned to the Naval Academy as first head of the Department of Aviation. From March 1948 until July 1949 he commanded he carrier SICILY, after which he again returned to the Naval Academy, where he served this time as Commandant of Midshipmen. On February 12, 1952 he assumed command of the attack carrier CORAL SEA, operating in European waters, and from December of that year until June 1954 served as Chief of Staff to Admiral Jerauld Wright, USN, Commander in Chief, U. S. Naval Forces, Eastern Atlantic and Mediterranean, and later as Deputy Commander in Chief.

V. Adm. R. B. Pirie, USN, Ret.

In August 1954 he was assigned as Deputy Chief of Staff and Deputy Chief of Staff (Plans and Operations), and later served as Chief of Staff and Aide to the Commander in Chief, U. S. Atlantic Fleet. In March 1956 he assumed command of Carrier Division 6, which was deployed with the SIXTH Fleet in the Mediterranean from June to October 1956. He was Commander of the United States SECOND Fleet, and Commander Striking Fleet in the Allied Command, Atlantic, from July 3, 1957 until May 1958, when he became Deputy Chief of Naval Operations (Air), Navy Department.

"For exceptionally meritorious service...as Deputy Chief of Naval Operations (Air) from May 1958 to November 1962..." he was awarded the Distinguished Service Medal. He was serving in that capacity when relieved of all active duty pending his retirement, effective November 1, 1962.

26 November 1962

VICE ADMIRAL ROBERT B. PIRIE, U. S. NAVY, RETIRED

PERSONAL DATA

Born: Wymore, Nebraska, 4/18/05
Parents: Charles Bruce and Thelma Harms Pirie
Wife: Gertrude May Freeman of New York City
Children: Lieutenant (jg) Robert B. Pirie, Jr., USN (Class of 1955, USNA) and Sandra Pirie
Official Address: Wymore, Nebraska
Education: Wymore High School (1922); USNA (BS, 1926); Flight Training, Naval Air Station, Pensacola, Flordia; Torpedo Instruction, NTS, Newport, R. I.; completed Naval War College Correspondence Course in Strategy and Tactics

PROMOTIONS

Commissioned Ensign, 6/3/26; Lieutenant (jg) 6/3/29; Lieutenant, 6/30/36; Lt. Commander, 7/1/40; Commander, 9/17/42; Captain, 4/27/44; Rear Admiral, 7/1/53; and Vice Admiral, 7/3/57. Transferred to the Retired List, 11/1/62.

DECORATIONS AND MEDALS:

Distinguished Service Medal
Silver Star Medal
Legion of Merit, Combat "V"
Gold Star in lieu of Second Legion of Merit
Bronze Star Medal, Combat "V"
Presidential Unit Citation awarded USS FANSHAW BAY (Ribbon)
Presidential Unit Citation awarded USS LEXINGTON (Star)
Presidential Unit Citation awarded USS ESSEX (Star)
Presidential Unit Citation awarded USS BUNKER HILL (Star)
American Defense Service Medal, Fleet Clasp
American Campaign Medal
Asiatic-Pacific Campaign Medal, with silver star (5 operations)
World War II Victory Medal
Navy Occupation Service Medal, Europe Clasp
National Defense Service Medal
Philippine Liberation with two Stars

CITATIONS:

Silver Star Medal: "For conspicuous gallantry and intrepidity as Chief of Staff of Commander Task Group THIRTY EIGHT POINT TWO during the occupation of Palau and air attacks on the Philippine Islands, September 6 to 24; air attacks on Okinawa Jima, Formosa and Luzon, October 6 to 20; during the Battle for Leyte Gulf, October 24 to 26; and air attacks on Luzon on October 29 and November 5 and 6, 1944.

V. Adm. R. B. Pirie, USN, Ret.

(His) Task Group was under substained enemy air attack on four occasions, but by expert maneuvering of the formation and superior performance of our planes in intercepting and fighting off attacking aircraft, no major damage to any ship was sustained..."

Distinguished Service Medal: "For exceptionally meritorious service...as Deputy Chief of Naval Operations (Air) from May 1958 to November 1962. A dynamic leader and skilled technician in the field of aviation, Vice Admiral Pirie has been responsible for advances which contributed significantly to the effectiveness of the naval air arm as an element of sea power and which raised the level of Fleet readiness to unprecedented heights. In strengthening the Navy's weapons arsenal and improving fleet tactical doctrine, he vigorously sought better weapons and equipment based upon sound research and accurate evaluation of operational experience. Under his direction, significant improvements were achieved in aviation safety, a more efficient and economical program for aviation maintenance was instituted, and training and operating procedures were standardized. Exercising initiative and foresight, Vice Admiral Pirie established the first normal Navy organization for astronautics and led the Navy in the exploitation of space as essential to the perpetuation of sea power supremacy. Through his knowledge and understanding of aviation in general, and of the unique problems of naval aviation in particular, he made important contributions to aviation development as a respresentative of the Navy and the nation on policy-making boards and committees at interservice, national and international levels..."

Legion of Merit: "For...outstanding services to the Government of the United States...during operations against enemy Japanese forces off the coast of Luzon, Formosa and China, from November 7, 1944 through January 25, 1945. Assisting in planning operations against the enemy, Captain Pirie insured the effective employment of the full strength of the Task Group. As coordinator of operations he supervised the execution of missions by units of the Task Group, and contributed materially to their successful accomplishment. His courage under fire, leadership and devotion to duty were in keeping with the highest traditions of the U. S. Naval Service."

Gold Star in lieu of the Second Legion of Merit: "For...outstanding services as Assistant Air Operations Officer on the Staff of Commander Air Force, Pacific Fleet, from October 1942 to March 1943. Directly responsible for discharging all functions of Fleet Air Wing multi-engined aircraft squadrons (he) capably supervised the preparation of these units for combat, skillfully controlled their movements until reported for operational control by the fleet air wing commanders, and worked out the multitude of complex details involved in planning the rotation of personnel and aircraft..."

Bronze Star Medal: "For meritorious achievement...during the assault and capture of the enemy Japanese-held Southern Marianas Islands,

V. Adm. R. B. Pirie, USN, Ret.

from June 14 to August 1, 1944. Exercising strong initiative and decisive judgment in the planning of aggressive support missions throughout the amphibious operations against these heavily fortified islands, (he) rendered invaluable assistance to his Commanding Officers...to provide effective aerial cover for our surface units during critical stages of the campaign..."

CHRONOLOGICAL TRANSCRIPT OF SERVICE:

Jun 1926 - Aug 1926	U. S. Naval Academy (Instruction in Aviation)
Aug 1926 - Jun 1927	USS DOBBIN
Jun 1927 - Dec 1927	Naval Torpedo Station (Instruction)
Dec 1927 - Jul 1928	USS BARRY
Jul 1928 - Aug 1929	Naval Air Station, Pensacola, Fla. (Flight Training) (Designated Naval Aviation, 6/25/29)
Aug 1929 - May 1931	Fighting Squadron 3B (USS LEXINGTON & USS LANGLEY)
May 1931 - May 1933	Naval Air Station, Anacostia, D. C.
May 1933 - Jun 1935	Aide and Flag Lieutenant, Staff, Commander Aircraft, Base Force
Jun 1935 - Jun 1936	USS RALEIGH (Senior Aviator)
Jun 1936 - May 1938	Naval Academy (VN8D-5 Squadron)
May 1938 - Nov 1939	USS TEAL (Commanding Officer)
Nov 1939 - Jan 1940	Bombing Squadron 5 (USS YORKTOWN)
Jan 1940 - Aug 1940	Scouting Squadron 5 (USS YORKTOWN) (Executive Officer)
Aug 1940 - Sep 1942	Naval Air Station, Miami, Florida (Superintendent of Training)
Sep 1942 - Mar 1943	Staff, Commander Air Force, Pacific Fleet
Mar 1943 - Sep 1943	Pre-commissioning duty in the USS BAFFINS at Tacoma, Wash.
Sep 1943 - May 1944	USS MISSION BAY (Executive Officer)
May 1944 - Jul 1944	Staff, Commander Carrier Division 25 (Chief of Staff & Aide)
Jul 1944 - Mar 1945	Staff, Commander Carrier Division 4 (Chief of Staff & Aide)
Mar 1945 - Aug 1945	Staff, Commander in Chief, United States Fleet (Air Operations Officer)
Aug 1945 - Jan 1946	Office of the Chief of Naval Operations, Navy Dept. (OP-33)
Jan 1946 - Mar 1948	Naval Academy (Head Aviation Dept.)
Mar 1948 - Jul 1949	USS SICILY (Commanding Officer)
Jul 1949 - Jan 1952	Naval Academy (Commandant of Midshipmen)
Feb 1952 - Dec 1952	USS CORAL SEA (Commanding Officer)
Jan 1953 - Jul 1954	Deputy Commander in Chief Naval Forces, Eastern Atlantic & Mediterranean and Chief of Staff and Aide to the Commander in Chief Naval Forces, Eastern Atlantic & Mediterranean
Aug 1954 - Sep 1955	Deputy Chief of Staff and Deputy Chief of Staff (Plans & Operations) to the Commander in Chief, Atlantic
Sep 1955 - Feb 1956	Chief of Staff an Aide to the Commander in Chief, Atlantic

V. Adm. R. B. Pirie, USN, Ret.

Mar 1956 - Jul 1957   Commander Carrier Division 6
Jul 1957 - May 1958   Commander SECOND Fleet; Commander Striking Fleet,
                          Allied Command, Atlantic
May 1958 - Nov 1962   Deputy Chief of Naval Operations (Air), Navy Dept.
1 Nov 1962   Transferred to the Retired List

Navy Office of Information
Internal Relations Division (OI-430)
26 November 1962

Authorization

The U. S. Naval Institute is hereby authorized to make available to individuals, libraries, and other repositories of its choosing the transcripts of eight oral history interviews concerning the life and career of Vice Admiral Robert B. Pirie. The interviews were recorded on 19 May and 7 August 1972, 11 May, 15 October, 17 October, and 18 October 1973, and on 12 March and 3 May 1974 in collaboration with John T. Mason, Jr., for the U.S. Naval Institute.

The undersigned does hereby release and assign to the U.S. Naval Institute all right, title, restrictions, and interest in the interviews. The copyright in both the oral and transcribed versions shall be the sole property of the U.S. Naval Institute. The tape recordings of the interviews are and will remain the property of the U.S. Naval Institute.

Signed and sealed this 21st day of July 1990.

Robert B. Pirie, Jr., for Vice Admiral
Robert B. Pirie, deceased

DECLARATION OF TRUST

The undersigned does hereby appoint and designate as his (her) Trustee herein, the Secretary-Treasurer and Publisher of the United States Naval Institute to perform and discharge the following duties, powers, and privileges in connection with the possession and use of a certain taped interview between the undersigned and the Oral History Department of the United States Naval Institute.

1. Classification of Transcript.

   ( )a. If classified OPEN, the transcript(s) may be read or the recording(s) audited by the qualified personnel upon presentation of proper credentials, as determined by the Secretary-Treasurer of the U. S. Naval Institute.

   ( )b. If classified PERMISSION REQUIRED TO CITE OR QUOTE, the user will be required to obtain permission in writing from the interviewee prior to quoting or citing from either the transcript(s) or the recording(s).

   (✓)c. If classified PERMISSION REQUIRED, permission must be obtained in writing from the interviewee before the transcribed interview(s) can be examined or the tape recording(s) audited.

   ( )d. If classified CLOSED, the transcribed interview(s) and the tape recording(s) will be sealed until a time specified by the interviewee. This may be until the death of the interviewee or for any specified number of years.

2. It is expressly understood that in giving this authorization, I am in no way precluded from placing such restrictions as I may desire upon use of the interview at any time during my lifetime, nor does this authorization in any way affect my rights to the copyright of my literary expressions that may be contained in the interview.

Witness my hand and seal this _____ day of _____ 19__

Robert B. Pirie

I hereby accept and consent to the foregoing Declaration of Trust and the powers therein conferred upon me as Trustee.

Interview No. 1 with Vice Admiral Robert Burns Pirie, U.S. Navy (Retired)

Place: The Naval Institute, Annapolis, Maryland

Date: Friday morning, 19 May 1972

Subject: Biography

By: John T. Mason, Jr.

Q: Admiral, I've been looking forward to this series, you know, for about two years and I'm glad it's finally beginning because you have a terrific story to tell and I'm glad it's under way.

You were born where?

Adm. P.: Wymore, Nebraska.

Q: And what was the date?

Adm. P.: April 18, 1905, and I went to school in Nebraska. I graduated from the Wymore High School in 1922 and was given a principal appointment to the Naval Academy by Representative McLaughlin and by some quirk of fate passed the entrance examination. I think probably the academic board at that time gave me a little on one or two marks, and I entered on the 22nd of June 1922.

Q: How did you happen to turn to the Navy? I mean, coming from the middle of the country?

Pirie #1 - 2

Adm. P.: My father was a Scot —

Q: That's obvious, with Robert Burns!

Adm. P.: born in Scotland, and he came to this country with his parents in 1892. He was eight years old and when I was a small boy he used to delight in telling stories about his experiences as a small boy in Scotland. He was born in a small town, Banff, on the north coast, north of Aberdeen, on the seashore. And that was the beginning of my interest in the sea. He talked so much about it and was so wrapped up in that part of the world and the sea that it just got into my blood.

Q: It was a romantic thing for you!

Adm. P.: Yes. As a matter of fact, when I told him when I was a junior in high school, that I wanted to go to the Naval Academy he looked at me and he said, "Where did you ever get that in your head?" I'd never seen the Naval Academy. I had not been to either coast. I'd been to Chicago, on Lake Michigan, but that's about all. So I told him that I was really interested, but he didn't pay much attention to me until the beginning of my senior year when I said that "I want to tell you again that I want to go to the Naval Academy." And he said, "All right, if you insist on it, we'd better get to work and do some studying so that you can pass, but I'll get you an appointment."

Q: Did he have any political influence?

Adm. P.: He had a great friend Adam McMullin, who later was governor of the state of Nebraska, and my father, later actually worked for him as the purchaser for the state and as the Secretary of Labor of the state. Adam McMullin went to Representative McLaughlin and got this principal appointment.

I didn't have great difficulty after I once got in because I'd had a fairly good background. My mother and father both liked to teach us and take part - he, for example, was very good at geometry and my mother was very good at algebra, so they sort of prepped me.

Q: How many were there in the family?

Adm. P.: My brother John, who is two and a half years younger and who just retired as the general counsel for Pan American. He went to the Naval Academy the year I graduated in 1926 and he stayed two years and stood One in his class both years, and resigned. When asked by the officials why he resigned, he said, "because he wasn't learning anything!" He got a Rhodes scholarship right after that and went to Oxford and got a "first" at Oxford and came back to work in New York in a law firm, and he was doing nothing but Pan American's work so Trippe got him into Pan American, and he's just retired.

One of the interesting things about our childhood is the way my mother and father taught us painlessly a lot of the incidental facts that you get to store away in your brain. They played a game called "geography cards," and "history cards," and "literature cards," so that all of this basic knowledge of geography, history, and literature, and some mathematics thrown into it, we knew before we ever went to school and we didn't have to work. We would fight to get this game started in the evening and it was all a lot of fun, but meantime we were storing up a lot of facts that we put away in our brains, so we didn't have to study to get them.

Q: You said your father was director of labor for the state. Was he interested in labor relations?

Adm. P.: He was a machinist. His father had been an ironmonger in Scotland, came over, and was the master mechanic in the Burlington Railroad division, and my father and his two brothers went to work as apprentices and they put two sisters through school. But they went to work and never did finish high school. My father studied in a law office on his own time with a friend of his and took the bar exams in 1921 just before I went in the Naval Academy and passed and became an attorney.

Q: He certainly was an enterprising man, wasn't he?

Adm. P.: He had to work hard. As hard as he had to work on the railroad, you know, and then to pick this up. But they all worked in the Burlington Railroad. The other two brothers got to be heads of divisions.

Q: This really was a land of opportunity, wasn't it?

Adm. P.: Yes, it was great for the whole family. Well, I didn't have too much trouble with study. I was in the hospital about a month in my plebe year with pneumonia and laryngitis and one thing and

Pirie #1 - 5

another, which set me back a little. I stood about 150, I guess, that year in my class, but I didn't have any difficulty after that. I think I stood 42 of 465 when I graduated.

I had just turned seventeen when I came in, so I was one of the younger ones in the class. I wasn't very mature physically. I didn't weigh enough to make the varsity football. I played scrub football all four years and I tried to row on the crew but I got sinus trouble in the second year and had a sinus operation that sort of knocked the pins out from under me in the crew. But I was basically too light to row on the crew. They wanted somebody who weighed over 200 pounds, you know, so you could lose a little, and I never could get above about 175 while I was a midshipman.

Q: You had to be pretty beefy!

Adm. P.: Yes. My first class year I was company commander - well, let me go to the midshipmen cruises.

We made three cruises in the old battleships. I was in the Florida for my first cruise, and we went to northern Europe, Copenhagen Greenock, Scotland, and then down to Lisbon. Admiral McCulley was squadron commander. On the second cruise we went to northern Europe again. I was in the Wyoming, and we went to Rotterdam and Torquay, England, and back down to Lisbon, I guess. My first class cruise we went to the West Coast and we went to San Diego, San Francisco, Seattle through the Canal, not to Hawaii. I was in the Utah at that period — during that cruise. Yen Coney was the officer in charge of the midshipmen

men on the Utah on that cruise and by some chance he picked me to be his assistant. I got along well with him and I think he was responsible probably for my getting quite a high "grease" mark. What we called a "grease mark" is aptitude for the service - during that cruise and I was made a company commander. We had our stripes all year. We had eight companies in those days. I was with the Sixth Company and was company commander the whole year and we won the colors and my wife was the color girl.

Q: Oh, she was?

Adm. P.: Yes, and we're still married, which is unusual in this day and age!

Q: Was she an Annapolis girl?

Adm. P.: No, she was from New York City. I met her through my mother's sister who was living in New York at the time.

Q: Tell me, did these cruises confirm your ambition to be a sailor?

Adm. P.: I wasn't too crazy about the battleship life. It was pretty rough work. These were all coal-burning ships, and I spent half the time down in that damned fireroom because I was big and there weren't but about 30 or 40 percent of those people who could take this punishment down there, with the heat and the dirt, and mess. It was bloody. But I spent half of every cruise down there and I didn't care much about that. They were hard working cruises. There was not much goofing off during that period because they put you to work.

Q: They were all three coal-burning?

Adm. P.: Yes. We fired battle practice and learned what the guns were all about. We did it ourselves, you know, and that was interesting. But I was real gung-ho for the Navy. I liked the Navy and nobody could ever get that out of me. I never thought about resigning or getting away from the Navy. It never occurred to me in my life. I didn't have much trouble with sickness. I got a little puny when we first got to sea. We had a very rough crossing the first year, and I never will forget we had a great big basketball fellow, who was a grown man - I was a little kid compared to him - and he was a great basketball player who made the team his plebe year, and he got so seasick he was paralyzed, and I spent most of that cruise taking care of that bugger and he resigned the moment he got back.

Q: The Navy was not for him!

Adm. P.: Not for him, at all. He was a burley great big fellow, but he just was paralyzed by mal de mer.

Q: Did you develop an interest in aviation while you were at the Academy?

Adm. P.: Well, we had what they called "aviation summer." Half of my class stayed back from first class cruise and took an aviation training. It was the first group that they gave any kind of aviation

Pirie #1 - 8

training and they did it in an F5L. Then the other half of us stayed after we graduated for three months and took this training, and this was in F5Ls again. We did a lot of ground school work but we had about maybe ten flights during the summer.

Q: Just flights as observers?

Adm. P.: No. We did navigation. We went all the way down the Bay and back and that sort of thing, fired guns, and did everything that the crew was supposed to do. We took the part of crewmen. That interested me quite a bit, but I went to the Dobbin in September.

Q: Tell me how you went to the Dobbin.

Adm. P.: My class voted to assign ships at graduation by drawing lots vis-a-vis doing it by class standing, so I drew No. 463 out of 465 and there were only three ships left when they got to me and the Dobbin was the most desirable as far as I was concerned, and that's the reason I went to the Dobbin.

Q: What was your class standing, by the way?

Adm. P.: 42. Anyway, when I got to the Dobbin I was assigned as assistant gunnery officer. There were four classmates - four of us went - and I was assigned assistant gunnery officer, and the gunnery officer was Forrest B. Royal of the class of 1915, who was a very fine naval officer. He came from a naval family and he took me in tow and I really had a very instructive and hard-working year.

The minute I got on board we went to Guantanamo and G

We were down there two and a half months in the fall and got back about the middle of November and by that time I'd convinced my fiancee that we ought to get married and we were married at the Little Church Around the Corner in New York on th 25th of November 1926 and went out to Chicago to see the Army and Navy game where we cleared a 21-to-21 tie with Army at Soldiers Field. Our team that year was national champions.

Well, we got back to New York for the December and Christmas period and then we went south and stayed four months in the spring at Guantanamo and Gonaive, so the first year I was in the fleet I spent six and a half months in Guantanamo and Gonaive.

Q: That must have been hard on your bride?

Adm. P.: Oh! Well, I got back in May and I got orders to preliminary flight training at Norfolk.

Q: You had put in an application?

Adm. P.: No, I just got orders. Everyone in the class had to go and take so many hours of instruction, or whatever was required for your solo, and then let you solo, and that's when I really got the bug. I got an instructor at Norfolk called Mike La Porte, a chief petty officer who later was one of the best pilots in early Pan American days and finally retired as a chief pilot with Pan American and was quite a character. Mike was a good instructor and I got very much interested. Then I had orders to torpedo school and I went to Newport, and, of course, my whole thought once I got through with that early flight training was to get to Pensacola, but they didn't take anyone in less than two years in those day. You had to spend two years in the fleet.

So when I left the torpedo school I got orders to the USS Barry and I was assigned as torpedo officer -

Q: She was a destroyer?

Adm. P.: A destroyer in the Atlantic, and we again spent four months in the Guantanamo-Gonaive area and fired all the practices. We had such a transition in officers and shuffling around that I had practically every job on the ship before I got through, including navigator and gunnery officer. I had every job except chief engineer.

Q: That's certainly one of the advantages of being in a destroyer!

Adm. P.: I learned a lot. My skipper was "Plug" Holt of the class of 1910, and the division commander was John Barleon. We were the division flagship. I learned a lot and that time that I spent in the destroyer before I went to Pensacola really got me hep with everything connected with the sea and I never had to worry again about any phase of seamanship or navigation because I had plenty of it.

So I got orders to Pensacola and got there in August. I had a little difficulty right in the beginning. My instructor was Bob Hickey and I was his first student in primary seaplanes and I think we were fighting each other a little bit for about seven or eight hours, but I eventually -

Q: You mean there was a personality clash?

Pirie #1 - 11

Adm. P.: No, not personality, but just he didn't know much about instructing and I was, you know, gung-ho and tightened up and didn't get relaxed, so we struggled for a little while, but I never had any difficulty after I passed that solo test. I went breezing through without any trouble.

Q: Tell me about Pensacola.

Adm. P.: Pensacola at that time -- a great many of the people, of course, were out of my class because this was two years after graduating, and I had about eight classmates including myself in my particular group. We had a lot of quite senior officers in our class. We had a good many that were lieutenants and lieutenant commanders, then we had some commanders, and some captains going through at that time because they were short of rank in the aviation organization. One of the ones that I remember most vividly in my class was John Hoover, who was out of the class of 1907, and he was then a commander and John really did the course. Many of these senior officers sort of halfway did it. They did the flying -

Q: This was after King had been there?

Adm. P.: King had been there the year before. We had Zaugbaum. As a matter of fact, I flew Zaugbaum on his last flight. He had to drop a bomb and hit the Massachusetts from a big boat and he hadn't done it so they told me I could do the flying for him and I flew Zaugbaum on his last flight before they gave him his wings. We had a great many of those senior fellows, but in my group we had Admiral Jim Russell and Ford Taylor. The rest of the people – I don't think many of them are living. In the class right after us was Fitzhugh Lee and P. D. Stroop, who are very close friends. We had quite a congenial group.

Q: I imagine these older fellows added something to it?

Adm. P.: Oh, yes, very interesting. They had a struggle. Most of them had a harder time getting through the flying than we did. It was a little tougher for them to pick up after ten years. The older you get the more difficult it is, because you tense and tighten up.

They had primary seaplanes for about 45 or 50 hours and then we went to primary land planes, and my primary land plane instructor was D. S. Cornwell. He retired as a rear admiral. He's a fine man and he taught me a lot about planes. He was a real good flier himself. Then we went from there to observation planes Vought, land planes. They had UOs and the first O-2Us at that time, and we did navigation and radio and maybe a little gunnery, and then from there to "big boats," so-called. These were – some were boats, but most of them were twin-float big ten-ton seaplanes, torpedo planes, which was a course that lasted about 30 hours, and from there to fighters. Most of the people who were not going to get into the carriers were going to battleships or going to big-boat squadrons left at that time. They got their wings and went to sea. And those of us who went into fighter planes – well, they gave them a little, say, ten hours in fighters, but they then picked the guys who were going to be fighter pilots –

Pirie #1 - 13

Q: A matter of selection?

Adm. P.: Yes. They selected them out and they went to sea, and we stayed and took another 40 hours or so of flying and then left.

Q: Did you have gliders anywhere along the line?

Adm. P.: No. No gliders. It was all powered airplanes. We got the first NYs. They'd had Jennies. The NY was a Navy type that was both land plane and sea plane for primary training, and we had in fighters Curtiss Hawks for the most part. The head of the fighter squadron was Dave Rittenhouse, who was quite a character in those days, and the instructors that I remember the best were Eddie Ewen, which was quite a famous name in later years, and Cornwell.

It was very interesting and I fortunately stood One in my class so I got my choice and I picked VF-3 in the Lexington.

Q: Is there anything interesting to say about the facilities at Pensacola?

Adm. P.: It's hard to realize but in those days there was no such thing as a runway. There were no brakes on these airplanes. You steered with a tail skag. You came to rest and it was a steerable tail skag, but there were no brakes on the airplanes and there was no voice communication. The instructor used a gosport, you know. There was no electrical –

Q: It was a pretty uncertain way of communicating, wasn't it?

Adm. P.: Oh, no. They were pretty good. They could shout pretty well over those gosports, you know. You could hear everything they said. To get into the business of when I first saw brakes on an airplane and two-way voice radio - that came later.

Q: Did you have parachutes in those days?

Adm. P.: Yes, we all wore parachutes on every flight. We had enough fixed gunnery to, you know, just have a smattering of it and know what it was all about, not time to really have any proficiency.

Q: Were there many casualties in the class during the period of training?

Adm. P.: You mean attrition?

Q: Yes.

Adm. P.: I think we only got 30 percent through in those days - only 30 percent of those who went to Pensacola got through. There was terrific attrition in the early stages.

Q: Was it due to the rigorous course or was it that the aptitude hadn't been selected or hadn't been determined?

Adm. P.: There wasn't enough thinking in the young minds about flying. They didn't have the same sort of instinctive feeling that the young fellows do nowadays, and it was difficult for them to pick it out. I'd say the instruction was pretty tough and they didn't take any nonsense, and you had to perform emergencies and that sort of thing to the instructor's satisfaction. I don't think the instructors were as good. They didn't have instructor schools. The instructors were amateurs in addition to the student being an amateur, so putting the two together I think made it poor caliber. I think if you took those same people and put instructors who had been to instructor school and knew what they were doing, you'd get a lot more through, and I think that the kids today, or in the last twenty years, grew up with airplanes around them and knowing a lot about everything. A great many of them had had flights before they got there. That all contributed.

Q: Back in 1928 it was kind of an exotic thing, wasn't it?

Adm. P.: Right, flashy. Everybody thought you were a fool to go into aviation in those days. I never will forget both the skipper and the division commander of the destroyer when I left said, you're making a great mistake.

Q: This was a dead end, was it?

Adm. P.: A dead end, you're not going to amount to anything, and this type of thing.

Admiral Halsey was there at the time I was there. We had old Cory Field and it was all sand, of course, and weeds - I suppose somebody might call it grass, but it wasn't much grass. And then they had Station Field, which was a very small field right by the balloon hangar. All of the fields that are used today were built in World War II and subsequently.

Ground school at Pensacola in those days didn't amount to very much. We just learned a few things about engines and a little bit about the airplane. They had a building that we went to the first two months where we overhauled and rebuilt an airplane and put it together completely, so we'd learn what the rudiments of the thing were about. We got a chance to overhaul both an airplane and an engine and learn that way, by doing it ourselves.

Q: And I guess that stood you in good stead on many occasions?

Adm. P.: Right. We knew quite a bit about it. We flew half a day and went to ground school the other half day, and we always had some kind of an inspection or something we had to go to on Saturday mornings. We had Saturday afternoon and Sunday off.

Q: Did you play hard in that off time?

Adm. P.: Yes, we did. We had a lot of athletic facilities. I was very much interested in golf and I played quite a bit of golf in those days.

Q: That's second nature to a Scotsman, anyway, isn't it?

Adm. P.: There was the Pensacola Country Club and another one out west of town. The station had no golf course at that time.

The admiral in command at Pensacola was Admiral Raby and the commanding officer was Warren G. Childs.

We traveled across country after and drove up through Nebraska. That was the first time my wife and I had driven across country, and in a new De Soto. It was the first year that the De Soto automobile was built. These roads were not all paved in those days, a lot of them were gravel and rock, and they wore a set of tires out and I ran out of money out in the middle of New Mexico or somewhere and had to wire my old man for money to buy new tires. We arrived in San Diego about the 1st of October 1929 and I immediately got into the process of carrier qualifying and I qualified on the Langley, which was our first carrier. We had flying F-3Bs, Boeing fighters, biplanes. My first squadron commander was Samuel P. Ginder, and I was assigned Number 3, which was flying wing on him, and my administrative job was office manager.

Q: Office manager?

Adm. P.: Yes. That year we won the Shiff Trophy, which was the safety record. We went to Panama and had some kind of an exercise down there and then back again.

Q: Was Admiral Reeves there?

Adm. P.: Admiral Reeves was the commander of the battle force, aircraft battle force, they called it, and he was later relieved by H. V. Butler. They were the two admirals in command of the carrier wings at that time.

Q: He was a great exponent of aviation.

Pirie #1 - 18

Adm. P.: Both of them were. Reeves was a great advocate of aviation and was one of the early time airmen. We, of course, had regular gunnery and bombing competition exercises during that time. It was during that period that I learned to do fixed gunnery and bombing.

Q: How many hours a week were you required to fly?

Adm. P.: I would guess that we flew on the order of 35 or 40 hours a month in those days. The flights weren't too long and we didn't have too much endurance in those airplanes, you know. We would just go out and see where we could get away and do our bombing on targets on the land.

We went around in that cruise to Panama and ended up on the East Coast with a huge exercise and we flew the aircraft from the Saratoga and Lexington around all the large cities on the East Coast. At the end of that period, the Lexington went into overhaul at Norfolk and all the aircraft and pilots from the Saratoga and Lexington went back on the Saratoga. We were sort of blocked in. We couldn't do any flying because there were too many aircraft on board.

We got back, I'd say, in early July, about the 1st of July and the Lexington didn't get back until about the 1st of September. We had a large exercise at that time off Monterey with the first real amphibious landings. The troops came from Fort Lewis at Takoma and they were in transports and brought down from that area, and we met them. We did a sort of an air support exercise to support the troops ashore. They were all Army troops. My memory is that there were no Marines involved in that landing.

At that time the commanding officer of the Lexington was Captain E. J. King and the exec was John H. Hoover.

Q: Quite a pair!

Adm. P.: Yes. On the 1st of July Sam Ginder had been relieved by Gerald F. Bogan, lieutenant commander, and he had been in command of Squadron One at Pensacola before that and had given me my solo check, as a matter of fact. I spent a great deal of time serving under Bogan in later years.

Q: At some time in the series, I hope you'll give me a picture of Bogan.

Adm. P.: Yes. Well, he was a rough tough guy. He'd had a lot of experience in the Far East. He'd been to Vladivostok, he'd spent a lot of time in destroyers, and was an experienced seaman before he ever went to flight training. He went to flight training quite late, I think as a senior lieutenant.

We had a fine group of people in gunnery and bombing and we won the "E" for excellence in gunnery and bombing in that year.

Q: When you were in the Lexington?

Adm. P.: The Lexington VF-3 squadron.

Q: Tell me about landing, arresting gear and so forth.

Adm. P.: Well, the arresting gear was physically the same as the arresting gear today. It wasn't anything like as large because it didn't require the size machinery or size wires and what not, because the force didn't amount to much. You might say by comparison with aircraft today we were flying gliders and free balloons. Our landing speed was probably 45 knots and with wind over the deck that cut it down. Your real problem was to keep from floating over the wires. You had to get down into the gear and get caught. We had barriers, of course, before the angled deck and that saved us. We didn't have brakes in those days. We only had tail skags and when we came on board the carrier they put a wheel on instead of the skags so you wouldn't tear the deck up, but no brakes. We got brakes right at the end of that cruise, and they were makeshift brakes put into the planes. We also did not have two-way voice radio until about the time I left VF-3 in the summer of 1931.

About the 1st of January 1931 the Langley was ordered to the East Coast and our squadron was ordered from the Lexington to the Langley. We had one scouting squadron on board that I think came from the Lexington too - one scouting squadron and one fighter squadron were put on the Langley and we went around to the East Coast. We had a cruise through the canal and into the Caribbean where we had some war games, and about that time I got a telegram from Ralph Ofstie, who was the head of the flight test section, asking if I would like to be an assistant flight test pilot. I immediately accepted and I was ordered to Anacostia where the flight test section was located.

Pirie #1 - 21

Q: How did your bride react to this?

Adm. P.: She didn't worry too much about my flying in those days.

Q: But this was a dangerous operation, wasn't it?

Adm. P.: It was a little. We had two or three experiences while I was in the flight testing that were quite hairy.

I was detached from VF-3 in June and arrived at Anacostia and reported to flight test about the 1st of July 1931.

Q: Before you tell me about that, Sir, I want to ask a question. You said that the Lexington had put in at all the East Coast ports and the Langley had come back to the East Coast. Was this in the nature of public relations?

Adm. P.: No. You see, there were no carriers besides those. They were the only three carriers we had, and there was some feeling that we should have a carrier on the East Coast, but they didn't want to separate the Lexington and Saratoga because they had a lot of things going back and forth, you know - competition - and facilities were better out at North Island than they were at Norfolk for handling this outfit at that time, so they wanted to get the Langley back. As a matter of fact, one of the reasons was the trouble in Nicaragua. At the tail end of that war game we did some gunnery at Guantanamo, finished up our gunnery year. We were flying from Hicacal Beach, and in the midst of that we were ordered to go to Nicaragua to try to take care of Sandino. They were having so much trouble with him at that time.

Pirie #1 - 22

We were all loaded and ready to go and got down there and swung around the hook for about two or three weeks and they never would let us go ashore and get him. They never would let us get into the action. The Marines were in there and we would have, of course, been supporting the Marines. We never saw any action. We just went down to swing around that hook.

Q: Thinking in terms of public relations, was there a conscious effort in naval aviation circles to get public support?

Adm. P.: Yes, I think there was a good deal. We went to the air races every year at Cleveland in those days. One squadron would go and we had some other air stunt teams. This effort that I told you about on the East Coast in 1930 where we took all of the planes from the Lexington and Saratoga and flew them to all the large cities, New York, Boston, Philadelphia, Hartford, and then stacked down over Washington, Baltimore, Richmond, they all got a chance to look at what carrier airplanes looked like. With these you've got to remember that the Langley was the first carrier, and the Lexington and Saratoga were the second and third carriers. They were the first large ones that we had a large number of planes on. They were converted battle cruisers. The public didn't know much about carrier aviation, so I think that was a great effort to publicize them a little bit. We did the same thing on the West Coast with San Francisco, and I'm sure later they did it at Seattle. I don't know that Seattle had ever seen a carrier plane, except for going over them on the ground, but never saw them fly from carriers.

Pirie #1 - 23

Q: Well, aviation had some very astute people in the Bureau of Aeronautics, people like Admiral Moffitt, who understood public relations.

Adm. P.: Yes, and so did Reeves. Reeves was a great one for public relations and he understood it fully.

Q: Did you get out to the races?

Adm. P.: No. VF-1 I believe went both years while I was in. I'm sure they did. VF-3 went to the races the year I left, in 1931. We'd won the "E" in gunnery and bombing and we were picked to go and they went from Norfolk to Cleveland in September, but by that time I'd been detached.

It was interesting that while I was assistant flight test officer we had to do a good deal of transport flying and we had to check out the transports, and those of us in the flight test had to take some transport flights if there weren't enough officers in operations to take care of it. I was the junior one in flight test and I was the junior one at Anacostia up to that time, so the airplane that I got usually as a transport was a Sikorsky amphibian. We called it the "praying mantis." It looked like a praying mantis. It went about 85 knots full speed and landed at about 70. Well, I got the job of flying the mechanics from VF-3 from Norfolk to Cleveland for VF-3 at that time, so I joined my old squadron out there for one day and watched them do their thing. "Their thing" was a nine-plane loop at night with the wings tied together with flares on them.

Q: Spectacular!

Adm. P.: It was spectacular in those days.

The flight test section was quite interesting in those days. The flight test officer was Ralph Ofstie, as I said. We had Admiral J. F. Bolger, who was then a lieutenant and a big-boat pilot, as we called them. He was an expert in multi-engine planes and he did practically nothing but that, and he was the gunnery officer. Fred Trapnell was the third senior, and I was the fourth. There were only four of us and we got, as an engineer from MIT, Theta Combs. All of these officers made flag rank.

Q: Tell me about some of the new types you tested.

Adm. P.: Well, the airplanes were quite interesting. At that time we had a considerable number of amphibious planes because small amphibians for use on battleships and cruisers preferably as rescue planes on big carriers. It was the day when the amphibian was of great interest to us because it could land in the water or on wheels on land, so we had about half a dozen of those built by Loening and later by Grumman. The first airplane Grumman built was one of these amphibs. Most of the ones I remember were Loening.

Q: It was the great day of the amphibious, wasn't it?

Adm. P.: That's right. Then, we had several new fighter planes and torpedo bombers. During my time the first BM-1, the first real heavy dive bomber that could carry a 1,000-lb bomb, came into being. I did a lot of test work on that. My first project was the F-4B3. The F-4B3 was a bi-plane but it was a monocut fuselage, metal, the first metal-covered fuselage. There were a number of those bought for naval aviation. As a matter of fact, the Air Museum at Pensacola has one on display that's quite interesting. It's very interesting to note the cost of that airplane and engine with the bomb racks, with the fixed guns, the thing was invoiced at something like $50,000! And now a comparable fighter airplane costs $15,000,000.

Well, the F-4B3 was my first project. During our time we also tested the planes for the Akron and Macon, the dirigibles. We had three airplanes, one built by Curtiss, one built by Fokker, and one built by Berliner-Joyce. Trapnell and I did most of the test work on those. As a matter of fact, Trapnell in his second year went to a squadron on the Akron. I gave all the photographs of all the airplanes we had in the test section at that time to the Naval Historical Section in Washington, and probably we could easily get them or get duplicates from that.

Q: What relations did you have with the aircraft companies?

Adm. P.: We had to go to what they called mock-up boards. I was on almost all of those. When you got ready to build an airplane and make a contract in those days, the company that you were giving the contract to had to build a mock-up, so-called, of the cockpit and all of the controls and that sort of thing. Then they had a board that consisted of experts in engines, ordnance, and everything, and they had one of us flight test officers. So I went on most of these mock-up boards and so

Pirie #1 - 26

got to know practically all of the aircraft industry.

It was interesting that the first flight I had to Hartford, Connecticut, after I got in was with an amphibious float for an O-2U, and I had to go to Chance-Vought to have something done to this airplane. I was there one day and I asked Gene Wilson, who was there as head of Chance-Vought at the time, if he'd take me to Pratt and Whitney. Pratt and Whitney was a brand new company, just beginning to build aerial engines. They took me over and the man who was told off to show me around was Bill Gwinn, who has just retired as chairman of the board of Pratt and Whitney, of United Aircraft. That was 1931.

We had some very interesting big boats in those days. We had five or six in competition that ended up in the Consolidated flying boats that were the forerunner of the ones used at the beginning of World War II. I had to do quite a bit of flying as a co-pilot in those days with Bolger in making measurements of various kinds. Our knowledge of flight tests was pretty mediocre compared to what it is now, and I learned as much from Trapnell as from anyone. He was a student of aerodynamics and taught me a great deal about flying in those days.

Another thing. After the experience in those airplanes, you never were afraid to get into any kind of an airplane from then on.

Q: If you survived!

Adm. P.: Another very interesting plane we had was the Pitcairn autogyro, the forerunner of the helicopter, which came during that period. We had three of them. As a matter of fact, there's a picture of three of them in formation among the photographs I gave to the Naval Historical Section.

Q: What did you think of the autogyro?

Adm. P. It was quite interesting. It had, of course, some great faults. The rotor wasn't driven. You had an engine. That was a free-wheeling rotor, and after it got to turning you got the web. It had small wings and so you took off with the engine pulling you, there was no connection between the engine and the rotor. That came later. It was interesting and it was, as I said, the forerunner of the helicopter.

Q: What use was envisioned for it at that time?

Adm. P.: Observation. It could be used for slow-speed observation.

Q: Was the Navy enthusiastic about the idea?

Adm. P.: No, it died a-borning. About that time old Igor Sikorsky was working on the helicopter, so it never did amount to anything. They never did buy more than those three.

Q: Did Sikorsky produce a prototype of a helicopter at that time?

Adm. P.: No, not at that period. It was a little later.

Grumman Corporation came into existence at this period and I got to know Mr. Grumman and Jake Swirble and Bill Swindler, who was the chief engineer, and spent a good deal of time with them. We got the first two Grumman two-seaters one was a fighter and was was a scouting plane, so-called. We did all the test work on those airplanes at the time.

In January 1933 Bogan and I were taking the two Grumman airplanes to the West Coast for carrier trials and on our return we stayed overnight at St. Louis and when I retracted my gear, it was a mechanical retraction of the wheels, the bull gear let go and the wheels were just flopping in the air. It was very cold at the time. I had a chief petty officer named Bailey with me in the back seat. He tried to get out on the wings and kick those things down so I could lock them, but he just couldn't quite do it. He, of course, had a parachute on and was trying to kick these wheels down so I could get them locked, but he couldn't hack it. Bogan went back to the field and came back in some sort of a transport airplane that had written on the side. "There's a barge in the Mississippi River at such and such a place. You can go and land alongside of that." Well, in that cold weather, I wrote him a note and threw it down across the field and told him that I'd rather take a chance on landing on the field than I would freezing to death and, besides, that would lose the airplane if I landed in the water.

So, we burned the gas out and I asked Bailey if he wanted to jump since he carried a parachute. He said, no, he'd stick with me. We landed and all it did was bend the propeller in a little bit undercarriage and we got a new propeller and bull gear and put them on and we flew on to the coast. That was the first wheels-up landing in the Navy because they were the first retractable landing wheels that we had. I got a commendation from the Secretary of the Navy for landing that one on its belly. Claude Swanson, Secretary Swanson.

Q: When you deliver planes like that for the carriers, did you test them on board the carriers, too?

Adm. P.: No, we turned them over to the fleet out there and they did the landings on board. We'd done the landings on the carrier suitability unit which was then at Norfolk -- it's now Patuxent, but we had the deck on the field at Norfolk and we used it.

There were a couple of other hairy instances. I had some hairy ones all right.

Q: Tell me about them.

Adm. P.: We had a Berliner-Joyce fighter that I flew to the West Coast in early 1932.

Q: What kind?

Adm. P.: Berliner-Joyce. Henry Berliner and Temple Joyce started this company. By myself, a solo flight across there in those days was something that was -- it took me three days. I took that out to the fleet and flew around with it on the carriers. I think it was the Assistant Secretary of the Navy for Air and he had been flying a Curtiss two-seat biplane that was the fastest thing we had and he wanted a better airplane so they bought for him from Lockheed one of the first Lockheed Orions, a low-wing monoplane, and I got the job of testing it.

It was very interesting that the spec for high speed was

for about 214 miles an hour, and it would only go 208, and this made Ingals furious! When he was told that it would only go 208, he said he didn't believe it. So I said, "All right, come on over here and we'll go out together and try it." So we let him fly the thing over the speed course and he found out it would only go 208! That was an interesting experience. It was very badly unstable longitudinally because - when the wheels were down - because of the big wheel wells which they didn't cover up in those days, and it lost a lot of life. If you tended to use too much rudder right or left, the nose would drop rapidly on you.

Luddington Airlines bought some of these airplanes at that time and when I was coming back from this flight to the West Coast when I took the Berliner-Joyce fighter, the United Airlines people, Patterson, asked if I'd ride with the airline and make any comments I had about their airplanes and their methods of operation in those days. So I took a 40-B4, which was an old biplane with four or five seats in the fuselage, up to San Francisco, and there they had a larger Boeing airplane, but it was a biplane. I got as far as Chicago, and then I got into a Ford Transport in Chicago and rode that to New York. I got into New York late in the afternoon. I'd have to wait about an hour to get into a Ford transport - I guess it was Eastern in those days - but the Luddington Line had one of these Orions going out in a few minutes and I said wouldn't it be great to get in that and get back an hour or so earlier. I'd been gone for a week and was anxious to get home.

But I thought about that test, about how unstable it was, and Trapnell and I both said that somebody was riding for a fall, they would get in trouble and have that nose go down. So I deferred and waited and went in the Ford transport. The Luddington airliner did exactly that. The pilot going in to Camden, New Jersey, hit that rudder a little hard and the nose went right straight down and right into the ground and killed everybody on board. I came that close to getting in that, but my experience with the Orion had taught me.

Q: You had to have an extra kind of sense when you were a test pilot!

Adm. P.: Another interesting thing was that in the final conference on buying these airplanes, Admiral Moffett conducted the conference himself at his office with all of his top aides of the Bureau of Aeronautics, but he always insisted that the test pilots be there. So I had many an hour in Admiral Moffett's office, and he asked piercing questions, as did his aides, about the flying qualities of the airplanes and what we knew about them.

Q: Tell me about him.

Adm. P.: He was a great man. I almost got in the airplane with him when he was killed. I flew him up there in a Bianca monoplane with about four or five people, and as I got out of the airplane with them and walked over to the Akron, and they started up the ladder and Moffett said, "Why don't you come and go on this flight with us, Pirie?" I didn't like the looks of those damned gas bags in those days. I just didn't have any confidence. I said, "No, thanks, Admiral. I think I'll go back to Anacostia." So they went up and he was killed that night in the Akron.

He was a wonderful man, and, of course, his real staunch support for naval aviation against all the rest of the Navy at that time was magnificent.

Q: That took real courage!

Adm. P.: Real courage because he was put upon by the people who didn't really believe in it, and we didn't really come into our own even though basically we had the background, World War II is where we proved real worth of the carriers.

Q: Did you have anything to do with Ralph Barnaby anywhere along in your career?

Adm. P.: Yes, I knew Barnaby during this period. He was in the Bureau at that time and I got to know Ralph real well.

We did catapult testing as well as all the other flight testing from a barge at the Washington Navy Yard in those days. All the amphibians and float seaplanes had to be thoroughly tested with weight increments and whatnot, and that was a fairly interesting part of our test procedures.

Q: That was one place where - one area - where the battleship officer and the naval aviator sort of came together, was it not?

Adm. P.: We had observation planes, so-called, in battleships and cruisers.

Q: The regular line officer was interested in that, wasn't he?

Adm. P.: Yes, later on. They didn't take to it very kindly at first. They thought the ship did better gunnery observation and better scouting itself, and they didn't trust what the aviator saw. It took a long time for them to accept -

Q: But they got tangible results!

Adm. P.: They got real results once they got started.

We had several other fighter aircraft come along about that time, but the Boeing fighters were the most successful ones until the Grummans got started. The Grumman single-seat fighter came the year after I left the test center, but the initial experience with the two-seat fighter was enough to prove that they could do the job. They had biplanes, small single-engine biplanes, until the F-4F, which was at the beginning of World War II.

Q: Admiral, who was giving the principal impetus to the development of new types of planes at that time? Was it the military, or was it commercial aviation?

Adm. P.: No, I think it was the military. I think the people we had in the Bureau of Aeronautics at that time were all vitally interested. We had people like Admiral Radford, Admiral Salada, Admiral Kelly Turner, Admiral McFall, Jock Clark. These people all contributed to the development of better military fighting airplanes.

Q: I was thinking in terms of the postal service beginning to go in for air mail delivery and so forth and the commercial lines signed up for this. Maybe that gave an impetus to the development of new planes?

Adm. P.: Of course, airmail-carrying had a great deal to do with the transport development and subsidization by the postal department paid for them in the early days. The Boeing representative in Washington when I was in the test section was James P. Murray, who later was a vice president of the Boeing Corporation, but Jim Murray flew the first air mail in an old Ford B-4. I got to know Jim and we were very close friends all the rest of our lives. He died here recently. We got to know all the contractor representatives and all the heads of the principal aviation concerns. Glenn Martin, of course, was in Baltimore and spent a great deal of time around the test section. We had several airplanes being tested in those days and we saw a good deal of him.

Dutch Kindleberger, the head of North American, and Burdett Wright, the head of Curtiss-Wright. The Renschlers were the people at the head of United Aircraft and Chance-Vought Corporation. Charlie McCarthy, Gene Wilson, Jack Horner, the head of Pratt and Whitney. Igor Sikorsky I met in those days.

Q: What about Bill McCracken? Did he have anything to do with it?

Adm. P.: Bill didn't have anything to do with us per se. I got to know Bill, not well at that time, but later on. I got to know him quite well when I was on the NACA, the National Aeronautic Association.

It was a very interesting period in the development of aviation. One of the things that finally was responsible for our getting Patuxent River as a test station was that we had several of our planes come apart in the vicinity of Washington and some spin in. The first BM-1 bomber was being tested by a classmate of mine named Ed Ritchie and it came apart about 8,000 feet right over Anacostia. It was a defective tail that had sympathetic vibrations and finally fell off, and when he jumped out his parachute caught on the plane and he was killed. But that plane hit up on Oxon Hill, right above there. It was real dangerous and a lot of it was in a school yard. What kept them from killing some school children I'll never know, but I had the job of going up and picking that whole thing up and reconstructing what had happened, and we found that it was this tail. What it was was a single-point suspension and it allowed the tail to rock. They rebuilt it and just put a two-point suspension on the tail so that it couldn't move and that cured the problem on that plane.

Q: Tell me about reconstructing a plane after an accident. That must be a very difficult thing to do, isn't it?

Adm. P.: Oh it is, but you've got to geographically find where the pieces are. I found the pieces of this tail were quite a way from where the rest of it hit, so I knew that the tail was the first thing that came off. You could almost draw a line from the flight path. We were watching it when it happened, so we knew what the flight path was. We found the fuselage and the engine and the wings and then you go back down that line, and here was the whole tail about a quarter of a mile down the line. That told us that it was the tail that had come off first because of the problem. We ran some other tests.

When we got the second BM-1 I had to run the stem test on that and it was a flat spinner. We knew it was a flat spinner and the center of gravity was too far aft. I said to Ofstie after I'd run these first tests that this thing was so flat it didn't have to go round half a turn before the horizon went out of sight. And, you know, when you do a spin you pull the plane up and stall it and the nose goes down, and it starts to spin. Well, when the nose comes up and you can't see the horizon that's spinning flat. It's very dangerous. You can't get it out of its spin. Well, it was going flat in half a turn and I told Ofstie I didn't want any more of that, this was a dangerous airplane and we're going to have a lot of trouble unless they correct this.

The Martin Company decided that they would take it on and they spun the thing in and Ken Ebel, who was not a real test pilot but was working in the engineering department, a National Guard pilot, did this then, and he couldn't get it out and he got out at low altitude and the wing hit him in the shins and broke both of them, I think, but we got him out of the water. It just shows you that once you get in difficulty in one of those things, you've got to analyze them and be careful.

The same thing happened to me in a Grumman - a similar experience - in a Grumman two-seater. The wing alignment was quite difficult and you had to do it almost every flight in this airplane. I was flying this day and it was wing heavy on one side. I did the ten-turn spin to the right, which we were required to do, and it came out all right. When I did the ten-turn spin to the left I put the controls over and nothing happened because it was out of line. I blew it out with the engine. Fortunately the engine took. In a lot of those cases there was so much force within the fuel system, within the piping, that it would get a vapor lock and you couldn't get the engine turned on, but I was fortunate that I blew it out. You learn a lot by these things.

Another thing on the BM-2 Martin dive bomber, they had long tanks along the fuselage, right alongside of the two cockpits, like say 12 feet long, and when the thing sat on the ground at an angle the fuel force at take-off point for the pipe was in the middle of the tank. If you were low on fuel and you were accelerating, the fuel would all go to the rear end of the tank and expose that point and stop your engine. How did we find this out? I was on a flight in an F-4B3 and came down in the middle one afternoon and Ofstie was standing on the line and he said, "We've just done some stability tests on this thing. Trapnell and I have just finished and would you take it up and do it." I had my parachute on. I just got out, went over and got in this airplane. They had the engine running and I took off toward the south. There was a big bank 50 feet high in those days between Anacostia and Bolling Field, and the thing quit on me when I got about 100 feet in the air and I was going right into that bank. So I pulled the stick back and let it go, stall, and she came right down flat, and I had a 1,000 pound bomb on this damned thing. It was a dummy bomb and it came right up between my feet and there I was sitting with these wings crashing outside.

Q: And it blew the tires, I suppose!

Adm. P.: Oh, yes. My landing gear just went to hell. So that's the way we found out that this was a defective fuel system.

Q: That's a pretty hairy way of finding out!

Adm. P.: The reason was that if they'd have filled that, if they'd have gased that thing and had that tank half full, some fellow would have had disaster later on because of this defective system. So we later just put the pipe in the back, at take-off point in the back of the plane so that we knew that it wasn't going to get into this kind of a situation.

Q: As you relate these things, I almost gather that the outstanding requirement for a test pilot is to be a very observing person?

Adm. P.: Yes, you've got to be wide awake the whole time. I had quite an experience on a Curtiss fighter, F-11C, or some such designation. It had a brand-new engine that Pratt and Whitney had just delivered to put into this fighter and we had it loaded with lead used as weights to take the place of various pieces of equipment like guns and whatnot, and it was loaded to maximum, and they wanted to run a quick test on the flight deck at Norfolk. So, I get in this airplane and go down to Norfolk, and made three landings in the gear and let someone else, I think, Jimmy Thach who was in that section make a couple and then I got back in the airplane and started back for Anacostia and right over Mobjack Bay, down in the south Chesapeake, this thing quit on me. Fortunately, I had 6,000 feet. I made a dead-stick landing in a little corn field or pasture. The cam drive gear broke so that the engine just quit. No valves moving. And the man on whose farm I landed was Elliot Moreman, who was a graduate of the

Naval Academy in the class of 1910! So I stayed there two days. They brought me down a new engine and put this second engine in, and the second engine had never even been checked out on the test stand for fuel consumption.

I didn't want to put too much fuel in the tank of this thing because it was a small field and I was worried about getting out. Of course, I took the weights out of the thing, but it still was a very small field. So I took off and I started back for Anacostia, and five miles south of Anacostia this thing quit on me again, and I landed in an alfalfa field on some farm. I got back after three days but they had to tow this thing in and they put the thing on the test stand, of course, and found out it was using about three times as much fuel as it should have been using.

I had another experience with an experimental engine in a Curtiss Hawk. I went to Long Island to get it. The inspector was old Smoky Rhodes who'd been the chief petty officer of the NC-4 and he was my instructor in Pensacola on big boats. The propeller on this thing turned in the opposite direction. Instead of rotating clockwise, looking from the air, it rotated counter-clockwise. They had a terrific amount of torque in those small airplanes and you had to be very careful as you took off getting into the air, that you didn't ground loop. So this was quite an experience getting that thing off.

Well, they fueled this thing up full and we started back – it was an experimental engine, of course – I started back for Anacostia and I got right, oh, I was 8,000 or 10,000 feet over Camp Perry up there north of Havre de Grace when this thing quit on me. I was trying to get in to the race track at Havre de Grace. Well, this was an old airplane and it had sort of dead fabric on the wings and it came down like a rock and I ended up landing on old Senator Tydings' front yard in about six feet of water and turned over on my back. I was in mud, and, oh, it was a mess! That's the way we found out that engine had an excess of fuel consumption.

Q: What percentage of the planes that came to you for testing had defects, serious defects?

Adm. P.: Most of them were unstable in those days. Stability was a matter of trial and error. While we were using the NACA at Langley Field, we used their wind tunnels and whatnot, the state of the art hadn't developed to perfection yet like it is now. So we were doing a lot of this by trial and error. We didn't know the NACA people very well. As a matter of fact, McAdoo was the test pilot who did a lot of the testing for the commercial companies that had to pay for demonstrations, you know. He did a great deal of that and his successor was G   .
Well, we got to know them quite well because they were up there doing a lot of it and we exchanged ideas.

Q: What would be the time element involved from the drawing board through the test center for a new plane?

Adm. P.: A lot less than we have now. And they, of course, bought two or three of a type instead of buying one airplane. They would buy from two or three manufacturers and have a competition.

Q: They could afford to then!

Adm. P.: You could afford to at $50,000 a copy. It was interesting in that respect. We had two or three fighters in every competition, and the planes for the Akron is the one that I remember best because those three we had right there and we took turns flying them, and talked the situation over with regard to hooking on the Akron.

Q: Did you fly from the Akron?

Adm. P.: I never did fly from the Akron. Trapnell did most of that and then he went to the squadron, as I said.

Q: Was there any interchange with foreign manufacturers? The British, for instance?

Adm. P.: Not at that time. We did have some exchanges with the Air Force. When they had a new airplane that we wanted to look at, we'd get hold of it and fly it and vice versa.

Q: You spoke of moving the test center from Anacostia to a country area like Patuxent. In your time there, did you avoid flights over the city of Washington?

Adm. P.: We did to the best of our ability, but we took the real dangerous testing, spin testing and dive testing, to we'll say, to full 10 Gs, that kind of thing where there was a chance of an airplane failing.

some part of it failing, we took those to Dahlgren in the late part of my time at the test center. The second year I was in the test section, my friend Lieutenant Commander G. F. Bogan came from Fighting-3 to the test section as head of the test section - he was head of it the second year I was in it.

Q: Were there interested government people who came down to observe some of these tests?

Adm. P.: People from the Bureau. We always had a good many of them around when we had anything like a demonstration or any serious testing going on. And the engineering duty only people were designers and those types from the Bureau were always there when we had some important evolution.

Q: Did you have anything to do with Captain Diehl?

Adm. P.: Yes. I knew Walter well in aerodynamics. I still see him. He was a leading aerodynamicist and I guess he's probably one of the greatest in the country today, if not the greatest. He understands the business thoroughly. And he was the aerodynamicist in those days.

Q: I suppose it was a great help in that time to have a man like Dave Ingalls, who was in the government.

Adm. P.: A great enthusiast, yes, and sold it. As a matter of fact, he came there with Coolidge, I believe, and was there with Hoover during this period. But I think he'd come when Cal Coolidge was in.

Q: I think you're right.

Adm. P.: And you know Cal Coolidge said that he didn't think too much of aviation in the early days and he said, "Why don't you aviators get one airplane and take turns flying?"

Q: Save money that way!

Adm. P.: But Ingalls was a great help. Of course, he hadn't quite come along yet --

Q: He was in the Bureau, wasn't he? After Moffett?

Adm. P.: After Moffett, but I can't remember where he was when he left the Lexington.

Q: This was a time when there were a lot of flights over the ocean and so forth, and over the north pole. This gave great impetus -

Adm. P.: Yes. Byrd was around in those days but I didn't - we didn't see much of him at Anacostia.

Q: Did you see anything of Lindberg there?

Adm. P.: No, he didn't show up around our place. Of course, he took off from New York.

I guess it was just about the time that I went to Anacostia to the test section that they dedicated Floyd Bennett Field. He'd been Byrd's pilot, you know. They had a big celebration up there to dedicate that field in New York.

Q: Admiral, I wonder if you could say something about this whole period in time, how it relates to the total development of naval aviation?

Adm. P.: This period was the early beginning of carrier aviation, and so the craft that we were flying were sort of World War I outgrowths. We hadn't yet gotten into heavier, sophisticated airplanes and we hadn't been in many monoplanes, which eventually became the type airplane that we fly in combat today.

It was also a very interesting period so far as the development of large big boats, seaplanes, was concerned, and the PBY of World War II came directly from the work that we did in those days, 1931 to 1933. The development of the fighter airplane and of the attack airplane also began to evolve in that period because we were thinking in terms of getting a bomber that could deliver a heavy load. This BM airplane built by Martin was the first one that would carry a 1,000-pound bomb. We were used to bombing with 100-pound bombs.

The development of the large machine gun came along about that time. We were using 30 caliber machine guns and 50 caliber were just being developed. The development of the World War II fighter airplane bomber airplane and torpedo plane was just in its infancy at that time. Thinking about the monoplane, the Buffalo Brewster was the first really and was started about that time. The F-4F hadn't been thought of and it was the best fighter we had at the beginning. The SBC and BT that we had at the beginning of the war hadn't really been developed and the torpedo plane hadn't been germinated in their thinking at that time. The beginnings of those aircraft all took place three or four years after I was in the test section. I'll say a little bit more about that when I get to the period just before the war, 1939 and 1940, and what went on at that time when I was in the Yorktown.

Q: I suppose that the development of new types of planes was contingent upon the growing concept of the use of the carrier in the fleet, was it?

Adm. P.: Yes. The idea was what are you going to need, what is a carrier for, and how was it going to be protected, because we had no radar in those days. You were depending on sight, the human eyeball, for warning you of anything coming in on you, and the development of scouting techniques and going a long distance from the carrier - we thought it was a real kind of a feat to go a hundred miles from the carrier, in those days, and it was and get back. People got lost all the time. We had a hell of a time with searches and that sort of thing.

The development of gunnery and dive-bombing tactics, however, was a product of this period, and the development of the fixed gunnery techniques that we used at the beginning of World War II all came from this group of people who started out in these early carriers. The development of dive-bombing tactics, all this took place at this time and we all learned how to bomb and shoot well and we could teach the younger people how to do it. You see, two-way radio came along at this period and gave us voice communication which was a great advantage to us. Well, just maneuvering around the carrier talking to each other in the air. We used to have to do it all by hand signals before that.

Q: At this point the carrier had not yet been conceived of as a central unit in the fleet?

Adm. P.: No, in a supporting role. I think the concept of using the attack carrier for offensive operations was really started about Reeves' time, and Reeves was an advocate of it. Up to that time, the battleship and the cruiser had been the pieces de resistance. They only thought in terms of those as real offensive weapons.

Q: Reeves himself didn't have wings, did he?

Adm. P.: He was an observer, I believe. He went to Pensacola but he took an observer's course.

Q: You mentioned various things that were coming on at that time, what about the cargo plane development, the transport planes?

Adm. P.: Of course, the Ford Trimotor was <u>the</u> transport at that time and it was the basic transport plane until we got the first Douglas DC-1. I flew the Ford quite a bit. I think we made more progress at that particular time in the development of the seaplane and we didn't have much to do with transport land planes. We took what was available. Then the DC-1 came along, the Douglas workhorse, and that became the basic aircraft, but that was quite a bit later, as late as the beginning of World War II, you know, the only thing we had for flying the Atlantic and Pacific was the big Boeing seaplane.

Q: Why did the seaplane have such an impetus at that time and later fade from the picture?

Adm. P.: Well, I think that there hadn't been a land plane developed that would go long distances and the seaplane would go quite long distances, and the handling, the building of landing gear and retractable landing gear, those kind of things, hadn't developed yet. And the fields hadn't developed. We didn't have runways. The field at Anacostia when I was flying at the test section was all dirt, just a dirt grass field. We spent half our time out there with tractors pulling our planes out of the mud.

Q: And it was vulnerable to weather!

Adm. P.: Everything. We didn't fly for quite long periods when we'd have bad weather like that because the field wouldn't stand it. And you couldn't handle it. We didn't have the facilities anywhere. So the seaplane was more attractive from a standpoint because you had the closed harbor areas where you could take seaplanes off and land them and you could handle much greater weights.

Q: Was it perhaps true that the concept of the seaplane was much more readily understandable by the naval officer who had a general aversion to flying?

Adm. P.: Very much so. They thought it was the Air Force's business to fly big bombers and whatnot. The B-17 came along and was the forerunner, basically, of the transport airplane. That took place in the mid 1930s, the concept of getting a large bomber built.

Pirie #1 - 48

Q: How did the idea of the seaplane fit into Moffett's concept of aviation?

Adm. P.: I think we all thought and I think he did too in terms of the seaplane as an important part of our business of being able to fly around the globe, go anywhere that we were supposed to go. I will relate in talking about my next duty I was on Admiral Johnson's staff when we flew the first seaplanes to Hawaii, the first formation. It was a Consolidated seaplane and that was quite an episode. The first ones that went.

You know, in terms of how you were going to use them hadn't really developed as a global thing yet, but we knew that if we were going to do scouting and have any real military capability we had to develop this big airplane, and that's how the seaplane evolved and how we got the PBY for the beginning of World War II.

Q: Then was it perfectly natural for the seaplane to fade from the picture when land planes became speedier and -

Adm. P.: That's right, and I was in on that when I was with DCNO and had to kill the jet seaplane that Martin built, the P-6M. But that will be another episode.

They don't have that usefulness once you get fields that can handle large airplanes on steel mats, and they can handle huge ones today in that kind of environment.

A great many friends of senior aviators at that time became lifelong friends and had a great deal to do with my career later on, like L. B. Richardson, who was the wartime Assistant Chief of the Bureau of Aeronautics.

Q: Certainly, career-wise, it was a strategic time to be there, wasn't it?

Adm. P.: It was. Of course, Admiral Moffett, Admiral King, Kelly Turner — and I got to know all these people I was intimately associated with like Bogan and Ginder, Ralph Ofstie, and all of the squadron commanders in those days, the wing commanders, Bradford, Salada, all of the individuals who were mixed up in World War II as flag officers were all people with whom we were associated in those early days.

Q: Was Wu Duncan involved there?

Adm. P.: Wu was there. Wu was in the carriers when I first went and he was around the Bureau of Aeronautics. Matt Gardner, Ballentine, Admiral Halsey, although I guess I didn't know him so well then as I did later.

Q: What about the Whitings?

Adm. P.: Yes, I knew Ken Whiting quite well, and I knew his older brother, F. E. M. He was around the Naval Academy at the time I was on duty there. Ken Whiting was skipper of the Langley —

Q: When you were on her?

Adm. P.: No.

Pirie #1 - 50

Q: Were you involved with Charlie Mason at all?

Adm. P.: Yes, I knew Charlie very well. I didn't get into the training command as a training pilot, and Charlie spent an awful lot of time in Pensacola and Jacksonville and various other places. He built Jacksonville at the beginning of the war, or just before. So I didn't really serve with Charlie until later, but I knew him quite well.

Q: Well, perhaps you want to talk about the next phase of your career when you went as aide and flag lieutenant to Alfie Johnson?

Adm. P.: At the end of my tour in the test section, I had orders to the USS California as an aviator on a battleship and was all set to go. My wife had gone to New York to be with her family for a week or two before we took off for the West Coast. She was going out by train because she was pregnant and carrying our son, Robert, who was born in September of that year, so I was living with a couple of my classmates for a week before leaving, and I got a telephone call Saturday morning from Andy McFall, who was the detail officer in the Bureau of Aeronautics at the time, and he said, come on over, I want to see you right away. I arrived about eleven a.m. on Saturday morning and McFall said, "You're going as Alfie Johnson's flag lieutenant. Your orders have been changed."

I said, "Who's Alfie Johnson?"

"He's assistant chief of the Bureau of Personnel, but he's just been selected for promotion." This was going to be his first flag job as what they called Commander, Aircraft Scouting Force — which was the big boats, the flying boats.

So I got my orders changed and I proceeded to California and I met Admiral Johnson at the train and that was frankly the first time I ever saw him, and I became his flag lieutenant. I was with him for two years and it was a very interesting and enjoyable experience. We had a great staff. The chief of staff was Marc Mitscher - oh, I'd forgotten, in the early days Marc Mitscher was always around the Bureau of Aeronautics and I got to know him in those early days.

Marc Mitscher was chief of staff, Salada was operations officer. George Henderson was the engineer. Nicholson was the engineering duty only officer. Bud Hall, G. B. H. Hall, was the communications officer. Jack Perry, John Perry, was the flag secretary, and I was flag lieutenant.

Q: That was quite a galaxy!

Adm. P.: The supply officer was a fellow named Wilson, and we had a chief warrant officer named Parker, who was the best man in aviation supply that we had for many years.

Q: Alfie Johnson was worthy of a staff like that, however, was he not?

Adm. P.: He was a fine man. He didn't know too much about aviation. We had a little trouble with him sometimes, but he was quite a character.

Q: Had he been to Pensacola?

Adm. P.: He was an observer, yes. He had observer's wings. He spent a lot of time in the early days in the Wright and was mixed up with the Billy Mitchell trial and he had a lot to do with those captive balloons and stuff like that, but he hadn't done any real active business in flying. He hadn't been around the carriers. He was on duty in Washington during this period.

Q: At one point he was captain of the Kearsarge?

Adm. P.: He had the Richmond as his command. And he had command of the Colorado. It was a very interesting cruise, and this was when we were beginning to get these seaplanes and we made some pretty interesting long flights. The first time we tried any real distance flying was when we flew down to Panama from the East Coast in PB-2Ys, and then they flew from Panama to Acapulco, refueled, and flew from Acapulco to San Diego. Then they got ready for this flight to Hawaii. Kneffler McGinnis was the skipper of the squadron.

Three of our staff flew. Mitscher flew with McGinnis, and George Henderson flew with a lieutenant named Davis. McKenna, one of the pilots in that squadron, got sick and had appendicitis and had an operation about ten days before the flight, and Jack Perry flew that airplane. He was our flag secretary.

Q: I've often wondered why Mitscher flew almost anonymously on that flight with McGinnis. He wasn't advertised as being there.

Adm. P.: Well, he was a very modest man in the first place, but he

Pirie #1 - 53

wanted to go on the flight. He was one of the real pioneers. I'm not sure in my own mind just exactly why, but there was some question about whether they were really going to go.

Q: Whether they had fortitude enough to go!

Adm. P.: Whether they had fortitude enough to take off, and Pete was going to see to it that they did! He was quite a guy.

Well, we made - we took some of the patrol planes up the coast to San Francisco and Seattle and went to Alaska for the first time. That might have been the following year. One of the most interesting things was that we went out to Hawaii. We went to Midway for the first time. We were the first Navy that had been to Midway since 1912 when they'd withdrawn, and this was 1934 in January or February. We went ashore and, it was rough. We went through the cable entrance. There was a cable station, as you know, and they had these commercial cable people there, but we made a quick survey of using this and how we would use it, and then we held a fleet exercise there, and the next year we took the patrol planes out there.

Q: Our interest in those little dots in the Pacific was really growing, wasn't it?

Adm. P.: Just started. The first real glimmer. We never had been at Wake, but we did Midway and that's how Midway's use got started. We built there, and the next year built a camp on Midway and we took our staff out there and we ran the patrol plane operations from Midway and did all the scouting in the fleet war games where the carriers and the rest of the fleet were attacked and we were the sort of defenders.

Q: Since you mention Midway, Wake, and various places in the Pacific and Alaska as well, I'm forced to ask about weather reports. What kind of weather reports did you have to deal with?

Adm. P.: We had to do our own. Weather reporting in that part of the world was almost nil, and your own meteorologists had to make their own estimates based on observations that they could make from the ships or from the airplanes.

Q: Just local observations?

Adm. P.: When we went to Alaska the first time with Admiral Johnson we went to Ketchikan, Sitka, Seward, Cordova, but we did not go to Kodiak. I can tell you a lot about going to Kodiak for the first time later when I had the USS Teal and I took the original survey party in to Kodiak that surveyed all the bases.

Q: Did you have better weather reporting off of Alaska?

Adm. P.: No, zero practically. We did our own maps. In 1939 when I had the Teal, Trapnell had a squadron and we went out there together and were there two or three weeks at one time when I was tending him and we had to draw our own maps. As a matter of fact, we were weathered in at Yakutat one time for something like five days, and Trapnell and I drew our own maps and we predicted within one hour when the stuff would lift and we could get out of there. It was that kind of business.

Q: Perhaps you were just as well off, then, doing you own?

Adm. P.: Yes. I tell you it was frightening out in the Aleutians. Jim Russell, if you ever get him back here, he was in the Aleutians at the beginning of the war, and he can tell you some hair-raising experiences. We didn't even have a radio beacon, you know, we had nothing. No radio aids of any kind. The weather reporting was just horrible, but we gradually caught on and did a lot of our own. We learned to do it ourselves.

This experience of going up there the first time with Admiral Johnson and the staff, of course, it was a virgin country and the fishing and the shooting was just terrific. All the staff loved to fish and shoot. We had great times. We bought a lot of fishing tackle in a sporting goods store in San Diego, and Admiral Johnson had never done trout fishing, if he'd done any at all, which I doubt. We took him to the Russian River and he caught the largest rainbow trout that had been caught and that was a disaster for all these fishermen. They thought they were great and old Alfie caught the biggest - a 33-inch rainbow trout! And we froze it in a block of ice, and we had a chaplain, a Lutheran, and he was a great bragger about his ability and what not and he never could catch much of anything, so we got a little one, about two inches long, and froze that in the same block and showed this thing in the sporting goods store window. The largest trout caught by the admiral and the smallest one caught by the chaplain!

Well, we had the experience later of taking the patrol planes

Pirie #1 - 56

to some of that part of Alaska and pioneering, but this originally was looking it over with the idea of what we could do. The Midway experience was great and we did French Frigate shoals and that proved to be quite interesting.

Q: Who in the Navy was giving impetus to this surveying?

Adm. P.: Well, the CNO - you know this kind of thing was just beginning to be really thought about. Yarnell was at Pearl Harbor in those days as commandant of the district, and I think he probably had a great deal to do with it. He was a great friend of Alfie Johnson's and I stayed at the Yarnells' two or three times during this period.

Q: What kind of installations did we have at Pearl?

Adm. P.: We had Ford Island and we had good seaplane facilities around the island, good beaching facilities and what not, and good hangars. We did a reasonable job there. The field was built as a real field and later on the Air Force used Ford Island before Hickham was built.

We made a couple of other very interesting cruises during this period. We went down through the canal in the Wright and picked up the seaplane squadrons from Panama, three squadrons I believe, and a couple of small tenders. We went along the coast of north South America to Cartegena, Colombia, Maracaibo, and Trinidad, and then we went up through the Lesser Antilles. We went to St. Vincent and St. Lucia, Martinique and Guadeloupe, and then to San Juan, and then to Santo Domingo, over to Jamaica, Guantanamo and Jamaica, and back down to Panama. It was very interesting doing the whole island bit. That was a fascinating thing from the standpoint of meeting people and doing the thing there which was to get those squadrons broken out of Panama and spending some time cruising.

Q: When you went down the west coast of South America, you were in Johnson's stomping ground?

Adm. P.: Right. His father's was one of the original survey ships on the West Coast.

Q: And his mother was born in -

Adm. P.: His mother was a Chilean. But his father was the one who did the original thing up at San Francisco and Monterey. We stopped at Acapulco, of course, but we had to make a couple of other stops – after we got the PB-2Ys, they could make it, but with the earlier planes we had to stop at Cabo St. Lucas, just inside the tip of Southern California. We stopped there and then stopped at Acapulco and then we stopped at some place in Nicaragua and then on in to Panama, Bahia Honda.

There was hardly anything in Acapulco in those days,- one or two saloons.

Q: Tell be about Admiral Johnny Hoover.

Adm. P.: Johnny Hoover relieved Mitscher the second year I was on Admiral Johnson's staff. We made some of these cruises down the West

Coast and Admiral, then Captain, John Hoover had a passion to catch a giant ray - a manta, and he went off in a motor whale boat with a 50-gallon steel drum as a float and he had a steel chain and a big harpoon, and the first time he harpooned he hit this old big manta - he was in a whale boat and he hit this manta in the back with this harpoon and that manta took the barrel and everything and went out of sight in about three seconds!

Q: Almost took Hoover with him!

Adm. P.: So he decided he was going to undertake some more stringent steps to catch this, so he got a bigger harpoon made in the blacksmith's shop and a bigger chain and he chained it to the king post on the motor whale boat. And he hit one of these big devils about 15 feet across, and there was the damnedest floundering around you've every seen, and that old manta came up under the whale boat and cracked the keel, but fortunately they got away. They broke that chain and let that guy go, but he broke the keel on that motor whale boat. They were lucky to get back alive.

Q: Did that cure Hoover?

Adm. P.: He didn't fool around with that manta any more! He loved to fish. We did a lot of shark fishing, for the big sharks off Midway and down in Bahia Honda and Acapulco.

This was a real interesting cruise because of the developments that were going on. We had the first flight of the seaplanes to Hawaii.

Pirie #1 - 59

It was a period of real development, looking now toward World War II and getting everybody ready.

Q: It was kind of watershed time?

Adm. P.: Some of the planes had a very difficult time getting from Hawaii out to Midway because they didn't have enough range in those days. As a matter of fact, they'd been flying with most of their mixture controls closed. Nobody had ever opened the mixture control and gotten any real fuel consumption, and one of the exercises we had in getting out there was to get people thinking about really flying and using their planes to the maximum of their capabilities.

Q: Then a mental factor was involved, wasn't it?

Adm. P.: Mental.

Q: You intimated that with McGinnis' attempt –

Adm. P.: The rest of those boys we had a hard time getting off to go to Midway from Hawaii. Two of the squadron commanders said they wouldn't go, they couldn't make it, and they just ordered them to go. We had eight or ten of them scattered all over between Hawaii and Midway and we picked them up with seaplane tenders and finally got them either in to French Frigate shoals or Midway and made that flight out there and back.

Q: How good was their navigation at that point?

Adm. P.: It was pretty good.

Q: To find a tiny spot in the ocean?

Adm. P.: Well, the radio aids were not very good but we could navigate pretty well. We had fairly good sights and sextants and ways and means of getting those distances. Afterwards, of course, you got radio aids which helped with beams and so forth.

We were in the Wright most of that period but when we had the exercise in 1935 at Midway we went out in the Northampton - no, the Chester - and transferred to an old submarine tender, the Beaver, did our thing out at Midway in the Beaver and then came back to Hawaii that way. As a matter of fact, we lost one patrol plane with Vandenberg and Skelly at this exercise, and Admiral Johnson insisted on flying back, so he and I flew back with John Dale Price to Hawaii so that Alfie could go and see these widows. He didn't want to ride back in the ship. He thought it was so important to do this and we got back to Hawaii and did that business and then waited for the ship to catch up in three or four days. The Wright was our flagship, however, during most of that time.

Interview No. 2 with Vice Admiral Robert Burns Pirie, U.S. Navy (Retired)

Place: The Naval Institute, Annapolis, Maryland

Date: Monday afternoon, 7 August 1972

Subject: Biography

By: John T. Mason, Jr.

Q: Last time you dealt with your tour of duty with Admiral Alfie Johnson and I think you want to conclude your remarks on that at this point. You told me, off tape, that there was another expedition to Midway and this time there was a fleet war game.

Adm. P.: In the spring of 1935 we had a fleet exercise that involved operating all of the patrol planes in the Pacific, that is, in Hawaii, from Midway. They had never flown out there before and it was quite an exercise getting them out. We only had one squadron that really had the legs to go out without any difficulty and it was a new PBY squadron. We had airplanes scattered all over the islands, French Frigate, and we picked them all up with seaplane tenders, but we got them all there one way or another and had this exercise. They did the scouting from Midway. It was the first time that an exercise had been held out there in modern history because the Navy left there in 1912.

Q: The first time we realized that the island had any —

Adm. P.: Had any strategic or tactical significance. This was before anything was built. We set up a tent camp on the beach and had a small seaplane tender inside which acted as a logistics ship. We were there for about ten days. The objective of the enemy force was to get in and take Midway, and it was our job to scout and report so that the carrier planes could get after the enemy force coming in.

It was a fine exercise and that was the first one, as I say, that was held —

Q: Was there any similarity between the action at that time and the action with the Japanese some time later?

Adm. P.: Well, they were trying to do the same thing, but at the time the Japs came in we had a base at Midway and had land planes and some defensive forces. We had none at that time, in 1935.

In 1935, then, I returned after that exercise and I was detached and ordered to the USS Raleigh, a cruiser that was the flagship of the destroyer force, Pacific. I was in the Raleigh a very short time when the senior aviator, Clark Lewis, who was a great friend of mine, had a heart attack and died and I became senior aviator in the Raleigh.

Q: How many planes did she carry?

Adm. P.: Two, and they were air catapults in those days. We got the SO-C seaplane at that time, which was the one that we had in the battleships and cruisers at the beginning of the war, and inducted them into

Pirie #2 - 63

the fleet.

This was an interesting period. I spent most of the time on the West Coast, but we had a fleet exercise in the spring that took us around to the Atlantic and I was detached in June of 1936 and reported to the Naval Academy -

Q: Was this something you were seeking, this assignment at the Naval Academy?

Adm. P.: I think Commander McFall, who was the head of the aviation detachment here and also the director of athletics, asked for me to come and I was the chief engineer and material officer of that squadron. We were then based in the Reina Mercedes the squadron for flying the midshipmen in the spring and fall and during the summer. I also worked in the athletic office with Commander McFall and tried to help him with public relations. We had no PIO in the athletic department at that time, so he had me acting in that capacity.

It was a very interesting tour and during that period I flew a great many of the midshipmen principally in the classes of 1938 and 1939 and we got to be great friends later.

Q: How many recruits did you make?

Adm. P.: We got a good many aviators recruited out of that group. As a matter of fact, two close friends and admirals now on the active list, Admiral Cousins and Admiral Bringle, were in the class of 1937 and I first met them at that time, as midshipmen.

I not only enjoyed the aviation relationship and flying the midshipmen and trying to get them interested in naval aviation, but I enjoyed the contact with the athletic department. It was during this period that initial steps were taken in trying to recruit athletes and our initial steps were taken to form the Naval Academy Foundation, which actually wasn't incorporated and formalized until the early 1940s. But we were working toward that end because we could see that we had to have some kind of an organization to get proper athletes to have a major athletic program here.

Q: Is this an idea that had its origin in your fertile brain?

Adm. P.: No, Rip Miller and Tom Hamilton, who were both here during that period, worked on this and the initial head of the foundation was H. McCoy Jones of the class of 1919, who was a civilian. I eventually relieved him in the early 1960s when he gave up as head of the foundation and I took over as president.

Q: What was the impetus for developing this outreach program?

Adm. P.: Any collegiate athletic program that was going to be on a major basis, playing the major teams in the Ivy League and in the Big Ten and in the South where we were principally involved, was going to have to get into the business of recruiting some athletes because you couldn't play with just the people who walked through the doors.

Q: Couldn't compete with Notre Dame that way!

Adm. P.: We couldn't compete, and so we had to get into the business of putting boys in prep school and making the program go. Now it's beginning to come to fruition.

Q: How did you make this idea tie in with the concept of training men for leadership and becoming naval officers?

Adm. P.: One of the most important parts of leadership is physical as well as mental and moral leadership, and you've got to have an athletic program to develop leadership qualities, and this was a part of that program. It's as much a part of any leadership program as mental and moral parts.

I don't think I've got much more to say. I made a great many friends during that period of several of the senior officers who were very kind to me in my later life in the Navy and who helped me a great deal.

Q: Were there any innovations in terms of public relations at this time?

Adm. P.: No, not particularly. We were only in the initial stages and all I did basically was to try to handle the press at the games and see that they were adequately taken care of and whatnot. That was about all we did. We just didn't have any large advertising of teams or anything of that kind. Our sole effort was to try to handle the press as best we could.

Q: Who was superintendent at that period?

Adm. P.: The superintendent was David Foot Sellers and I believe he was here during that whole period.

Q: Was he all for promoting these views in the area of athletics?

Adm. P.: Yes, I believe that he was. The real enthusiasts were then - Captain Griffin, who was the director of athletics, and Commander McFall.

Q: Going back once more to the aviation setup, wasn't that a fairly new thing at the Academy?

Adm. P.: We had had some aviation indoctrination training starting with my class, which is 1926, but we hadn't had adequate airplanes. We had patrol planes assigned here at the time -

Q: That was largely in the summertime?

Adm. P.: Yes. We flew in the spring and the fall somewhat, but then we took one class in the summer and devoted the whole summer to it, the second class, and we flew them on daily missions. We went down to Langley Field and visited the NACA and gave them a good ground school indoctrination. Starting the next year, which was about 1938, the year I left, they had a fleet squadron come up and do the training and that continued for several years - until the war started. In 1938 I was ordered to command the USS *Teal*, which was stationed on the West Coast but was spending a considerable amount of its time in Alaska.

I left in early June and I reported to the USS *Teal* in Sitk

Alaska, on the 15th of June 1938 and I relieved then - Lieutenant Cruise in command. I spent the remaining twenty months in command of that ship in Alaskan and Aleutian waters.

Q: What was her purpose in being there?

Adm. P.: Seaplane tender. This was a seaplane tender and we tended for squadrons that were mostly Seattle-based. The base at Sitka was just being constructed at that time. There was nothing yet at Kodiak. As a matter of fact, I took the initial survey party in to Kodiak in the summer of 1939 when the original surveys of Woman's Bay and a base for Kodiak were made.

I was there in the summer of 1938 when we tended a squadron from Seattle that came up and flew out to Kodiak and I took this plane guard out in the Gulf of Alaska. In the early fall I went down to, via Seattle, to Mare Island for overhaul. The ship hadn't been overhauled for about five years and we had an extensive overhaul. We got out shortly after the first of the year, in January, and went back by Seattle for a short period and then went back to Alaska for the winter.

Q: That must have been a rugged experience!

Adm. P.: Most of - all of the transits to and from Alaska from Seattle I made through the inside passage, and I originally took pilots who were great authorities on the inside passage and on shiphandling, Ray Farwell being the first one and O'Donnell the second one. During the latter stages I made a couple of the passages myself, but the weather was so bad, mostly fog, and the navigation aids were so few that it was better and more economical to take a pilot than it was to try to do it yourself, because it took so long doing it yourself. You had to stop and anchor in bad weather, if you could anchor. When I first took the Teal I had no modern navigation aids. I had a standard magnetic compass, a deep-sea sounding lead, and a radio direction finder that didn't work.

During my overhaul at Mare Island I got a deep-sea sounding apparatus and a gyrocompass and a radio direction finder that worked. From then on my navigation trials weren't as great. However, we had no radar in those days and the principal means of navigating the inside passage was to blow your whistle and get the distance that you were from the banks by the length of time it took the sound of the echo to return. I learned whistle navigation from Ray Farwell and O'Donnell during that period because we were in fog most of the time going to and from Alaska.

Q: The seaplanes weren't able to operate very much in wintertime, were they, up there?

Adm. P.: Yes. We had a squadron up there that whole winter. The weather in southeast Alaska is quite moderate. It isn't until you get over inland and get over the mountain ranges that you get into this freezing cold weather. We had sort of moderate weather. We'd get a week when we had snow on the ground and temperatures below freezing, but then we'd get a week when it would thaw and be moderate. It wasn't that bad. As a matter of fact, from a standpoint of fog there was less fog in the winter than there was in the summer, and there was less real heavy, steady rain. In the summer months in the Sitka area, southeast west particularly, it rains all the time and visibility is low and it's quite difficult operating.

Q: At that point in time, did you visualize the use of the Aleutians and Alaska and that area - ?

Adm. P.: Yes, that was what was being done. We had survey parties up there and several of these seaplane tenders took survey parties into the Aleutians. I never took a survey party out to Dutch Harbor or Adak, but the Gannett and several of her sister ships had. The Sandpiper, I believe, had taken survey parties out there and done the initial surveying in the Aleutian Islands.

Q: Was the Coast Guard in evidence when you were there? Were they assisting in any way?

Adm. P.: Yes. The Coast Guard was in evidence in southeast Alaska and out at Kodiak and in the Aleutians, but not on a permanent basis. They weren't permanently stationed up there. They were only there interim at that time.

As I said, I took the initial survey party in to Kodiak. The weather in Kodiak at the time I was in there in the summer, September of 1939, was vicious. They had three williwaws that blew up without warning and would blow up to 100 knots. They blew about half the time and the other half of the time you had dead calm, and you never knew when they were coming. I had a standard order with my crew to call me when the wind got to 25 knots. The first time that they called me in the middle of the night, I ran out just in time to see both whale boats and the motor launch break the moorings and lines and fly through the air. They went high and dry on the beach and we had to go and cut logs and roll them back down and get them in the water as soon as the wind abated. The weather was quite an experience in those days.

Q: How many hours does one of these things last?

Adm. P.: Oh, it would last twenty-four hours. We had planes up there that we were tending at that time. They kept one crewman on each plane at all times, but when they got any kind of a warning they'd get out and get on them. They had to keep these airplanes turning over in order to take some tension off the anchor cable and keep them from blowing ashore, but we didn't lose a plane during that time in all this weather.

Q: Was ice any factor at all in the winter?

Adm. P.: At altitude it was, but not on the surface. We weren't bothered by ice in the areas in which we were operating on the seacoast. It's surprising how moderate it is on the seacoast.

It was a very interesting experience. The shooting and fishing was really great in those days. We used to feed the crew with salmon and trout, ducks, and deer. We had a great time not only hunting them, but eating them.

Q: Were you required to report very clearly on weather conditions and temperatures and what-have-you to Washington? Were they taking interest in studying this whole area?

Adm. P.: Yes. They were just beginning to get good meteorological records up there, but no stations except Dutch Harbor were giving much if any reports, and it was quite difficult to get enough reporting to the west of the Alaskan coast to make a real estimate of when this weather was coming through. They now have much better reporting and can make a good estimate of when bad weather is coming.

Q: Did you carry a weather man on board the Teal?

Adm. P.: No. We had to do our own. There was no meteorologist of any kind at that time. I had three warrant officers, two bo'suns and one machinist, an engineer, and about fifty men in the crew.

There were no radio aids for flying west of Sitka, none at Kodiak and none out in the Aleutians, and so the flying was really hazardous in those days and we had to be very careful about when we launched and recovered airplanes.

Q: Did you have any spectacular experience during that period of time?

Adm. P.: Mostly bad weather, yes! The Gulf of Alaska was a frightful place when the wind blew so hard and I only had about six or seven men in my ship that could really take it. Everybody else went down when it got bad. So it was quite some experience and it vaccinated me from weather forever! I was never bothered by it much from then on.

Q: Were there any other units of the fleet up there at that time?

Adm. P.: We'd have other seaplane tenders that were based in San Francisco and Seattle come up occasionally, and we'd once in a while have our admiral come up in a cruiser or something on an inspection, something of that character, but there was no real - they were mostly familiarization and very little of that.

Q: Did you have any contact with the Japanese or the Russians?

Adm. P.: None. There was a Russian church in Sitka. Old Father Kashiveroff, who got to be a very great friend, was one of the oldest and it was one of the oldest churches in Alaska. We spent a good deal of time talking to him. They had a Russian church also in Kodiak and one at Dutch Harbor.

The principal industry, of course, in Sitka was fishing and all of the rest of the businesses revolved around fishing mostly. They had four or five University of Washington graduates who headed up the oil companies and the fisheries, and we made friends with them and spent a lot of time with them, both in summer and winter. There wasn't anything to do in the winter except play cards.

Q: You must have learned a lot of valuable lessons in the period in Alaska, lessons that you didn't want to repeat?

Adm. P.: There were great lessons on seamanship and navigation that were to stand me in good stead the rest of my time in the service, and my shiphandling, which were invaluable.

Pirie #2 - 73

In the fall of 1939 I was ordered to Bombing 5 in the Yorktown and I reported in in San Diego in October to Bombing 5, then commanded by Lieutenant Commander Ward Harrigan.

Q: She was operating in the Pacific?

Adm. P.: The Yorktown had just come to the Pacific that year. The Yorktown and Enterprise.

Q: Who was the skipper of the Yorktown?

Adm. P.: The skipper of the Yorktown at that time was McWhorter and he was relieved by Gunther. The squadrons were relatively new and were just beginning to do their extensive dive-bombing and gunnery training, and it was a very interesting period.

Q: Were there new-type planes on the Yorktown?

Adm. P.: They had BT-1s, the first monoplanes, dive bombers, and I spent about three months in that squadron and then was ordered to be executive officer of Scouting-5, which was in the same ship, commanded by Lieutenant Bob Hunter. We had a fleet exercise that took us out to Hawaii in the late spring, and when we got out there they decided to relieve the fleet and, without warning, we were left in Hawaii and did three or four months' training in the Hawaiian area and I was detached --

Q: They based the fleet there, didn't they?

Adm. P.: Yes, they based the fleet out there in the summer of 1940.

Q: Why that sudden decision to base in there?

Adm. P.: I don't know, unless it was the difficulties going on out in the Far East.

Q: The political situation?

Adm. P.: Political. We did get a lot of excellent bombing and gunnery training in at that time. My squadron commander was relieved - Bob Hunter was relieved by Curtis Smiley in June or July, and in late September I was detached and ordered to Naval Air Station, Miami, which we were putting in commission to train carrier pilots.

Q: Before you tell me about that, let me ask, since you were with a scouting squadron, how far afield did you range? Did you have any observation missions and that kind of thing?

Adm. P.: We made the longest flights away from the carrier — up to that time it had been in the area of 100 miles or 150 and we started going 200 miles in those days, which was a pretty good piece for carrier airplanes of that vintage. They were fairly long flights. We also had some interesting exercises in antisubmarine warfare, which were the first ones that I'd ever done from a carrier. They took a destroyer division of four ships and the carrier and put it in a square 100 miles on the sides with two or three submarines and we exercised in detecting and the simulated sinking of the submarines. It was the first time that we had done such a joint exercise from the carrier with surface ships.

Q: One judges then that the role of the carrier was changing considerably, was it not? I mean the concept of the use of the carrier?

Adm. P.: Of course, they were all new. This was all new at the time, and we knew we'd have to protect ourselves against submarines so this was just an exercise. Later we had anti-submarine warfare carriers that did nothing but work on this, but this was in the initial stages of the carrier and it was all experimental.

We also had the old Utah converted to a target ship and we bombed her quite a bit with water-filled bombs in those days, besides having practice on fixed targets. We actually dropped on her. They'd armored the deck so she could take all the -

Q: Were you using any kind of bomb sights?

Adm. P.: We were dive bombing and it was all done without sights.

Q: Did the fleet have any bomb sights at that time? The Norden sight hadn't come in yet, had it?

Adm. P.: Yes, the Norden sight was in being at that time in the patrol planes for high-altitude bombing, but we didn't use it for dive bombing.

During this period I was fortunate to have an opportunity to train a couple of those great pilots of World War II. I had as my wing man in Scouting-5 Stanley Vejtasa and Fritz Falkner. Vejtasa became quite famous for shooting down seven Japanese airplanes in one flight, and Falkner had quite a great war record too. We had the time and the opportunity to teach these young fellows how to shoot and it paid great dividends.

Q: So it was advantageous to have the fleet suddenly based in Hawaii?

Adm. P.: It was. We had the time to do a lot of things that we might not have gotten done on the West Coast. It was a very interesting period and I enjoyed getting back into the carriers again. It was real sad to have to leave but I preferred going to Miami to train the carrier pilots than going to command a naval reserve air station.

Q: And it was a stepped up program, wasn't it?

Adm. P.: It was a new program, and we took - I reported in at Miami in October and we started training in November. We moved what was the advanced training squadron from Pensacola to Miami and we flew out of tents, some temporary tents and so forth, until we got our principal hangars and parking areas completed in January or February of 1941.

This was a very interesting period in training these carrier pilots in Miami. We had the fleet airplanes that had been cast off principally, the older obsolete carrier aircraft, as our principal training aircraft, but later in the period got many SNJs and other aircraft to supplement these obsolete carrier planes.

Q: How many pilots were you training at a time?

Adm. P.: During the period that I was there from October 1940 til

Pirie #2 - 77

I left in September 1942 we trained 2,500 Marine and Navy carrier pilots. We had the individuals for about two months and it was principally gunner, dive bombing, and navigation training. We had a landing and take off at Opa-Locka every twenty-six seconds from seven o'clock in the morning till one in the morning. We had on board at any one time I would say 300, maybe 200. It was a very interesting period because we had the time and good instructors to really teach these boys how to shoot and dive bomb, and they were the backbone of the Navy and Marine Corps in the fighter and bombing squadrons during the war.

Q: Where did these fellows hail from?

Adm. P.: They came from all over the country. We had cadets from the cadet program and we had some regular naval officers, a few of them, and some reserve officers, but they were principally aviation cadets, both Marine and Navy.

Commencing sometime in the spring of 1941 we took Royal Navy reserve trainees because the regular training establishment that the British had was over crowded and they couldn't do very much training in the British Isles because of the war, so they farmed it out and we trained RNVRs in quite some numbers for the rest of the time that I was there.

Q: The Royal Navy carrier was somewhat different from ours. Was there any difference in training techniques?

Adm. P.: No, not basically. The carriers were about the same. They had the same kind of landing gear.

Q: Weren't they smaller?

Adm. P.: No. The Illustrious and the Formidable, their principal carriers, were about the same size as our Yorktown and Enterprise. They were quite substantial ships. The Royal Navy liaison officer who first reported to us was Lieutenant Commander Charles Evans, who had quite an illustrious career in the Mediterranean as a squadron commander and was very much decorated when he came to us at Miami.

My skipper at Naval Air Station, Miami, was Commander Gerald F. Bogan. He was promoted to captain during the period that we were there.

Q: Tell me a little about him.

Adm. P.: Well I'd been in a squadron in the Lexington with him, Fighting-3, and then I was in the test section - the second year I was in the test section he was head of it. So I knew him quite well. He also had been in the Yorktown as executive officer when I was in the squadron on the Yorktown. He was a great pilot and a great fighter. I'll have more to say about him because I served with him a good bit of the time during the war.

Q: Were there any specially new techniques being employed in Miami at this point? Were there any lessons being learned from the European battlefields being applied?

Adm. P.: Our fighter tactics and methods were all taking advantage of what we could get from the British, but their contacts had been with the Germans and after we got into the war our principal fighting was with the Japanese. I was operations officer initially when I went to Miami and after I'd been there about three months I was ordered as superintendent of training, and had responsibility for the training of all these reserve pilots.

Q: How extensive was night training as a part of the whole program?

Adm. P.: We did a good deal of night flying, both basic night formation flying and getting them used to night navigation and getting the pilot generally attuned to night - to being up at night. We didn't do carrier qualification as such and had to depend on them getting their carrier qualification after they got to sea.

Q: How extensive was our knowledge at that time of Japanese night techniques?

Adm. P.: It was pretty meager. As a matter of fact, one of the great criticisms that we had later of the intelligence system was that we had an assistant attache, Lieutenant Commander Frank Bridget, who had been giving good reports on the capabilities of the Japanese and very little of it was getting to the troops in the field. We had a meager knowledge of their capabilities and just how good they were.

Q: You mean you couldn't pry this loose from Intelligence in Washington?

Adm. P.: I don't know where the bottleneck was, but there was a considerable bottleneck between what was being reported by him and what was actually getting to the people in the field. This was confirmed after the war by his wife who was with him and knew what he was doing and what he was reporting in most cases. He was captured on Bataan and made a prisoner and lost his life at the end of the war as a prisoner of the Japs.

Q: Admiral, this was I believe before the advent of the jeep carrier used in antisubmarine and convoying and so forth, but was there any anticipation in the training program of this sort of thing, and the need for flying at night in order to observe at dawn and dusk the German submarines in the Atlantic?

Adm. P.: No, I don't believe so. The small-carrier concept hadn't yet germinated and we didn't have any at that time. We had, of course, just gotten the Ranger and the Wasp. I don't believe that the first Hornet had yet been commissioned. The carrier building program for the Essex-type carriers hadn't started, and none of these small-carrier conversions had taken place. The first small-carrier conversions were tankers, the Sangamon and the Santee class were the first ones and they were taken on the North African invasion and then later went to the Pacific. Then they started the conversion of the merchant ships, which took place mostly up in Tacoma in the beginning. And then what we called the Kaiser coffins were all built in Oregon and we commissioned those at Astoria.

During this period the war started and we had a lot of ship sinkings, tankers particularly, going on in the Gulf Stream, right off

Pirie #2 - 81

the Miami and Palm Beach coast, and as a result had to do something to assist in trying to observe and looking for the German submarines in the area to try to protect our shipping. We were ill equipped to do that because we didn't have the aircraft that lent themselves to this nor the techniques nor were the pilots trained. We did get depth charges and put them on the scouting and bombing planes and our pilots took turns - after doing a great many instruction hours, they would go out and fly at night, in dusk and dawn, out there trying to help protect against the submarines. We had some real great sinkings in that area. Most of the tankers were huge fires and very sad sights to see.

We then got a group of Air Force aircraft that were ordered down to assist in antisubmarine warfare, and they were completely inexperienced. We had to teach them what little we could about anti-submarine warfare, what to look for, and how to go about it. These were Lockheed aircraft, twin engine, with a very bad ground handling characteristic, and one of the distressing things that happened early in their period with us, an aircraft crew came in and they had five 300- or 400-pound depth charges on board and they ground looped in the middle of the runway and the aircraft caught on fire. The crew all got out but they left the aircraft in the middle of the runway and the depth charges went off and blew a lake in the middle of our runway where we were trying to have a landing and take-off every twenty seconds. It put us out of commission for a couple of days while we got that hole filled in - at least on half of our field. We had one half dedicated to landing and one to take-off, so we had to revise our operations for that period. But it was a hole about - about 200 feet in diameter and about 50 or 60 feet deep right in the middle of this runway!

Q: At least you knew the depth charges worked!

Adm. P.: They all worked!

Q: In retrospect, did you notice any spurt in the effectiveness of the training as a result of sending these pilots out on actual missions against the German submarines?

Adm. P.: No. Of course, this was just sort of a fringe effort and outside of the fact that a submarine could see an aircraft up there I don't think that the effort did much good. And the pilots, of course, were all pretty tired of it because they were flying a hundred or so hours a month in training and this was extra work, so to speak, and so they didn't take too much liking to it.

We had all the administrative people that we could muster go out and take a couple of hours of this kind of flying. I took several flights myself and saw several of the ships hit out there by submarines and burning, and it was a pretty sad sight.

Q: Was there any new element added to your training in the light of the experience we were having with the Murmansk convoys and contact with the Germans there and so forth?

Adm. P.: There was not much in the way of carrier aircraft that got into that. Most of those aircraft that were trying to assist up there were land-based seaplanes and the carriers didn't get into that convoy protection role.

Q: What was the casualty incidence training under these circumstances?

Adm. P.: Our casualties were remarkably light in the period of training down there. We did have a good many in the early days because we didn't have shoulder harness, and we had a good many casualties due to bad landings or spinning into the ground while landing or taking off. They would have head injuries from their head going forward and hitting an instrument panel or something. We worked very hard to get shoulder harness, which we built ourselves initially. The British had some shoulder harness at the time but they didn't have excess to give to us and we weren't geared up to manufacturing it through our supply system, so we built our own and we saved many a life and many people from bad injury because we put the shoulder harness in those aircraft in, I'd say, the summer of 1941. From then on we didn't have any of these serious injuries from bad landings or low-altitude spins.

The casualty rates among the RNVRs were a great deal higher than our boys, but it was principally because their manpower was not as good as ours at that time. But you've got to realize that they'd been in a three- or four-year war by that time and their manpower was pretty well depleted and these weren't the best physical specimens.

Q: Their pilots were going into the RAF. Once your men completed the course at Miami, what sort of assignments did they get?

Adm. P.: They all went right to carrier squadrons. The Marines, of course, were formed into the Marine air groups and the ones that fought the first part of the war got into - well, we had a Marine squadron in the <u>Yorktown</u> in 1940 that I got very friendly with. It was commanded by Major Vern McGee and he's still living, but that squadron was the squadron that was on Wake Island when the Japs took it, and most of them lost their lives. I think there are a few of them still left.

The Navy pilots all went to fighter and scouting and bomber squadrons, and they were in our carriers at the beginning of the war.

Q: A job like this must have given you a great sense of satisfaction that you were doing something that was tremendously valuable in the war effort?

Adm. P.: Yes, it did and it was very interesting and a busy time. We worked hard and, as I said, we got 2,500 out by the time I left in September 1942, and they were all well trained and were fine individuals. A great many of them today come up to and say, "You signed my flight designation." And I did sign a good many of them.

Some of the personalities that were instructors in that group at Miami were "Jumping Joe" Clifton who had been a great football player for Navy, Bagdanovich, a Marine named "Fish" Salmon. Some of the more distinguished students that we had down there who completed their training at Miami who now come to mind are Paul Thayer, who is now the chief executive officer, I think chairman of the board, of LTV Corporation. He had a distinguished career during the war.

There were a good many of the obsolete aircraft that we had

that were being given to our allies to beef up their air forces before we got into the fighting. In order to conserve the instructors we used student pilots to do the ferrying. We had some pretty interesting flights with them.

Q: What was the ferrying route?

Adm. P.: Going back and forth to the West Coast or to New York where we took some of these aircraft that were going to Greece. The aircraft were not as well equipped for weather flying as they are now. We were going in some fairly unseasonable weather and we had some problems with these young neophytes, but we had to use them to keep from using the regular instructors.

Q: When they were ferried to New York, then they were put on board ships?

Adm. P.: Yes, they'd put them on board freighters and take them to Europe, and we'd have to get back usually by train. There were no commercial airlines in those days.

Q: Wasn't there some attempt to fly them across by different routes, places way up in Greenland? Bluie East or somewhere?

Adm. P.: Oh, they had that late in the war, quite late, after we got in the war. They got those two or three fields up there and they flew fighters across. The Air Force flew quite a few, but no in those earlier days.

Pirie #2 - 86

Q: How closely did Washington, the Department, maintain contact with the development of the training program?

Adm. P.: Very. We were in close liaison with the training division of the Bureau of Aeronautics, and we maintained a close liaison with Pensacola, where the basic training was being done and where we were getting the product. We were well coordinated with them. It was about this time that they opened up Corpus Christi, and they took over some of the advanced training late in my time at Miami.

Q: Was there any attempt to keep abreast of the new models that were being tested and so forth? These men were being assigned directly to carriers where some of these new planes would be placed. Was there any attempt to coordinate the two?

Adm. P.: We didn't have any of the new ones, but, of course, the F-4-F had just got into service. At the very beginning of the war we had Brewster Buffalos, which were transferred to us when the F-4-Fs began to come in and the SB D was the principal dive-bombing and scouting plane at that time. And then they had the Douglas Torpedo plane. So they had the transition when they got to their squadron and they had operational training units that they set up to transition people into the airplanes, but they didn't have too great difficulty transitioning into those aircraft at that time. It wasn't until sometime later that we got the F-6-F, the real fighter that did most of our fighting during the war.

Q: You were there when Pearl Harbor happened?

Adm. P.: Yes.

Q: Was there any noticeable change in things at that point?

Adm. P.: We were going just as fast as we could go, we couldn't do any more than we were doing, but we did take over some other fields and we got an acceleration in the building of the outlying fields and we got more help, more reserve officers came on active duty and we got a good deal more assistance and more instructors so that we were able to do our job somewhat better. But we couldn't fly any more in actual hours than we had been flying at the time.

The logistic problems connected with this kind of an operation were rather staggering to the establishment. It was hard to visualize. I remember hearing President Roosevelt on radio say something about that we were going to have an air force of 50,000 airplanes and that number so staggered the imagination that hardly anyone could believe it. It was the same way with the regular supplies system and the logistics system that we had at the time. They weren't geared to handle the kind of an operation we were getting into. It was hard to get anyone to believe that it was going to get as big as it was going to get. We had to go out and salvage spare parts from all the other air stations, and I just used to take an old chief and give him a truck and tell him to go to San Diego or Norfolk and go into the Supply Department, which we had authorization to do, and get these parts off the shelf and bring them back, because if we tried to do this by the old system we were used to the war would be over before we ever got the parts there. I never will forget telling the supply officer he'd better get some tanker trucks to handle oil, lubricating oil. He couldn't believe this. He'd been dealing in 50-gallon drums, and I told him he'd have a stack of 50-gallon drums that would make the pyramids look sick in the middle of that field and that he'd better get some tank trucks because we would be using that much oil. He couldn't believe it. And the only time we'd let him bring his tank trucks down to our operating line was between one o'clock in the morning and seven in the morning. He also couldn't believe that - that he was going to have to do this loading in the middle of the night. There were all sorts of things.

I'll talk about logistics at Pearl Harbor and some of these other places later. It was difficult to get the system geared up to do the great volume and gigantic number of things that were going to happen.

Q: Some of you, obviously, had the vision and the initiative that was necessary. How did it come about?

Adm. P.: We knew it was coming but it was difficult to get people geared up to do it or think about it. I got to Pearl Harbor right after this with Admiral Towers and they didn't have but one dock and it would only take a small ship, at Pearl Harbor where we were going to have to take all these damned carriers and do all the logistics, loading and so forth. Nothing. We survived some way.

During this period training simulators were inducted into

the system because we were trying to do as much training as we could without the actual use of the airplanes, the Link trainer being a big example. The Link trainer was in existence before this but we expanded the use of the Link trainer a great deal. We got a good many more of them. Every kind of training device was put to use, and Admiral de Flores who headed up the synthetic training device division in the Bureau visited us many times, and we started innovating bombing simulators and gunnery simulators and navigation simulators to do as much training on the ground as possible to keep from using the few airplanes that we had then.

Q: Louis de Flores was a pretty imaginative fellow, wasn't he?

Adm. P.: He was a wonderful man. I got to know him very well and we became very close personal friends during this period and he was a lifelong friend. A great man and he was reponsible for the training devices center that we now have at Orlando. He was the originator of that whole concept.

A great deal of the training that we do today on the ground in simulators to keep from using very expensive aircraft in the air -- in other words, an aircraft costs 15 million dollars and it costs many thousands of dollars an hour to fly, and the more you can do on the ground the more economical it is to train an individual, whether he's a pilot or a navigator-bombardier -

Q: And the end result is the same!

Adm. P.: And the end result's the same. Our training of the mechanics and the individuals who take care of the aircraft, by the same token, it's a lot better to have simulators to train them than it is to have an active airplane that you have to take apart and put back together again each time when you're trying to teach them what the systems are. This is very sophisticated today and we have these kinds of flying simulators that are in trailer trucks that we use at all of our centers to train pilots. You could fly a whole mission in a simulator, thereby doing ninety percent of the training on the ground and ten percent in the air.

Q: Did you have any emotional crack-ups among these boys? I mean as a result of the constant pressure, the almost overflying?

Adm. P.: In any flight-training program you always have a few individuals who are not capable of simulating the training, of taking it, and that come a cropper for one reason or another.

Q: A medical check was kept on them?

Adm. P.: We had good checks with our doctors and, as superintendent of training, I had a board which sat on each case and when a student was brought up that they didn't recommend for continuing, and we gave a thorough study of each one of these cases because it was important to us to get as many through as we could. We had good medical advice and I don't think during this period lost too many, but you were bound to have a few that went by the boards for one reason or another.

Q: How did it balance out? The number of pilots you were training and turning out and the number of carriers that were being built?

Adm. P.: We were ahead of the game at that time because we were getting an excess before the carrier building program got up, but then we, of course, later --

Q: It's easier to train a man than to build a carrier!

Adm. P.: Yes, and we were building a tremendous number of these satellite bases which took over later on. We were turning these pilots out in huge numbers, as you know, after we got into the second and third year of the war. And we got a large number of these small jeep carriers and we had to have a lead.

Q: Did you have any other foreign nationalities, other than the Royal Navy people?

Adm. P.: Not as students.

In the summer of 1942, after the war had started, my commanding officer, Captain Bogan, was informed that he'd be ordered to command the Saratoga. He sent for me and asked me whether I'd like to go to the Saratoga with him about the first of October. I told him I'd like very much to go, that I'd prefer to go as an air group commander and fly, but that if I couldn't go flying I'd like to be air officer and navigator. He told me that he would ask for me and it was tentatively arranged that I would go with him to the Saratoga. He was detached about the first of October and at about the same time as he was detached I received detach orders to report to Admiral Towers in San Francisco on a certain date, which I believe was about the 10th of October -

Q: And that took priority over Bogan?

Adm. P.: Yes. - as an assistant operations officer on the Commander, Air Force Pacific, staff, and that I was to meet Admiral Towers in San Francisco and proceed with him to Pearl Harbor. Air transportation was at a premium in those days and I had to ride a train from Miami to San Francisco. I joined Admiral Towers there and we flew out. Admiral Towers and his aide, Lee Loomis, flew in a Boeing seaplane to Pearl and arrived I believe on the 15th of October 1942.

Our predecessor as Commander, Air Force Pacific, had been Admiral Halsey, who had been ordered to relieve Admiral Ghormley at Noumea. At this time the Guadalcanal campaign was in its most intensive stage. The logistics were of rather staggering proportions because we had so little to do such a lot. I was the only operations officer with Admiral Towers at the time we took over and had the job of handling both the carrier aircraft and the patrol planes' logistics. I must say they were in horrible shape at that time. We, for example, only had one small dock at Pearl Harbor and no plans to build any more. There were not enough aircraft and we were getting constant pleas for additional aircraft from the carriers and from the land-based units in Guadalcanal, particularly the Marines.

It was shortly after we got out there that the Wasp was sunk in the area, and Captain Sherman, who was the commanding officer of the

Wasp, and two of his officers were ordered to the staff. Captain Sherman was ordered as chief of staff and Captain Soucek and Commander Beakley were ordered as operations officer and assistant operations officer, respectively.

Q: Which Soucek was that?

Adm. P.: Apollo. He had been the exec of the Wasp and Beakley was the air officer.

In November, after they reported, Admiral Towers sent Captain Pennoyer, who was EDO officer on the staff, and myself down to the Solomons not only to get first-hand information on the situation as it existed down there, but to try to use every method we could to get the forces in the field to salvage as many aircraft by cannibalizing one aircraft and building another, and thus tide us over until we could get production aircraft flowing out to them.

Q: I take it this was not a general practice up to that point?

Adm. P.: All they'd been doing was screaming for aircraft and not paying too much attention to cannibalizing and making the most of what they had, because there were no more. I mean, until we got production lines going, they had the aircraft that we were going to have to fight with. So if you had three aircraft on the field, one with a blown tire off the runway and a couple of them shot up or something, you could cannibalize, tow them over into the bushes, put a tent over them, and build an aircraft out of the three that were damaged -- or the two that were damaged - and it was absolutely essential that something be done about this because we were just about to run out.

Q: It seems to me that this is the sort of thing that enterprising Americans would do anyway under the circumstances?

Adm. P.: Well, it was a pretty tough go down there, I'll tell you. They were working under some of the worst conditions you ever saw in your life. It rained, mosquitoes, bugs, terrible, and all the time being under attack, Japanese battleships throwing 14-inch shells in to the field all the time. It was really bad. But let me relate a few things connected with this trip.

On the way down -

Q: How did you go?

Adm. P.: We went in a four-engine seaplane that was being delivered to Admiral Halsey as his personal plane, and it was flown by Lieutenant Commander McCants, who was an ex CAP and whom I knew quite well. I was then a Commander, and Captain Pennoyer and I got in the airplane with McCants and we had no other passengers, just his crew, and started for Noumea. That was our first stop. We stopped to gas at Canton and at Suva in the Fijis, and as we were coming in to Suva I was sitting in the right-hand pilot's seat, flying at about 8,000 feet, and McCants was taking a rest, and I thought I saw something shining. I thought it was a mirror or something shining on the ground, and I got to looking closer, and there was a British battery down there in the islands firing at us! These damned tracers were going by the tail. They were poor shots fortunately, but this seaplane was the first one that they'd seen of our PB-4Y seaplanes and they looked just exactly like the Jap big four-engined seaplane.

I got hold of McCants right away and we got out of there and got away from them and got into Suva.

Q: You didn't attempt to communicate?

Adm. P.: We couldn't communicate. We didn't have any recognition signals or anything. We let the British know so that they could tell their friends they'd better get some recognition capability.

We then flew from there to Noumea and one of the things that Admiral Towers asked me to do was to go into the NATS terminal, Navy Air Transport terminal, and see what they were carrying down in NATS pipeline in the way of spare parts. We were getting a lot of complaints that they weren't getting parts. So I went into the NATS terminal and there was a JG there and I said, "What are in those crates? And he said, "Mimeograph paper." I said "Mimeograph paper! Do you mean to tell me that they're carrying mimeograph paper down here when we need spare parts so bad." He said, yes - "Admiral Turner is down at Guadalcanal and he's got to write operations orders and we've got to get mimeograph paper for him."

When I got back to Pearl Harbor and told Admiral Towers this he almost went crazy, but this is all there was in this terminal. Anyhow we got that straightened out a little later.

Pennoyer and I then flew up to Espiritu Santo and our first attempt to get up to Guadalcanal was in an Air Force airplane and it ended in our getting lost and my having to bring them back in to Espiritu after about nine hours with practically no gasoline left. It was fortunate that we knew a little bit about the code words and hieroglyphics or we'd have never gotten back. We were going right out into the great big blue Pacific, 150 miles north of Espiritu, and I got this guy turned around and headed south, and we got some direction-finding signals. They wouldn't send out direction-finding signals so we could get home. We got back finally and we went out the next day - next night - in a Marine airplane. General Woods was the Marine aviator commander on the island and he was the one that we dealt with principally, although Vandergrift was in command of the whole operation. But we dealt with Woods and talked to his engineers and people and to the squadron commanders and told them how important it was to salvage as many of these airplanes as we could because there just weren't going to be any more airplanes, no matter what you said there was nothing anybody could do about it, even the Almighty, at that time. So they just had to salvage as many as they could. They went to work right away and did a better job of salvaging the airplanes and we got a lot of use out of those that looked like they were wrecked.

Q: The Seabees were already at Espiritu, weren't they, building runways and the like?

Adm. P.: Oh, yes, they built those. There were three strips already built at Espiritu, and, of course, this one field at Guadalcanal, Henderson, was all we had at the time and it was hotter than a firecracker.

Q: Tulagi wasn't built yet?

Adm. P.: Yes, Tulagi was built. One of these big night actions took place just the night before we got in there and they had sunken ships and damaged ships and a hell of a mess in there. I think it was Savo where a couple of cruisers had been sunk and a couple more of them were damaged and taken over to Tulagi, and several destroyers had been messed up in this thing.

I went up to the front lines with then-Colonel Cooley and Colonel Snedeker, a classmate of mine. We went up and visited Louis Puller while we were up there, and he'd just had that big night action where he killed several thousand Japs in that valley the night before. It was quite an exciting time for us, you know, getting to see this close to the action. Puller was out in the sun. He only had a sergeant with him in this dugout in the side of the hill and he had on a pair of fatigue pants and was barefooted. That's all he had on and he had four or five bullet holes that I could count in his torso and he had some more in his legs. He wouldn't even go back to a dressing station. They were these little things that the Japs were firing. They were about the size of a beebee or a .22 - I've forgotten what caliber it was. He didn't pay a damned bit of attention to them at all.

Q: You'd think he'd be bleeding.

Adm. P.: No, he just put some iodine on them, I think. I don't know, but he was a character, a great man.

Q: Chesty Puller!

Adm. P.: This was a great experience for us to go down there and see the war at first hand. We saw quite a bit of the action. We were there two or three days and then returned to talk to Admiral Fitch at Espiritu Santo about these logistic problems, then back by Noumea, and we flew back on a MATS aircraft which were then Martin twin-engine seaplanes. We got back on the 6th or 7th of December.

Interview No. 3 with Vice Admiral Robert Burns Pirie, U.S. Navy (Retired)

Place: The U.S. Naval Institute, Annapolis, Maryland

Date: Friday morning, 11 May 1973

Subject: Biography

By: John T. Mason, Jr.

Q: It's certainly good to see you in blooming health, Sir. I have for some time been looking forward to a continuation of this fascinating story. Last time, when we broke off, you had just departed from Guadalcanal, having made a very hasty trip there with Captain Penoyer at the behest of Admiral Towers and were on your way back to Pearl Harbor. You stopped at Espiritu Santo to talk with Admiral Fitch. Do you want to say something about that? You were talking about logistics.

Adm. P.: Captain Penoyer and I spent some 48 hours with Admiral Fitch and his staff at Espiritu Santo discussing the logistic situation and the problems we had at that stage of the game.

Q: They were pretty serious ones, weren't they?

Adm. P.: They were very serious, as related particularly to aircraft and aircraft spares. The aircraft industry at that time was not yet in full gear, and we were forced to make do with what we had and to try to improvise and cannibalize aircraft in the front line particularly at

Guadalcanal because there were no replacements in sight for a period of six months.

Q: FDR's goal of 50,000 planes was far off in the future, wasn't it?

Adm. P.: It was in the future at that time. We did not yet have the F-6F and the fighter planes that were being used at the time were principally F-4Fs. The Patrol planes that we had were pretty well worn out and the crews at that time had been down since the beginning of the war. Most of those who got out of the Philippines were still in the Solomons Islands area doing patrols. We hadn't yet been able to get aircraft and crews trained to replace them. This was all discussed with Admiral Fitch and his staff and we told them what time schedule they could expect to get replacements and get some relief in the situation. We also discussed with him the necessity for carefully monitoring what we were hauling by air in the Naval Air Transport line that we had coming down to the Pacific, which was pretty thin at that time.

Q: This was your experience with the mimeograph paper?

Adm. P.: Yes, and we would try to monitor it at the Pearl Harbor end and ask them to be sure that they didn't order any non-essential items to be transported by air from the continental U.S. down to the South Pacific. We tried to get a hand on exactly what was being transported by air.

At the end of that visit we returned to Pearl Harbor and made our report to Admiral Towers and intensified our efforts to accelerate crew training and the relief of some of those squadron personnel and aircraft that had been in the South Pacific far too long.

Q: What was the situation in Pearl itself, the facilities there? Were they rapidly improving?

Adm. P.: At that time we didn't have one dock that could take a large aircraft carrier. The only dock we had was alongside the administration building and supply department, and it would only take a small jeep carrier or a seaplane tender. We got the construction of adequate dock facilities started at that time.

It was a period in which we were having to make do with what we had. About six months later things began to flow in a more orderly fashion and we were getting the necessary aircraft and aircraft spare parts to relieve the situation.

Q: I suppose the policy had been made very clear, however, to the command in Pearl Harbor that first priorities were Europe?

Adm. P.: That was part of our problem, because they were getting ready for the invasion of North Africa and that did take a large percentage of what we had and the fighting in Guadalcanal and the Solomons was pretty much on a shoestring.

During the next three or four months we worked hard to get the situation in hand. Early in March Admiral Towers sent for me and told me that they were being pressed to release some of the regular senior officers on the staff to take combatant ship and aircraft jobs and replace them with Reserve officers and that I was the only commander or captain on the staff who hadn't swum away from a sunken aircraft carrier and he was going to give me an opportunity! They wanted to send me as executive officer of a carrier, and I got orders to report to the USS Baffin's commissioning detail at Tacoma, Washington, and I arrived there about the 1st of April and reported to Captain William L. Rees, who was her prospective commanding officer.

Q: These were for the jeep carriers, were they?

Adm. P.: This was one of the converted C-2 hulls, and we spent the next three months getting that crew in shape and getting ready to go aboard. We got on board about the middle of June.

Q: Where was this? In Tacoma?

Adm. P.: In Tacoma. We actually got on and took her to Bremerton for the last two weeks of outfitting. The night before we were to go in commission, which was the 1st of July, we got orders to turn the ship over to the British. In was the first of some ten small carriers turned over to the Royal Navy. It was quite a disappointment to us that instead of commissioning the ship we took it to Vancouver and turned it over to the Royal Navy.

Q: Did they have a ready crew for her?

Adm. P.: They got a crew there later. They weren't all there right at the time. They had a nucleus. But we took our old crew off and marched them down to a train and we departed for Astoria, Oregon, where we had orders to put the fifth of the Kaiser small carriers in commission, the USS Mission Bay. We spent another three months getting that ship's crew trained to take this type carrier. We got on board, my recollection is, about the 1st of October and went in commission and set out with the Guadalcanal, which was the sixth ship, under the command of Captain Dan Gallery. The two of us set out for San Diego for training.

Q: You knew you were destined for the Atlantic, did you?

Adm. P.: Well, we were told at that time we were destined for the Atlantic and we were to get our training with an air group to get the flight deck ready - the air department ready - at San Diego. So we spent about a month to six weeks. About the 1st of December we departed with the Guadalcanal for the East Coast via the Panama Canal.

Q: Did you have any qualms about going into the Atlantic and deserting the war in the Pacific at that point?

Adm. P.: We weren't very happy. We would have preferred to stay in the Pacific and get into the war in that area, rather than going into the Atlantic.

Q: But you had an intimate knowledge of what the problem was in the Atlantic when you were in Miami, didn't you? I mean the pressing need for -

Adm. P.: Yes, for escorts for convoys and fighting the submarine war.

Our small carriers at that time really were just getting some real control and sinking a good many submarines, and improving their worth in that antisubmarine war.

We arrived in Norfolk about the middle of December –

Q: May I ask you to lap back because you've passed over a very interesting incident, it seems to me, the war games, the attack on the Panama Canal as you went down?

Adm. P.: We didn't have an air group on board. We had no airplanes at that time. We were to get our air group on the East Coast.

As I say, we arrived about the 15th of December and we got orders to be ready to depart to shadow a large convoy on the 25th of December, Christmas Day. Actually, on Christmas Day the wind was blowing so hard at Norfolk that they couldn't get us away from the dock and we actually sailed on the 26th of December. What I mean by shadowing is staying in the general vicinity of the convoy to give it antisubmarine protection. This was a very large convoy of about 200 ships.

Q: Going to the UK?

Adm. P.: Going to the UK. A part of them going into the Med and Casablanca and a few of them breaking off to go up to the UK. There were a good many ammunition ships and tankers, and there were several small LCIs which had a real rough passage and they were stragglers a good deal of the time.

Pirie #3 - 105

We didn't encounter any German submarines on that passage and there were no submarine attacks on that convoy. All of them arrived safely at their destinations in either North Africa or the UK.

Q: What sort of a complement of planes had you acquired by that time?

Adm. P.: The squadron that we had on board consisted of 12 fighter aircraft, F-4Fs and 9 attack aircraft, TBMs for carrying depth charges. The squadron that we got had had one very successful cruise on one of the earlier small carriers and had sunk five or six German submarines during one passage to Europe and back shadowing convoys.

Q: So they were experienced?

Adm. P.: They were very experienced and very good. It was under the command of then Commander Avery.

Well, as I say, we didn't encounter any and we got in to Casablanca about the 15th of January. We were to spend four days getting some rest in Casablanca. We took on fuel the first day from a small gasoline tanker - a French tanker - and about noon we received orders to get ready to get under way as soon as we'd got our gasoline and go after a German submarine that they had spotted off the Portuguese coast.

We got this small French gasoline tanker in the early afternoon and completed fueling about 9:00 or 10:00 p.m., and about ten o'clock we got under way. About one quarter of the crew had had a chance to get their feet on shore for three or four hours, and that was the end of it. I remember distinctly getting under way that night, because the French pilot who came on board was drunk and the captain told me to take him down and put him in the boat, we'd take it out ourselves! It was a very black night.

We went up searching for this submarine off the Portuguese coast, never found it, and our escorts - six World War I type destroyers - we then went by the Azores and sent them in to get fuel, and headed back for our East Coast via Bermuda. It was one of the worst passages I've ever, the worst weather, I've ever seen.

Q: Mid-winter in the Atlantic!

Adm. P.: Oh, it blew 65 knots all the time, never a gap. The wind never stopped. It just went from southwest to northwest to southwest. It was right on our nose and those ships really were just like corks. You couldn't stay in the bunk. The motion on the ship would throw you out. In the middle of this passage we were just making barely steerageway, 5 knots, for a good part of this journey. We got out about halfway between the Azores and Bermuda and the captain sent for me in the middle of the night and said he'd just gotten a message that there was a German submarine within fifty miles of us. He wanted to know what I thought about launching, and I said, "Well, I don't know. You might launch them but I don't know how you'd ever get them back. It would be precarious just to catapult them." So he said, "Well, I'll wait till daylight."

At daylight I went up to the bridge. It didn't make much difference, daylight or dark. The weather was so bad that you had no visibility at all and the wind was blowing so hard that the spindrift was very heavy and you didn't have 100 yards' visibility.

Q: Didn't weather like that destroy the effectiveness of the enemy submarines, too?

Adm. P.: My philosophy was that if he had any sense at all, which he probably did - he was down 100 or 150 feet, getting away from that surface -

Q: It would be pretty hard for him to launch torpedoes under those circumstances?

Adm. P.: Well, he couldn't see and the sound apparatus on those ships at that time hadn't been perfected to the point where he could do it on the sound.

Along about ten o'clock in the morning the skipper said, "I'm going to launch," so we sounded flight quarters. Our procedure was that the first crew that got to the airplane on the catapult was the first one to go off and, to my great astonishment, they were fighting to get in this airplane. Even in that bad weather they were real gung-ho aviators, and they were sort of down in the mouth because they hadn't gotten a shot at a German submarine on this trip, while they'd had such a great success on the previous one.

Anyway, we launched four or five airplanes and four torpedo planes and they flew for about three hours with no success, then we had the job of recovering them. The ship would be in a level position both fore and aft, so that you could take an airplane on about five seconds out of every minute. The first fighter plane got on without an difficulty, and the second one was just in the landing area when the stern went down and he was in a stalled attitude and went down absolutely vertically, his wheels tore off, and buried this thing about 18 inches in the middle of the flight deck. We had to go out there and dig him out and get some steel plates over the deck --

Q: Was there fire attached to it?

Adm. P.: No, no fire. We just had to dig him out and that plane was gone. The wings were all damaged and everything. So we threw that airplane overboard, got the plate on the deck, and got the last six airplanes down on board without any great difficulty, to my amazement.

Q: Let me ask how the Mission Bay performed? They were purported to be sometimes in danger of cracking in two in bad weather, those Kaiser carriers.

Adm. P.: Well, we called them Kaiser "Coffins." We had many cracks in the hull. I can remember sitting during this period, on this passage in very heavy weather between the Azores and Bermuda, at the mess table in the wardroom and my chair was close to the bulkhead on the port side. I felt my feet getting wet and I looked down, and, sure enough, there was a big puddle of water. I said to the steward, "Why are you leaving this water?" He said, "We've mopped up the deck here. That's coming in from over there." I went over and, sure enough, there was a crack in the hull. We took the sheathing off and there was a big crack, ten feet long, in the hull and salt water was coming in through the side of the ship. We stopped those by drilling a hole at the end of the cracks so that the cracks wouldn't go any farther. We had several more in real cold weather. A little later on all the ships had this same experience.

Q: Did the knowledge of that cause any apprehension among the crew?

Adm. P.: Oh, they used to talk about it, but I don't think that any of them ever had a cracked keel. These cracks were all in and around the waterline or above. They used to pop the sides of the hangar and you heard these popping noises in rough weather.

We stopped and fueled those escorts at Bermuda and then went on up to Norfolk. When we got to Norfolk we didn't get inside. They gave us orders to go to New York and pick up fifty P-47s and take them to India. The Wake Island, another ship of this class, and ourselves loaded 150 P-47s each at Staten Island. We spent four days in New York. It was very cold, the middle of February, and we took off for India around Cape Horn.

Q: Where did you stash all these planes?

Adm. P.: On the flight deck. We had some in the hangar, but most of them were on the flight deck.

Q: Did you have any room for operational planes?

Adm. P.: No operations. This was dead deck. We had a destroyer escort down about the latitude of the Panama Canal, and from there on we didn't have an escort. We stopped at Recife, Brazil to fuel for one day, and then went to Capetown and fueled. We got an escort of two British destroyers as we approached Capetown because there were some raiders and submarine attacks going on in that area.

We stopped at Capetown to fuel and then those escorts took us up as far as Diego Suarez, on the north end of Madagascar, where we fueled again, and then went on in with another set of British escorts to Karachi.

Q: Part of the time you were pretty vulnerable, then?

Adm. P.: Yes. We went at full speed.

Q: What was your speed?

Adm. P.: Fifteen knots or sixteen knots.

Q: Any zigzagging?

Adm. P.: Yes, we zigzagged when we were in an area where we might expect submarines.

We stayed four days in Karachi, unloaded, and gave the crew some liberty, then started back with another set of escorts and we stopped at Durban for one day to fuel, then stopped in Bahai, Brazil, to fuel on the way back. We got back to Norfolk about the 8th of May. It took us exactly ninety days.

Q: And that was purely a transport job?

Adm. P.: A transport job. When we got to Norfolk I was detached. I'd

Pirie #3 - 111

gotten orders to report to Rear Admiral G. F. Bogan as his chief of staff, and was given four days to get from Norfolk to Pearl Harbor, and I hadn't seen my family for six months so I stopped by one day, I think, at San Diego, then went up to San Francisco and got an air transport to Pearl Harbor and reported to Admiral Bogan on the Fanshaw Bay early on morning of, I think the 8th of May.

Q: May I ask you one or two questions about the Atlantic first? You didn't get involved in hunter-killer operations actually?

Adm. P.: We had no submarine contact whatever during that whole trip. The Guadalcanal went out ten days after we did and they were put on a re-fueling submarine re-fueling two other German submarines in the middle of the Atlantic and sunk them. I think he also got one or two other submarines during that trip. It just shows you the toss of the dice. We didn't get one submarine, and he, I think, got either four or five during that one trip that he made to Europe and back. It was on a later trip that he captured the submarine.

Q: What about the state of your pilots and their ability to fly at night?

Adm. P.: We were just beginning to start night flying. Some of the ships that had been doing this for six or eight months started to do night flying, particularly night launches. They'd launch them at night but not try to recover them at night. But six months later most of them were doing both day and night flying. The air groups that we had at that time were not night-qualified.

Q: One other question. I understand the Tenth Fleet, with headquarters in Washington, was sending in daily reports on German submarines and their locations?

Adm. P.: Yes. That's who we worked with. They were our operational commander.

Q: What can you say about them and their effectiveness?

Adm. P.: They were very effective. They were getting most of their information from radio direction-finding. In those days the Germans when they got on the surface to fuel and make reports, we had a good direction-finding system and that's the way they spotted most of these. Then they put a carrier task group to work on finding them.

Q: This was all a part of the turn of the tide, wasn't it?

Adm. P.: Very effective. At about that time these small carriers became very effective and really made a dent in the German submarine fleet. Of course, we had our large patrol planes at work in the coastal areas, but the small carriers were effective out in the middle of the Atlantic where the submarines were out of range of the large patrol planes. This was why they became so effective at this period.

At the same time that I was detached to go and report to Bogan, I was promoted to captain.

I reported to Bogan in early May --

Pirie #3 - 113

Q: This was something you really wanted to do wasn't it?

Adm. P.: Yes. I was anxious to get to the war in the Pacific, which was very exciting at that time. The fast carriers were really well organized and they had gotten several of the Essex class out there, and it was getting to be an exciting war rather than just a holding war. We were beginning to take the offensive.

Bogan was in command of a division of small carriers, all of the Kaiser class, and he had Admiral Salada with another division forming a group of eight small carriers which were to do the close air support and fighter defense for the invasion of Saipan.

We departed very shortly after I reported aboard, en route to Eniwetok, did rehearsal operations en route, and we were in Eniwetok about four days for conferences before proceeding to Saipan for the invasion.

Q: You meant to get a knowledge of the over-all plan?

Adm. P.: The plan. Admiral Kelly Turner was in command of the amphibious operation with his flag in one of the amphibious ships. General Smith, popularly known as "Howling Mad" Smith, was the senior Marine General, and there was an Army general in command of an Army division and another Marine general in command of the other Marine division. Three divisions, two Marine and one Army, had to be put ashore to conduct the invasion of Saipan.

Q: Harry Hill was in that picture, too, was he not?

Adm. P.: He was in the other group that was scheduled to do the invasion of Guam, and did a month or so later.

We stayed at Eniwetok and had conferences on Admiral Kelly Turner's flagship. One incident that took place while we were in Eniwetok: Admiral Bogan decided that he'd like to take a ride in a B-24 that was in the command of Commander "Buz" Miller. We called him the "one-man air force." He would take off from Eniwetok with a full load of bombs and go to Truk or one of the other Japanese islands and give them a good pounding with one airplane, and Bogan decided when he heard about it that he wanted to go on one of these flights with Miller. He didn't ask Turner or anyone for permission, just got on board with Miller and took off on one of these flights, which took some 16 or 18 hours. They were long flights, and after he'd taken off on this flight with Miller, Admiral Turner called a conference and I had to go to the conference to represent the escort carriers that were going to do the close support. Turner asked me when I came into the cabin, with all the Marine generals and all the brass there, what I was doing there, where was Bogan? I said he'd gone off with Buz Miller to try to destroy Truk. Kelly let out a loud oath and turned to somebody and said, "You get out a set of orders saying that no one in any kind of a command position is going to make any more of these one-man flights."

I had to finally go and meet Bogan when he got back and they were really shot up. They had hit not Truk but one of the other small islands being held by the Japs, and the Japs hit this B-24, knocked out one engine, and they had some fire on board, and killed a couple of the

Pirie #3 - 115

crew. So it was quite an experience. And I had to tell Bogan what Kelly Turner had said, that there would be no more people with command responsibilities going off on these skylarking flights.

Q: Turner was absolutely right!

Adm. P.: He was. They had an order out to the whole fleet after that.

Q: It left quite a hole in the plan if one of the -

Adm. P.: Right - one of the flag officers went out.

Q: And didn't come back!

Adm. P.: Well, the invasion of Saipan commenced with the landings on the 15th of June. Three or four days prior to that the fast carrier task group had attacked Guam and beaten it up pretty well to prepare for the invasion.

Q: This was under the command of whom?

Adm. P.: The fast carriers were under the command of Marc Mitscher, Task Force 38. The first Battle of the Philippine Sea took place at that time and the Jap air was pretty heavy there. They had a number of aircraft on Guam and Rota and Tinian. They had one field on the south end of Saipan which had been pretty well sanitized by the fast carrier task group, and we took over the business of providing fighter cover at that time. But there were a good many Jap air attacks the first three or four days. We were under fairly heavy attack the 15th, 16th, and 17th, and we were hit in the Fanshaw Bay I think on the night of the 15th or the night of the 16th by a bomb dropped by Judy, a dive bomber. We had avoided several Jap aircraft torpedo attacks, but this one bomb went through the after end of the flight deck and exploded in the hangar and started some fires. It unfortunately also killed most of the damage-control party on the Fanshaw Bay, and it ruptured the main fire main aft on the deck below the hangar deck, just forward of the after elevator, and poured a tremendous amount of water into the bomb storage and the magazines.

It was just at about dusk and it was then an hour later, after dark, the ship seemed to be getting tender and my boss, Admiral Bogan, said, "You'd better go down – "

Q: You were both on board the Fanshaw Bay?

Adm. P.: Both on board – see, I was his chief of staff.

Q: And that was his flagship?

Adm. P.: His flagship. He said, "Since you have just come from a same class ship, the Mission Bay, you'd better go down and see what's going on in the hangar."

I got down and found this large amount of water being discharged into the magazines from this fire main and I knew where to shut the valve off to isolate it, so I got the valve shut off and isolated this part of the main and got the flow of water stopped, but it had done a tremendous amount of water damage and the ship was in no condition to continue. Her air group had been sent to the other ships in the group, so we then transferred by boat to the White Plains, and the Fanshaw Bay proceeded back to Eniwetok for repairs.

Q: Admiral, when were you becoming aware of the fact that the operation at Saipan was going to take longer than had been anticipated.

Adm. P.: The schedule, as I remember, for the invasion of Guam was to take place about a week or some --

Q: I think originally the 18th.

Adm. P.: Just a few days after the invasion of Saipan, but the opposition by the Japanese was tougher than they anticipated and they had some considerable losses of aircraft in the fast carriers during the Battle of the Philippine Sea due to their coming back late at night and landing in the water, a good many of them, so he didn't have as much air power as he thought he needed for the other invasion and they delayed the invasion of Guam. That whole invasion force, the support ships and the troops were kept at sea and the thing was delayed for a considerable period. My memory is that the invasion of Guam took place about thirty days later.

We stayed there and did the close air support for the invasion. About the third or fourth day Admiral Bogan was not satisfied that we were doing as well as we should to support the Marines.

Q: Why did he feel this way?

Adm. P.: Well, from the messages that we were getting back and the movement of the troops on shore was not as fast as they had anticipated, and he just deduced that we weren't doing as good a job as we should be doing and he said, "you get in an airplane and go over to Aslito and take Joe Thomas with you - he was assistant operations officer - and go to the Marine general's headquarters and find out how we can improve the situation."

So Thomas and I got in this TBM and landed at Aslito. It was still under pretty heavy fire from the Japs, but we got into a jeep and went to General Smith's headquarters and discussed with him how we could improve the situation, principally through better communication signaling system, most of which had to be done by sight and not sound at that time. We did it by ground panels. I think we did considerably improve our support and got better support for the Marines and the Army in the field.

Q: Since communication had to be handled by sight, was the weather an asset in this respect?

Adm. P.: The weather was always clear, unlimited. I can't even remember any rain. Maybe we had some rain showers, but the weather was very good during this whole period.

We were under some considerable attack at night by large Japanese Bettys that dropped torpedoes, but fortunately none of them ever hit us. You could hear them going off in the water because the Jap torpedo was set to explode at the end of its run as they were no menace to us after they'd finished their run.

Pirie #3 - 119

Q: Did the Japanese use any kind of aerial illumination?

Adm. P.: Yes.

Q: I know they did at Guadalcanal.

Adm. P.: Not so much at that time but later, off the Philippines, they used a considerable amount, which I'll talk about later, a considerable amount of illumination. But most of these Bettys that were attacking us at Saipan were flying at very low altitude. It almost seemed like they were going to hit the top of our masts going over. We were darkened, so it was pitch black, black nights. They could almost touch us, but fortunately none of us ever got hit during this period.

Q: They hadn't adopted the kamikaze yet?

Adm. P.: No. That one hit on the Fanshaw Bay was the only damage that we received. Several of the ships in the landing force got hit with bombs, but not in our carrier task group.

Q: Perhaps that was just as well with the Kaiser-class carriers, the way they were built!

Adm. P.: One of the incidents that I remember very well took place was that on this particular radio circuit everybody in the whole fleet could hear what was going on, and Admiral Turner was berating a destroyer that they'd sent down to get a shore battery on the north end of Tinian that was lobbing shells into the south end of Saipan, Aslito airfield, and that general area, and causing a lot of damage. He was pressing the captain of this destroyer to get in closer and get that battery. Finally, the destroyer got in too close and a Jap opened fire on him and blew his bridge and did a considerable amount of damage, and the destroyer had to withdraw. That night he was in the damaged-ship convoy going home, and along about dusk Admiral Turner got on this same circuit to say a kind word, if that was possible, to this fellow about the damage that had been done. He gave him a good build-up for what he had done, what he'd accomplished, and Turner said he was sorry that he'd sustained this damage but he'd done a fine job. He ended up by saying,"God bless you," and this skipper on the destroyer had very poor, improvised radio communication because of the damage that had been done to the ship, and he came back and said, "Please repeat your last message." Well, Admiral Turner came on and went through the whole thing again, and at the end of the second transmission he said "and God bless you" and the skipper of the destroyer came back and said, "Please repeat all after God."! That made quite a hit with all the people in the fleet.

Q: How was Kelly Turner in an operation like that?

Adm. P.: He was good and tough and he was very effective. He had a fine reputation. He had, of course, been through the Guadalcanal invasion before this and was well experienced in what was going on.

After we had been there thirteen or more days, the air opposition had dwindled down to practically nothing and the fast carriers had practically wiped out most of the Japanese air opposition. What little there was was just a sort of a nuisance value, so we were able to give a lot better support to the troops. By that time they'd got moving real fast and were chasing the Japs to the north end of the island. We'd get up quite close to the island to start our air operations in the morning because the wind blew steadily - the trade winds - from one direction, which was about 075. We'd go out on that course doing our operations all day, so we'd get up pretty close and you could see some of the things. It looked like the 4th of July, with all these star shells and what not being fired by our artillery on shore.

Q: What were your immediate losses on board in the way of pilots? Were they heavy?

Adm. P.: No. My memory is that they were very light at this stage of the game, because there was no air opposition really and there was very little antiaircraft opposition from the Japs there. It was all ground fire.

Q: It was all concentrated in the artillery?

Adm. P.: Yes. Of course, we then got an Air Force squadron and a Navy or Marine squadron in business on the airfield on Saipan and they took over a good deal of the air cover that we had had to do with our fighter aircraft.

So, sometime early in July, we were ordered to (Admiral Salada took over this close air support) and we were ordered to proceed to Eniwetok and take over Carrier Task Group 38.2 with Admiral Bogan to relieve the flag officer who had had to leave because of illness. We got into the Essex as our flagship and we had two light cruiser conversion carriers

Pirie #3 - 122

with the Essex in our division. We were then ordered to proceed to the preparation for the invasion of Guam and we made most of the attacks on Guam to soften up the opposition prior to that invasion.

Q: What sort of opposition did you meet?

Adm. P.: We met considerable antiaircraft and considerable opposition from the Japs on shore. Our artillery fire was trying to get rid of their pillboxes and anything that could interfere with the orderly landing of the Marines. We stayed there in support of our battleships and cruisers that did the gunfire support softening these positions up.

Q: How far offshore would a ship like the Essex stand?

Adm. P.: We'd stay out fifteen to twenty miles, as long as we didn't have opposition that amounted to anything.

We stayed there during that invasion for, I'd say, ten days or two weeks, until they were well established on shore. Then the small carriers took over and we went back to Eniwetok to get ready with the fast carrier task force for the invasion of Palau, and then to proceed after support there, to the first attacks on the Philippines by the fast carrier task group.

Q: It sounds like an almost around-the-clock operation?

Adm. P.: Yes, we were at sea practically the whole time.

Q: No rest?

Adm. P.: No, we didn't have any at that time. We got ashore maybe one day at Eniwetok, and then we proceeded to support the invasion of Palau, which was pretty tough. The Japs there had dug themselves into the caves and the sides of hills. While we had some of that kind of opposition on Guam, it was much tougher on Palau. The Marines had quite a rough time there for the first four or five days. But we didn't stay there. Some small carriers came and took over that air support, and we then proceeded with the fast carriers to make the initial attacks on Okinawa and the Philippines.

My memory is that we hit Okinawa first on the 12th of October, then after doing a considerable amount of damage there we proceeded down to the Philippines. There were four carrier task groups, 38.1, .2, .3, and .4, and 38.2, commanded by Admiral Bogan, was in the northernmost group, closest to the air opposition, when we made this initial attack on Okinawa. In other words, the four groups didn't operate in a fixed position, but with some latitude, but we were the northernmost of the four groups, on somewhat a north and south line.

We didn't get too much opposition during the day, but that night they mounted a tremendous attack with their Bettys, and they used very high-candlepower star lighting.

Q: Didn't they use some kind of parachutes also?

Adm. P.: Yes - I'm trying to think of the technical name for it. Illumination was fantastic, and they had a large number of these Bettys with torpedoes and bombs. We didn't have any night aircraft in the that time, so when they got within radar range the antiaircraft opened up on them. We had in our task group the Iowa and the New Jersey and several cruisers, in addition to the destroyers and our own 5-inch guns on the carriers, and they destroyed a tremendous number of these Bettys at night –

Q: The illumination worked both way, then, did it?

Adm. P.: Yes, it did, but we were relying on radar, with the influence fuse. At one stage of the game, one of our staff officers who was on the outside of the flag bridge opened the door and yelled at the admiral, "If you want to see a real sight, come out and take a look now." We went out, and it seemed like the whole sea was on fire from the burning of these Bettys. The gasoline fire on the water from these destroyed Japanese airplanes. We didn't get one hit in all that attack that they mounted, and we must have destroyed 150 of those –

Q: And not a single hit?

Adm. P.: Not a single hit on one of our ships.

Q: How do you account for that?

Adm. P.: Well, our antiaircraft was very effective and we got to them before they got rid of their weapons.

Q: And the influence fuse?

Adm. P.: Yes. We had the Independence with us, which was a night carrier, and in the subsequent days he would launch in the early evening, an hour before dusk, and have them in the air to the north of us, in the direction from which we would expect attack, and get the Japanese bellwether that was sent down to lead the rest of them in. By knocking that plane out, the rest of the Japanese attack planes had a very difficult time finding us at night.

Q: Disorganized?

Adm. P.: It disorganized them, by knocking down that one airplane. So the Independence really proved her worth after we got well.

Then we proceeded from those initial attacks on Okinawa —

Q: Let me ask you one question about the initial attacks. You said in the daytime when you made the attacks you got very little opposition from the Japanese, but then they sort of came out at night. Does this mean that they were taken quite by surprise and they didn't respond?

Adm. P.: I don't think they knew that we were going to hit Okinawa. These planes had to come down from the mainland to Okinawa. A good many of them flew from the mainland of Japan.

Q: Why did they choose to make their big stand at night?

Adm. P.: Because they didn't want to attack us in the daytime with the large air power that we had at the time. We'd gotten the F-6Gs by that time and they were very deadly for anything that approached within

50 or 60 miles of us.

Q: And they were counting on their illumination?

Adm. P.: Illumination and doing it at night so that we wouldn't get them in the daytime. There were some ships in a couple of the other task groups damaged and had to be taken under tow. A couple of cruisers. The air cover for getting them out of there was a significant part of the next four or five days' operations.

Then we went down and made the initial attacks on the airfields in the Philippines and we got quite a bit of air opposition at that time and had our combat air patrols and antiaircraft destroyed a considerable number of those Japanese airplanes, and I think during that particular period we broke the backs of the Japanese Navy, Air, and Japanese Air Force by the very heavy losses they took. A good many of them had been lost in the Battle of the Philippine Sea, but I think these initial attacks got what real experienced Japanese air they had left.

Q: You were, in effect, operating in two different theatres, were you not? The MacArthur area in the Philippines and the Nimitz one in the island-hopping?

Adm. P.: You see, MacArthur was down in the south. This was before the invasion of Leyte, when we supported him. He was down in New Guinea and Hahmahera and that area at that time, getting ready to move up north. Our support attacks on the Philippine airfields were principally to attrit the Japanese air and looking forward to getting ready for the invasion of Leyte.

Q: So you were in this theatre and then you - ?

Adm. P.: Yes. We were gone about thirty days from the time we left Eniwetok until we got back, when we went for the first time to Ulithi. The carriers stopped at Saipan to get bombs and ammunition, and the battleships and cruisers and most of the destroyers preceded us. They had very little opposition at Ulithi and we went inside the atoll there to anchor and reprovision and get ready to go again. We proceeded from taking these bombs and ammunition from Saipan down in to Ulithi.

We'd just been in there twenty-four hours when a typhoon blew up and caused us to get out, and it was some experience getting out of that inner lagoon.

In the meantime -

Q: Was that the first typhoon that you'd encountered?

Adm. P.: The first large typhoon that we'd encountered with the carrier task force.

In the meantime the Essex had gone back for overhaul and we had been in the Bunker Hill for a short period of time as the flagship and had just gotten into the Intrepid when we went in to Ulithi, when we were ordered to get out of Ulithi in the face of this typhoon. It was already blowing pretty hard and there were no significant landmarks for radar, and we hadn't had time to properly mark the channels. We were the first carrier out, preceded by four of our destroyers. It was almost a miracle that none of the ships ran aground getting out of there – that atoll and getting to sea. We got out to sea and rode that typhoon out, then came back in and finished our reprovisioning and supply, and then went back out to go after the Philippines again.

Q: It was safer in the open sea than it was in the protected lagoon?

Adm. P.: Yes. Oh, yes, by far. The problem in there is that anchors won't hold and you'll either drag anchor or break the anchor chain. The heavy typhoon winds can blow you up on the atoll and you'd be wrecked.

Well, we went back to proceed with the softening up of the Philippines and get ready for the invasion of Leyte.

Q: That brings a question to mind. I know that Admiral Nimitz had quite a problem with General MacArthur when units of the fleet were involved in MacArthur's operations. MacArthur never wanted to let them go again, and there was quite a problem there. Did you get involved in that with the carriers?

Adm. P.: No. I think General MacArthur thought that he should have more air support than he was getting from down in that area, but the problem of skipping over a good many of these islands required, I'm sure, in Admiral Nimitz' view all the air that he could get from the fast carrier task force. We were so intimately involved with our own jobs that those of us at the level we were were not conscious of any of this argument.

Of course, all of the invasion of Tarawa and Kwajalein and those islands had taken place before the Saipan invasion and they had then decided not to tackle Truk but to go right to the Philippines, and that was what we were involved in, getting ready for the Leyte invasion.

Well, we proceeded back again to the Philippines, and the principal invasion of Leyte took place between 20 and 29 October and during this period we had a great deal of air action, with the Japanese trying to damage the carrier task forces. It was during this period that we countered the first kamaikaze, and two or three of our carriers were pretty badly damaged.

Q: There's been no intimation of this technique before?

Adm. P.: No. We were hit in the Intrepid. One of the other light cruiser carriers, the Monterey, was fairly badly damaged too by a large kamikaze attack in the vicinity of Leyte. It was quite a large number. I would say thirty to forty of these kamikazes. We spotted them on the radar at some considerable distance, but the task force fighter direction had given one of the other task groups the job of dealing with them. They didn't have them on their radar, so by the time we got our fighter planes after these kamikazes they were already in their glide from like, say, twenty-five or thirty miles out at fairly high speed, and our fighter planes didn't make contact with very many of them. Consequently, the majority of them got into our task group. The antiaircraft destroyed a considerable number of them, but they did, as I say, hit two of our ships pretty badly. In the Intrepid the first one hit us - he came in at very low altitude and flew up from the stern and did a sort of a wing-over into the deck, and the bomb hit at an angle of about 30 degrees to the flight deck and entered the gallery deck, and went off in the gallery deck, just below the barrier area. It exploded just near an electronics repair shop - radar repair shop - and killed a good many people and started some fires. In the hangar we had fourteen or fifteen bomber aircraft all loaded with depth charges and bombs and fully fueled. It started a fire in the hangar and the principal fire party was dealing with that fire in the hangar when the second kamikaze came along not more than five or six minutes later. He tried to dive into the hole that had erupted upwards from the flight deck, a hole forty or fifty feet in diameter. He hit right in there and his bomb went down and went off and when it hit the hangar deck went straight through in the midst of those burning airplanes down below. This caused a real holocaust. All those planes caught on fire and the bombs went off and the gasoline was burning. It was a real nasty fire which lasted about five or six hours before we got it under control. We lost something like 150 officers and men in that thing, and it put that ship out of commission.

The other ship, the Monterey, had three hits. One was alongside and caused some damage in the hull of the ship, and one hit a 40-mm battery and knocked it off with the whole damned crew. Then he had one go off about 300 or 400 feet above the flight deck which scattered a whole lot of fire and metal parts and what not all over. He kept right on operating his aircraft during this whole business, and Admiral Halsey was so impressed with the action of that carrier that he personally got on the air and told the Monterey commanded by Captain Stan Micheals what a great job they had done and what a magnificent display of courage it was to see them operate.

Well, we had to go back -

Q: Let me ask you, Sir, what was your initial reaction to this new Japanese technique of desperation, Kamikaze?

Adm. P.: We could deal with them if our fighter planes could shoot them down. You must realize that very-low-flying aircraft couldn't be detected at that time until they were right on top of you so we had to depend on antiaircraft guns to shoot them down. But if we caught them at any altitude our fighter planes could deal with them. The problem was to have that air power of fighter cover over the task force at all times in order to ensure that they didn't -

Q: How did you look upon it? Did you look upon it as an act of desperation, as a final - ?

Adm. P.: Well, it became pretty obvious that they were desperate and that this was an act of desperation to try to damage us because they hadn't been able to do it with conventional aircraft and conventional tactics. So they had to fly into the decks because they weren't making any progress getting any hits with normal bombing or torpedo methods.

In the second of these two kamikazes that hit the Intrepid what was left of the body of the pilot rolled up the flight deck and was clear out on the bow. There was, of course, a lot of excitement and confusion going on and I was interested in trying to get hold of that torso, if I could, and see if we could get some blood samples to see if these boys had been drugged or taking any dope. But the sailors threw his body overboard before we could get to it.

Q: Was that ever determined?

Adm. P.: No. I don't think they ever found that there were any drugs or anything that wasn't normal given to these people.

Q: Just a national characteristic.

Adm. P.: We had to go back to Ulithi with the Intrepid and we were shifted to the Lexington, which had just come back from a kamikaze that hit the side of the ship. A side blow but it had done considerable damage around the after end of the island. They'd just been fixed up, so we shifted in to the Lexington at that time and went back for the attacks in November and December.

We got back to Ulithi in the Lexington before Christmas. By that time the Philippines had been well secured in the Leyte area and we were getting ready for the business of taking Luzon and Manila back. We spent about ten days around the Christmas period in Ulithi and we had a chance to get some rest and lick our wounds and get ready to go. It was at this stage of the game that the operations to take the fast carriers into the Philippine Sea were planned.

Q: Were you in on that planning?

Adm. P.: Yes, at Ulithi. I think at that time Admiral Mitscher had turned over to Admiral McCain, and Admiral McCain was in command of the fast carriers. We had four carrier task groups in this operation at that time, and we sailed from Ulithi before the 1st of January and went up and made some very heavy attacks on Luzon and on Okinawa. After getting them well softened up we proceeded to the straits into the Philippine Sea. We were not detected that night. We had three bogies, individual, on the screen that we launched fighters from the Independence to get, and they got all three of those Japanese aircraft proceeding down toward Luzon. As a result of this, the carrier task force was not detected.

We tried to fuel the morning after we got in. The weather was very bad and we couldn't get any of the ships fueled, and it was decided to proceed south and make another attempt the second day. By this time, we had taken into our task group a small carrier task group that had been working on the Manila area from inside. They'd come through the San Bernardino Strait. So we had a considerable number of ships to get refueled. We did fuel the next morning, still undetected by the Japanese, and then proceeded down to make the attacks on the Camranh Bay and Saigon area, where we caught a couple of large Japanese convoys, mostly tankers, and destroyed not only all of those merchant ships and tankers in the convoy, but all the combatant ships as well.

Q: You must have had a considerable complement of planes at your disposal?

Adm. P.: We had at least five carriers in every task group, including the small light cruiser carriers. So we had well over a thousand airplanes that we could put in the air at one time.

Q: And the Japs, apparently, had practically nothing?

Adm. P.: They had nothing left. We were getting very little opposition at any time.

We were in there and then went up and attacked Okinawa from the southwest, and then after five days, I think, proceeded back and into the Pacific and did some more work on the Philippine airfields. Then we proceeded back into Ulithi to resupply and get ready for the attacks on Tokyo, and the principal Japanese cities.

At that time, I was detached.

Q: This was in March, was it not?

Adm. P.: From the 1st of February our staff had not had any rest and recreation since the invasion of Saipan, so we were ordered home for a month and our task group taken over by Rear Admiral Davison. So we proceeded back by air to the West Coast of the United States. Then I was detached and reported to Admiral King's staff in Washington in late February.

Q: Perhaps, at this point, it would be well to stop and say something about Admiral Bogan and his effectiveness?

Adm. P.: Well, I'm in the first place prejudiced, but I think that he was the greatest carrier task group commander in the Pacific and did a magnificent job as a wartime commander. He had the intimate knowledge of what was going on in airplanes, having been a good pilot himself, and he was an excellent air warfare commander. He had great courage and stamina and did a superior job of handling the carrier task group.

Q: He obviously was the kind of man who commanded the respect of those he –

Adm. P.: He certainly did, of all the aviators. They were particularly, I think, fond of him and proud to be in the task group and he took superb care of them.

Q: You want to add something before we go back to Washington and Admiral King's staff. There are various things you want to add covering your period in the Pacific. One of them has to do with the Battle of Leyte Gulf.

Adm. P.: Yes. There are a couple of incidents which I didn't cover on discussing the fast carrier task force operations in the Pacific.

At the Battle of Leyte Gulf we had four fast carrier task groups in Task Force 38, including 38.2 where I was Admiral Bogan's chief of staff. The Japanese actions to try and interfere with the landings at Leyte Gulf are now well covered in history and consisted of a three-pronged effort, one through the San Bernardino Strait, one through a second force to come through the Surigao Strait, and a third and larger diversionary force to come around the north end of Luzon - come down from the north of Luzon and try to distract the fast carriers which were protecting and supporting the Leyte landings.

When the presence of the so-called diversionary force to the north of Luzon was detected, Admiral Halsey, commander of the Third Fleet, took action to take the whole of the fast carrier task force to the north to deal with this force, which consisted of five aircraft carriers and supporting ships.

Q: This was Kurita's?

Adm. P.: We at that time had three fast carrier task groups. One, in command of then Rear Admiral John Sydney McCain, was en route back to Ulithi for logistic resupply. Our carrier task group and one other had been sending our torpedo planes and our bombers into the Mindoro Gulf all during the day, attacking the Japanese force which was to exit the San Bernardino Strait. During this action, the Mushashi, the largest Japanese battleship at the time, and several other of the force had been sunk, but there remained in the force a number of battleships, cruisers, and destroyers which we had had contact with in the Mindoro Sea, but had lost contact with them late in the day. However, we sent night aircraft from the Independence to search for and report on their presence after dark. They were discovered coming through the San Bernardino Strait with searchlights shining on the trees on shore, and this was reported. The logical thing seemed to be to form a surface attack force consisting of battleships and cruisers and leave a number of them in the entrance to the San Bernardino Strait to deal with this force coming out. However, no orders from higher authority came to activate this force, most of which were in our task group.

I discussed this at some length during the night with Admiral Bogan and, while realizing the desirability of such action, he was not willing to send any message to higher authority on the subject.

Q: Why not?

Adm. P.: I believe that this was due to some differences which he had had with Admiral Halsey's staff on other operational matters. Admiral Burke, who was then chief of staff to Admiral Mitscher, confirms that he had the same feelings and had expressed the same idea to Admiral Mitscher, who also refused to recommend to higher authority.

Q: Where did Admiral Kinkaid come into this picture?

Adm. P.: Admiral Kinkaid was in the Seventh Fleet at Leyte in command of the naval forces making the invasion, and I believe history indicates that he had sent a request to Admiral Halsey and the Third Fleet for the protection of the invasion force.

It is probable that all of the Japanese surface navy, or the majority of what remained of the Japanese Navy, could have been dealt with in that one blow, had action been taken to provide a surface attack force to guard the San Bernardino Strait.

Q: Was there involved a certain degree of faulty intelligence which led some of them to think that there were many more units of the Japanese fleet than there were?

Adm. P.: I'm not sure on that point, but I do know that the Japanese in interviews given since the war indicate that the force to the north was called their diversionary force and it was put up there for the purpose of drawing the fast carriers and their supporting ships away from the Leyte Gulf, so that the two forces at San Bernardino and Surigai could get in without tough opposition and get at the invasion force, and hope to sink as many of the little carriers and the surface ships as they could.

This history of this battle is well covered in a new book called The Battle of Leyte Gulf by Edwin P. Hoyt and, in my opinion, quite accurately covered.

Another incident that I would like to mention is the great typhoon of 17-18 December in which several destroyers were lost and many other ships in the task force badly damaged.

Q: These were your own destroyers in your task force, were they?

Adm. P.: Some of them were attached to us. I think only one from our task force was lost.

Attempts to fuel early on the morning of the 17th of December 1944 were futile. No ship of the task force was able to get alongside either the tankers or the larger combatants to fuel. Unfortunately, a number of the destroyers had pumped ballast in order to take fuel and therefore were in an unstable condition. When it was apparent that we were not going to be able to get fuel to these detroyers, I made representations to Admiral Bogan that we should steam south across the path of the typhoon and get into the safe semicircle. He asked me what made me such a great weather prophet or oracle, and I replied that I wasn't a weather prophet or oracle but I brought out a copy of Bowditch and showed him the paths of all typhoons in history in that part of the Pacific Ocean, which were quite standard. After some discussion he said - told me to write a message to Admiral Mitscher and Admiral Halsey and recommend this course of action.

I prepared this message, which he sent, and that message is a part of the official court of enquiry, recommending that the task force steam south across the face of this typhoon and get into the safe semicircle.

Q: What was the response to the dispatch?

Adm. P.: This action was not taken. As a matter of fact, action was taken to steam due west and it turned out that this course of action got us right into the eye of the typhoon, where several of the destroyers foundered and were lost and there was serious damage to several of the other destroyers, cruisers, and light carriers. Two cruisers had their hulls cracked. They had serious fires in several of the light cruiser carriers where heavy tractors and machinery got loose in the hangar. It was a total disaster which could have been averted by getting the fleet into the safe semicircle.

Q: Admiral, at that point in time, how extensive and how accurate were weather reports in the fleet?

Adm. P.: Well, in the vast Pacific Ocean the exact pinpointing of the center of a typhoon of this character was not possible and the real severity of the storm could not be known from reporting stations. It was necessary to depend on man's knowledge of what was happening as events unfolded.

Q: Just common sense, once you got involved in a typhoon!

Adm. P.: A most unfortunate episode.

Another episode that I did not mention during the previous discourse on the Pacific war was a conference held on board the Lexington, Admiral Mitscher's flagship, at Eniwetok before proceeding to Palau. Admiral Mitscher had four carrier task group commanders, Admiral Fred Sherman, Admiral Jocko Clark, Admiral McCain, and Admiral Bogan, aboard the Lexington for a pre-departure conference at the time that some photographers were taking pictures for The Fighting Lady. There is a photograph in color of the participants in that conference in the "Fighting Lady" movie.

Admiral Bogan and I, I believe, were the last ones to arrive and as we started to walk into Admiral Mitscher's cabin, Admiral J. S. McCain walked out, and he had converted a green Marine fatigue hat into a chapeau which he wore that had the embroidered visor from an admiral's cap in black braid and cap device. It was a horrible-looking apparition.

Pirie # 3 - 141

When Bogan suddenly encountered Admiral McCain with this hat on coming out of Admiral Mitscher's cabin, without a moment's hesitation, he said, "Where's Stonewall Jackson?" which drew a good many laughs from several of the participants.

After being detached from Admiral Bogan's staff, I reported to Washington in late February –

Q: You left with some regret, didn't you?

Adm. P.: Yes, very much regret because I was in line to get command of a carrier at about that time and was looking forward to the strikes that we were about to make on the principal Japanese islands. We at that time had great predominance in air power, and I was anxious to be a participant in the demise of the Japanese.

Q: Which was now very apparent?

Adm. P.: Very apparent. However, duty called, and I relieved Captain Wallace Beakley as air operations officer on Admiral King's staff in March, and he was able to get to the Pacific and get his carrier command.

Duty on Admiral King's staff was very busy, very interesting, and most educational.

Q: What was your particular job?

Adm. P.: As air operations officer, I commissioned and decommissioned all aircraft unit squadrons, wrote the movement orders for all aircraft squadrons, everything to do with air operations. I was one of the ten

Pirie #3 - 142

watch-standers who stood twenty-four-hour watch in ten for Admiral King to take care of emergencies and handle the situation when the principals were not in their offices.

Q: Tell me what are the main duties of the watch officer, which you related to me off-tape.

Adm. P.: One of the main duties was to sit at Admiral King's desk while the charwomen were cleaning his office, which usually took place about 8 p.m., shortly after Admiral King's departure for the day, and on Admiral King's desk was everything that was going on in the war and with the Navy, including selectionboards, assignments of officers, flag officers, what he was going to say to Hap Arnold the next day, and a few other matters of some considerable significance that were of a highly classified nature.

I mentioned to Captain McDill, a classmate of mine who was the administrative assistant, that I thought possibly it would be advisable to have a sheet or some covering put over Admiral King's desk so that this would not become knowledge to any individual, other than the admiral himself. Captain McDill informed me that several people had made that suggestion to Admiral King with great regret, and that if I wanted to go in and tackle the "old man," I was welcome, but he suggested that I forget it, which I promptly did.

Q: Tell me about some of the interesting happenings in this job.

Adm. P.: It was a most frustrating period from the standpoint of one's personal survival because it was almost impossible to get quarters of any kind that were adequate for one's family, rationing, bus transportation, problems with automobiles. Living was quite difficult, and not a very happy period for any of us at that time.

Q: You didn't see much of your family, did you?

Adm. P.: I was working at that time 14 or 16 hours a day, so we generally tried to have driving squads, but seeing that I never made the driving squad for the homeward journey with any of my contemporaries and was usually trying to fight my way home by bus, and that was pretty difficult because they wouldn't stop.

Q: Wasn't there an extra bunk down on the Sequoia that you could occupy?

Adm. P.: I was one of those attahced to the Sequoia but I never had a set of quarters there! Admiral King lived on the Sequoia down at the Washington Navy Yard with some of his personal staff.

It was at about this time that Admiral King got the Navy to adopt the gray uniform with black trimming. When I arrived in Washington I had nothing but Khaki, and after the first staff meeting that I went to with Beakley, Vice Admiral Savvy Cooke, the chief of staff, asked me to remain for a minute and he suggested to me that I buy a gray uniform –

Q: Double quick!

Adm. P.: Yes – right now, which I did, and you may be sure that at the end of the war when they disappeared I got rid of those uniforms in a hurry!

Pirie #3 - 144

Q: As I recall, they were not very attractive?

Adm. P.: Not very practical either.

Q: By that time, King's staff was working pretty smoothly, wasn't it?

Adm. P.: Yes, we had quite an interesting time. When you have as much in the way of resources in material and men as we had at that stage of the game vis a vis our enemies, it wasn't too difficult. The end of the European war came along first and then followed shortly the end of the Japanese war and most of us were trying to find some more pleasant duty. I finally got to the Naval Academy as the first head of the Aviation Department in January 1946.

Q: Let's dwell a little on that period of duty, though, with King. As Op Air, did you get out into the hinterland very much? Did you travel?

Adm. P.: Yes, we had some conferences on the West Coast in connection with organizational problems.

Q: You mean with Admiral Nimitz?

Adm. P.: No, principally with the air commanders on the West Coast Admirals Montgomery and Bogan and with our naval air commander at Norfolk, Admiral Stump. Organizational problems for the transition from wartime to peacetime and setting up training units for, principally, electronic warfare, things that were coming into being at that time that required some organizational changes.

Pirie #3 - 145

Q: You were there during the time of Yalta, were you not?

Adm. P.: No, the Berlin Conference. Admiral King accompanied the President on several of these conferences but he didn't take operational staff people with him. He was accompanied by officers from the planning section, so I never had the opportunity to go on one of these conferences with Admiral King when he participated in the Roosevelt, Churchill, Stalin conferences.

After the war had ended and there was great interest in the atomic weapons, Admiral Blandy was assigned the task force command to conduct atomic tests in the Pacific -

Q: This was Bikini?

Adm. P.: Yes, I had a considerable amount of work connected with getting adequate ships for the housing of the scientists and the work of preparing weapons when the final decision was made to take one of our seaplane tenders and convert it.

Q: Did you have to bone up on the subject of atomic energy?

Adm. P.: No. I wasn't involved with any technical aspects of this, it was just logistics. So I wasn't involved in the actual atomic operations. I had considerable contact with Admiral Blandy and with Deke Parsons, who was the officer in the Navy most knowledgeable in atomic weapons.

Q: Since you mention logistics in this connection as Air Operations, did you have over-all involvement with logistics, too?

Adm. P.: As Air Operations, I wasn't involved in logistics as such. I'm not DCNO Air now, I'm air operations officer. No, I didn't have any real detailed logistics. Logistics were all run for the air part of it by DCNO Air, through DCNO Air's organization to the Bureau of Aeronautics.

Q: About that time was there not some sort of a hassle involving Admiral Radford and the plans for the postwar Navy? Weren't they being drawn up in some detail, reductions in forces and units and what-have-you, and they had a clash with Radford?

Adm. P.: Well, Admiral Radford came as DCNO Air during the early post-war period. I remember vividly having some contact with him.

Q: Tell me something about Admiral King himself.

Adm. P.: Well, I was a great admirer of Admiral King. He was a martinet and a great task master, but he was very fair and he was very smart, and, in my opinion, he made the greatest contribution to our winning the war and the early defeat of the Germans and Japanese of anybody. He was a man with a fine mind and great knowledge. I enjoyed working for him very much.

Q: Can you recall any specific incidents that would be worthy of biographical material?

Adm. P.: No. I found out early in the game that working in a big staff like that to try to get action taken on dispatches or papers that I was trying to move in a hurry, like moving squadrons or commissioning squadrons or decommissioning them and that sort of thing, that it would just take days, literally, to go around and get initials from half a dozen people between my level and Admiral King. So I finally just took the things up and got him to release them direct. Once in a while Admiral Edwards or Admiral Cooke or someone like that would ask me what I meant by bypassing them, and I'd just pass it off and try to get on with the business. But Admiral King was very good about that. He never once would ask me, if I'd bring something like that in for his initials, he never questioned the validity of doing it.

Shortly after I took over from Captain Beakley I received a memorandum on a very small piece of paper that said - my number was F-33: "F-33 Keep Dickie Byrd out of my office. EJK."

Q: Richard Evelyn Byrd?

Adm. P.: Yes. Admiral King had a habit of saying that if you couldn't get a memorandum on the face of one sheet of paper, then you were to come to him personally and have a conference. He didn't want to read more than one sheet. And he used memorandum pads all the way from size down to about one by two inches, all the way up to regular foolscap paper. But he didn't want any two-page memoranda or more. He wouldn't have anything to do with them. If you sent him a memorandum that didn't have your signature at the bottom of the page, he'd throw it in the waste basket, and you'd wonder where it was.

So one of the first ones I got was this "Keep Dickie Byrd out of my office." It was a little obscure to me how I was going to keep Dickie Byrd out of his office because I wasn't the guardian of his front office. But Dickie Byrd was becoming a damned nuisance with his Antarctic ideas and he was bothering Admiral King, so he thought since Dickie Byrd was an aviator I'll tell "the aviator" to keep him out of my office. That's the last I ever heard of it. I never saw him.

Q: What was King's relationship with the SecNavy?

Adm. P.: Apparently he had some differences of opinion, as you might expect, the civilian viewpoint not coinciding with the military in a great war, such as we were in. But my feeling was that he and Secretary Knox got along quite well, but I think he had some differences with Secretary Forrestal, mostly on logistic matters and personnel matters. I never saw any of this difference personally, but I understood that they had some differences.

Q: Tell me about some of the frustrations that you, as a fleet operational officer, encountered when you came back to the staff of Admiral King, meeting with opposition on this and that on the part of officers who really didn't know from experience in the field.

Adm. P.: Experiences in operating a carrier task force and particularly those that had to do with the defense of the carrier task force against air attack, which took place largely in the combat information center through a combat information officer and fighter director. The evolution of the CIC to what we have today has taken a considerable number of years, but some of the initial concepts of requirements for command and control from the combat information center were germinated during World War II in operating air defense.

As an example, getting information from the combat information center - accurate information - on a raid coming in - being detected and coming in was very difficult through the telephone talkers because they were about 50 percent or less effective. As a result, my boss, than Admiral Bogan, used to send me to the CIC when we had detected a raid, and had me communicate with him direct the information on what was going on in connection with the individual raid. As a result, I saw many shortcomings in the CIC as then operated, principally through confusion, noise, diversion of the individual by sight or sound and as a result a good many of the improvements which have been made in our modern combat information centers and command and control were generated at that period.

I found when I got back to Washington at the end of the war, after having been in a considerable amount of action in the CIC, that there were very few officers there who had had any experience or realized what the problems were, in order to get to a more efficient method. When I get to discussing postwar commands I'll have more to say about the evolvement of the modular CIC.

Q: There must have been other incidents of things that you knew about in the fleet and which men in Washington didn't know about in that sense, the operational sense, that you ran up against when you were air officer for King?

Adm. P.: Yes, there were a good many frustrations trying to deal with people who didn't have the experience of operating, particularly air operations, in wartime. I fortunately had a very sympathetic boss in Admiral King and was able to get to him direct on most anything that I needed to get done.

Q: He did have the other point of view then, he had the operational point of view?

Adm. P.: Yes, he understood.

One of the operational concepts that we developed during the raids on the Philippines and the Philippine air bases that may be of some interest was that the Japanese aircraft transfers from mainland Japan down past Okinawa to the Philippines were done principally at night with landings in the daylight. They didn't have many night landings, but they would time their take-offs from their departure point in order to arrive at Clark Field, for example, in Luzon, around Manila, at daylight. They landed just at daylight. We discovered that in the early part of the game through our night fighter flyers on the Independence, who were going in as single airplanes, not making any major attacks, but they observed this habit that they had of arriving at daylight.

Also, there were considerable numbers of take-offs of combatant planes going out of these fields at about the same time.

So we said that if we could get a significant number of our fighters over that field at that time we could really have a field day knocking these guys off.

Q: At dawn?

Adm. P.: At dawn, when they were coming in, and those who were trying to get out of the fields, too.

As a result, we devised a plan to take sixteen fighter aircraft off each one of our carriers at roughly 2:00 to 2:30 to 3:00 in the morning, so that at 4:30 or 5:00 when the sun came up, at dawn, they could be over those fields and let them have it, then come on home. Well, we didn't have in the aircraft any radar, any method of rendezvousing, other than just by sense or feel. It was black as a stack of cats, and you couldn't have anything except a minimum of light to show.

Q: The danger of collision must have been terrific?

Adm. P.: So it was terrific. Anyway, in the Lexington we had Freddie Bakutis, who was one of the great air group commanders. He was a fighter squadron commander. And in the Hornet we had Emmet Riera. They would rendezvous sixteen of their boys and go in over these fields, and we did a tremendous amount of damage and caught a lot of high-powered Japanese officials and bumped them off in transport airplanes, and caused real havoc with that system.

Q: Did they catch onto this quickly enough?

Adm. P.: They finally caught onto it, but we'd done a tremendous amount of damage by the time they caught onto it.

Q: Did we suffer drastically in the process?

Adm. P.: No, they were very fortunate. How these guys ever did it I don't know. It was fascinating to see them. Riera and Bakutis were the first ones off the catapult every damned time. They never delegated that to anybody else. They had a field day. You could see the exhaust from the engines once you got that close. They were most effective.

Interview No. 4 with Vice Admiral Robert Burns Pirie, U.S. Navy (Retired)

Place: The U. S. Naval Institute, Annapolis, Maryland

Date: Monday morning, 15 October 1973

Subject: Biography

By: John T. Mason, Jr.

Q: Well, as usual, it's good to see you this morning, Admiral. I've been looking forward to a resumption of this story. We're going back to Washington now, in March of 1945, when you became the Air Operations Officer on Admiral King's staff. You talked about this at some length last time, but there are other things to add, especially when Admiral Nimitz came on the scene to take over from King as Chief of Naval Operations.

Adm. P.: When the war ended the first noticeable thing that happened in Admiral King's staff in Washington was the immediate departure, through discharge, of all of the fine clerical and office help which we had. The WAVEs —

Q: You mean the people in uniform?

Adm. P.: The people in uniform, mostly WAVEs, who got an immediate discharge and either left us without help or with some type of incompetent help.

Q: It was simply that they wanted to leave the service, wasn't it?

Adm. P.: Yes. Once the war was over everyone wanted to get out, be finished with it, and go back home. They were in a position to get immediate discharges, and did, and we had some considerable amount of turmoil as far as the office and clerical staffs were concerned at that time.

Q: Was there any general realization that this was truly a crucial time, that we couldn't just drop everything and run?

Adm. P.: I think that this was quite true within the whole service. People who wanted to get out just wanted to go without any consideration for transition in an orderly manner. Certainly there was no orderly transition in Admiral King's staff. It was a disorderly transition. So it was quite an uncomfortable period.

Shortly after - I think in the late summer or early fall - Admiral Nimitz came and took over, relieved Admiral King, and during the subsequent three or four months most of the staff were involved in reorganizing the ComInch staff into what subsequently became the Chief of Naval Operations staff. I was not intimately involved in that reorganization. I knew a little bit about what was going on by virtue of contact with Admiral Radford, but didn't have any personal part in it. I was busy as Air Operations Officer at that time decommissioning squadrons and getting them moved into decommissioning areas. I was also quite involved, as I have said before, with the new training - operational training organizations particularly in electronics and electronic warfare, and had several conferences on the West Coast and in Norfolk with our air commanders on that subject.

Q: What was the overriding plan that you were working with? I mean how large a force did you anticipate maintaining and that sort of thing?

Adm. P.: My memory is that the attack carrier force was to be maintained at about 15 or 16 and the antisubmarine force at somewhere around 9 or 10 carriers. During this period the Coral Sea, the Midway, FDR were commissioned. They never did get to the war, but they had some operational features that were somewhat better than the Essex-class carriers and we worked on some of these advanced operational features.

The thing that I was principally involved in was fleet air electronics training units called FATUs, and commissioning and getting the FATU squadrons and organization started on the East Coast and the West Coast. They're still in existence.

Q: Where were they located at that time?

Adm. P.: In Norfolk and at San Diego —

Q: Did this require enlisting special personnel to supervise?

Adm. P.: No. It did require getting a training organization set up to get the enlisted men, and the officers, up to the proficiency that would be required to handle advanced electronics, which had come along in the late part of the war. We could see that electronics were going to have a great effect on the offensive capability of the airplane, in that were going to get missiles and things that we hadn't had during the war, and that an electronics capability would be a very important one and we were getting organized for it.

Q: Did this involve you then with the new set-up, the Operational Development Forces, later - Operational Test and Development Force?

Adm. P.: Well, Op-Tev For was set up during this period and was very heavily debated as to what form it would take and what would be involved in Op-Tev For at the time.

Q: It was concerned with electronics development?

Adm. P.: Yes. It was our opinion in the air organization that we should have our own test and development organization, and not have one organization for the whole Navy. But we lost that fight at that time, and it was all put together in one unit under Admiral Lee.

Q: Did you have any special relationship with Admiral Nimitz when he came on the scene?

Adm. P.: No, except that I'd known Admiral Nimitz for some years and considered him a personal friend. As I related, at one stage of my career when I had the USS Teal he was very helpful to me when he was Commandant of the Thirteenth Naval District in getting me some very much needed emergency repairs in Bremerton. We were friends from then on. But I didn't see too much of him during this period because, as I said, he was involved in this reorganization and I was not

Q: At this period, how influential was the thought that the Russians might be a potential enemy? How influential was that in the reorganization of the Navy and the maintenance of a certain level of efficiency?

Adm. P.: I don't recall that we were ever worried or involved with what the Russians might do at that time, particularly naval-wise.

Q: It was simply an internal point of view, as it were?

Adm. P.: Yes.

Q: Would you comment -- because it happened at this time -- on the dwindling of the Navy in terms of personnel? People just going back to private life, this hasty demobilization, and the policy. Would you comment on that?

Adm. P.: Of course, it hurt us a great deal because it practically put most of the ships out of commission, so to speak, until we could regroup and move people around to get a full complement even in our active fighting forces.

Q: How about the carriers? The pilots?

Adm. P.: A great many left, of course, and we had to amalgamate squadrons in order to get full units. We also got involved in mothballing aircraft. What do you do with all these airplanes that we had, and the idea of cocooning them and sealing them in tanks was born and started to be implemented at that time.

Q: How wise a policy was that?

Adm. P.: I think it was a good policy because a great many of the airplanes that we used during the Korean War came out of those tanks. They didn't last till the Vietnam War because they had become obsolete, but a great many were used during the Korean War.

Q: As a short-term policy, then, it was all right?

Adm. P.: It was, it was a good policy, but Aircraft become obsolete pretty fast.

Q: What about the training program at Pensacola as a result of the departure of so many pilots?

Adm. P.: Well, it had to be curtailed. The training program had to be drastically curtailed and bases closed to permit us to shrink back into a modest training program. We had hundreds of training bases, which all had to be decommissioned, closed up.

Q: Were efforts made to make the service more enticing as a way of life? Was an effort made to increase salaries and that kind of thing?

Adm. P.: I don't think at that period I ever heard anyone talk about trying to bring in inducements to keep either officers or enlisted men. We had more than we needed in total numbers and that problem never did come to the fore. As a matter of fact, the problem of inducements to get enlisted men to enlist or reenlist didn't really get any major attention until the mid-1950s or the early 1950s, 1953, 1954,

Pirie #4 - 159

as I remember.

I will relate, when I get to the time that I took command of the Sicily, the great predicaments we were in with regard to numbers and quality of the enlisted men, which was a product of the immediate post-war period.

Q: You, too, were anxious to get out of Washington?

Adm. P.: Right!

Q: So you found an opportunity and it was a splendid one in January of 1946. Tell me about that.

Adm. P.: In December I was asked by the detail officer if I would be interested in going to the Naval Academy to become the first head of the aviation department, and I accepted immediately and with great joy, and reported to Admiral Fitch, the Superintendent of the Naval Academy, 1 January 1946 to become the first head of department.

Q: What sort of licence did you have to set up this department?

Adm. P.: The only instructions I had from Admiral Fitch were that it being a new department I was to write the charter for it and the organization, and I had three or four officers who had preceded me who had done some considerable amount of work in setting the department up, which we did during the month of January, and started operating for the last term - the second term - of that year for the midshipmen.

Q: Obviously, you had some strong ideas yourself as to what should be done?

Adm. P.: I had some strong ideas about indoctrinating the midshipmen in aviation and in the necessity for teaching them a good many skills, which had never been taught at the Naval Academy, that had to do with wartime operations.

Q: What had they been taught up to this point?

Adm. P.: Practically nothing. We had aviation indoctrination which started with my class, back in 1925 or 1926 –

Q: That was a summer thing, wasn't it?

Adm. P.: It was a summer thing, and they had continued that. It was a smattering of what aviation amounted to at that time, but by the time the war came along there were so many advances and so many changes that took place in combat in the carrier task forces that had never reached the Naval Academy. It was getting to these advanced techniques and operational concepts that we found important to teach the midshipmen.

Q: It was rather late in getting this into being at the Academy, wasn't it?

Adm. P.: Well, everyone during the war was apparently too busy fighting and a great many of these things don't get back into the education and training system. I found when I got back here that there had been very little done to teach any advanced concepts and that there hadn't been

Pirie #4 - 161

too many of the officers back there exposed to real combatant operations during the war.

Q: It was rather awkward in a way, I would think, to start this whole program in the middle of the year?

Adm. P.: It was somewhat, but they gave us some time. They rescheduled and gave us some time to indoctrinate the midshipmen and teach them a little about these operational concepts, and we got it into the second term of that year and had classes in what's now Leahy Hall.

Q: Did you begin with the first classmen? I mean since they were ready to graduate.

Adm. P.: Yes. Aviation indoctrination was only - I don't think we ever had any second classmen - just first class.

Q: Try to summarize it all for them?

Adm. P.: Yes. One of the things that Admiral Fitch asked me to do when I first reported was to go to the heads of three of the professional departments, ordnance, seamanship and navigation, and marine engineering, and look over their curriculum and see if I thought it was up to date. He wrote each one of these heads of department and said that he had commissioned me to do this.

I got into immediate confrontation with each of these heads of department -

Q: I would think you would!

Adm. P.: - over coming to kibitz his curriculum, because I was about four classes junior in each case, and each one of them thought he knew more about his department than I possibly could.

Q: And I supposed they raised the question, what are your specific qualifications?

Adm. P.: Yes, well, my one qualification was that I'd been out there fighting during the war as chief of staff to a task group commander, and I knew a considerable amount about what the requirements were in each one of these areas. But it wasn't a very happy situation for the first two or three months.

Q: Did you come through with any special recommendations to Admiral Fitch?

Adm. P.: Yes, I made some considerable recommendations to Admiral Fitch, which I'm sure weren't very popular either. One that I remember specifically was the Mark 2 Plotting Board, which we as aviators had been using to navigate and work relative movement problems instead of using the old maneuvering board. When I went to the head of the seamanship department - seamanship and navigation - and told him that I thought they ought to be teaching maneuvering with this Mark 2 Plotting Board, he said, "We don't want any of your aviation gadgets around here." I said:

"Well, Captain, it isn't an aviation gadget. Down in Room so and so in your basement there are 500 of these stored, which were built by the Bureau of Ships. They have a different designation on them, but they're the same plotting boards."

He didn't believe it, and I had to take him down and show him!

We could work a maneuvering board problem in 15 seconds where it would take you at least that long to get the paper and the parallel rulers and a pencil out to get started working one on a maneuvering board. They were still teaching the red and blue azimuth tables. Very few people can remember those, and I asked him why he was still teaching those when they'd been obsolete for some years.

We finally got several of those improvements made.

Q: For the fall term, I suppose?

Adm. P.: Yes, Sir.

Q: Tell me about your own specific department.

Adm. P.: Well, after we got a curriculum drawn up and started classes —

Q: That was a short-order affair, wasn't it? I mean you went in January and the classes began in February.

Adm. P.: We took some of the things that had been taught in other departments, like in engineering and in seamanship and navigation, and ordnance — we took some of the things out of there and took them into the aviation department.

But the principal thing we did during the next three months was to get ready for the aviation indoctrination for the second class during the summer of 1946.

Pirie #4 - 164

Q: Was that done here, at the Academy?

Adm. P.: Yes, with fleet squadrons, and we had to get organized to take care of the squadrons here and do the -

Q: How different was that from what they had had previously?

Adm. P.: I think it was better because they had modern, up-to-date airplanes. They hadn't had aviation indoctrination, as such, during the war because they didn't have the facilities.

Q: As a result of this was there a quickening of interest in aviation at the Academy?

Adm. P.: Yes, I think we got considerable interest. We had an adequate number of volunteers for flight training from then on. It was also during this period that we got involved with sending volunteers to the Air Force. The Air Force Academy hadn't been started and the numbers coming from West Point were not adequate to fulfil the Air Force's needs and the Air Force was able in Washington to convince the powers that be to let them take as many volunteers from the Naval Academy as they could get. So a considerable number of graduates started volunteering to go in the Air Force.

Q: Was this related in any way to what was going on in Washington with the Department of Defense? The Air Force attempting to take over?

Adm. P.: Yes, they were trying to take all the air, including naval air, under their wing, and they were able to get them to agree to take all the Naval Academy Graduate volunteers they could get. I think there was a limit put on it in either 1948 or 1949 so that we wouldn't lose too many.

Q: Did the Navy enter into this agreement willingly?

Adm. P.: I don't think so, but I was not a party to that in Washington at the time and I can't tell you.

The other very important thing that we tried to do during this period was to get an Air Field authorized for the Naval Academy. That was my job and I spent a good deal of time on getting ready to appear before the Congress to get authorization for a Naval Academy airfield, and spent a lot of time up with individual congressmen who were friendly to that concept.

Q: You became a lobbyist, in other words?

Adm. P.: Yes.

Q: How effective were you in that role?

Adm. P.: Admiral W. Duncan was the Deputy CNO for Air and Admiral Fitch at first, and then Admiral Holloway, the Superintendent here. Working for them I appeared before the House and Senate Armed Forces committees as the principal witness to get an Air Field authorized for the Naval Academy. We had a great deal of opposition from the locals in the area north of the Naval Academy, what is now the entrance to the Bay Bridge, where we wanted to build the Air Field. They appeared in large numbers at every one of these hearings with hired lawyers, but in every instance we got a unanimous vote of the House Armed Services Committee and the Senate Armed Services Committee to build an Air Field at the Naval Academy.

Senator Millard Tydings was active in opposition to this project and, as a member of the Appropriations Committee, he used senatorial privilege and had it delayed to the point that it died a natural death in committee, and the airfield was never built.

Q: His attitude was built on the attitude of his - ?

Adm. P.: Local constituents, not the good of the service or the government.

Q: Did you attempt to work among your local people to change their attitude?

Adm. P.: Yes. We did a good deal of trying to indoctrinate them and tell them that we weren't going to ruin the countryside by having an airfield in the area, but we had very little success.

Q: I suppose it was largely the opposition - I mean what would happen in the air over the town?

Adm. P.: Yes, noise. The need for an Air Field had a considerable amount of validity for the immediate future. I would say today that there's probably no real need for it. We have an adequate field at Andrews Field that can be used by transporting the midshipmen back and forth.

The idea in the beginning was that it takes so long to transport midshipmen to another field, say, an hour or an hour and a half each way --

Q: Ground transportation?

Adm. P.: Yes, ground transportation - for the purpose of getting them to modern aircraft, that that became out of the question as a part of the regular academic routine, whereas it could have been done in the immediate vicinity of Annapolis and saved us a good deal of time.

It was a very interesting period also to me athletically. Admiral Tom Hamilton was the football coach.

Q: What was your personal involvement?

Adm. P.: I was on the athletic committee as a member. And it was during this period that we decided on having a civilian coach and had interviews with Don Faurot who was at Missouri, Bud Wilkinson, who was at Oklahoma, and George Sauer, who was then at Nebraska - no, he was a Nebraskan, but I can't remember where he was coaching. Anyway, they had all been prominent in the aviation program set up by Admiral Hamilton during the war and they were interviewed in order. Both Don Faurot and Bud Wilkinson turned the thing down, and George Sauer accepted and became our head coach to relieve, then, Captain Hamilton.

Q: What was the reason for the changeover from a naval officer to a civilian?

Pirie #4 - 168

Adm. P.: We had a committee meeting which was organized by Admiral Holloway, consisting of a number of very prominent ex-coaches and all-American players and others. I can remember Eddie Ewen, Billick Welchel, Pop Perry, and Slade Cutter, Buz Borries, Captain Hamilton, Whitey Taylor, among others, on that board. They made the recommendation to Admiral Holloway that we have a civilian coach. Then we interviewed and hired George Sauer, who had a certain amount of success. It's my opinion that he would have had a great deal more except for his assistants who were not the best influence on the midshipmen and eventually caused him to leave.

I was also head of the athletic committee and Commandant of Midshipmen when we hired Eddie Erdelatz some time later.

Q: What was the policy at that time in recruiting? For instance, football was paramount in the athletic program and our playing schedule was with major universities. What was the policy of recruitment of boys who were athletically inclined?

Adm. P.: In the mid-1930s, starting in 1936 I was here as a lieutenant and we informally organized what's now the Naval Academy Foundation under H. McCoy Jones, but it had no formal charter and no formal being. During that period there was a certain amount of recruitment and putting boys in prep school who couldn't otherwise make it. In 1944 a charter for the U.S. Naval Academy Foundation, Inc., was drawn up, and a formal organization of trustees put together, and after World War II that organization did raise money and put a certain number of promising young candidates for the Naval Academy who had athletic ability into prep school The remainder of the recruitment was done by the coaches and a few of what were called bird dogs. The bird dog organization was the brain child and product of Rip Miller, who had been here since the late 1920s and he had the organization for recruitment.

The Naval Academy Foundation, of which I am now president, has grown considerably since that time, and in the last ten years we've raised funds to make it almost a self-sufficient organization to put as many boys in prep school as we can get as candidates, who otherwise wouldn't have an opportunity to come to the Naval Academy because of lack of formal education or poor schooling in high school or preparatory school.

Q: How do you locate these prospective candidates?

Adm. P.: By any means. Anyone can nominate them. Most of them are nominated by the Athletic Association, legally. This is a system which is condoned and approved by the National Collegiate Athletic Association.

Q: Do you have scouts who go out?

Adm. P.: Blue and Gold officers and bird dogs all over the country, who are interested in Navy football, make recommendations. The coaches are the principal source of recommendations.

Q: How is this followed up? How are the appointments obtained?

Adm. P.: When we get a nomination we get a file on the boy, which consists of his school record, any college boards that he has taken, a physical exam to show that he is physically qualified, recommendation from five prominent people in his community, including his pastor and his school principal. And we get a confidential financial questionnaire made out by the parents to show what their financial capability is of putting him in preparatory school.

We then have within the Naval Academy Foundation a scholarship committee, and that scholarship committee meets and goes over each one of these records and either accepts or declines the boy. If he is accepted by our nominating committee, that record then has to be sent to the preparatory school, either of his choice or that we want to send him to, and they must accept him. Once he's accepted by the preparatory school, we take what we think the parents can pay, subtract that from the total tuition, and the school and the Naval Academy Foundation divide the rest of the cost. It's been quite a successful system.

We have, I think almost 70 boys into the Naval Academy Plebe class this last year. We have 80 boys in preparatory school this year.

Q: These preparatory schools are scattered throughout the country, are they?

Adm. P.: Yes, we have about 15 and they're prominent schools. We use Culver, Marine Military Academy, Marion Institute, Farragut, Northwestern.

Q: Well, they're not all congregated in this area?

Adm. P.: No, they're all over the country.

Q: Well, then how are the appointments made to the Academy? Are they congressional appointments?

Adm. P.: They get a congressional nomination, and if they cannot get a principal appointment they may come in under the alternate system, if they're good enough. And that's what our purpose is, to get them in a category where they are good enough to get in under the alternate system.

Q: Does the Foundation help them locate a particular congressman who might be willing to - ?

Adm. P.: We don't have anything to do with that. That's up to the Naval Academy authorities. We work very closely with the Dean of Admissions and the Director of Athletics, and the Executive Director of the Naval Academy Foundation, Rear Admiral Elliot Loughlin, has his office here on Maryland Avenue and works on a daily basis with the Dean of Admissions and the Director.

Q: Before the Foundation came into existence in the 1940s, all the elements of this program were in being?

Adm. P.: Yes. In 1944, as I say, we got the charter set up by Mr. H. McCoy Jones, and from then on we operated on a formal basis and had annual meetings. About ten years ago we increased the number of trustees to over 100. This is principally for fund-raising and we now, as I say,

Pirie #4 - 172

have raised enough funds to make it possible for us to put up to 100 boys in prep school every year.

Q: You have an endowment then?

Adm. P.: Well, that we have established.

So much for that, do you want to go back?

In early 1948 I was orderd to command the USS Sicily.

Q: After a pleasant two years at the Academy!

Adm. P.: A pleasant two years at the Academy.

Q: Were you sorry to leave at this point?

Adm. P.: No, I was interested in getting command of a ship at an early date, and I was selected to go to the National War College, but because I had not had a ship command at that time I was deferred -

Q: That was at the very beginning of the National War College?

Adm. P.: Yes, the first class, I think. First or second. Anyway, I took command of the Sicily in the Boston Navy Yard. It was just completing an overhaul, and the deplorable condition of the enlisted personnel situation became very evident to me immediately. They had roughly 125 enlisted men in that ship, the complement of which should have been around 700 or 800, and those 125 enlisted men consisted of ten chief petty officers and 115 second class seamen. No engineering force and no one with any experience except the chiefs and most of them were either cooks or bakers, none who knew anything about operations.

Pirie #4 - 173

Q: No wonder you found the Sicily laid up at the Navy Yard!

Adm. P.: It was so bad that they hadn't even been able to carry the dirt and debris out of the ship.

Well, Admiral Blandy was the Commander-in-Chief of the Atlantic Fleet, and they sent me enough crew to move from the Boston Navy yard to Norfolk. I got a few engineers - I think there were enough to stand two watches and enough to run the navigation and CIC to get to Norfolk.

I went up to call on Admiral Blandy after I arrived in Norfolk and pleaded with him to give me enough crew to go out as far as the Chesapeake light ship so I could dump all the debris overboard and wash this horrible mess down, and he said to me:

"Don't worry. I'll fix you up sooner or later and get you out."

As a result of that conversation, they got me a skeleton crew. I think it amounted to some 300 to 350 officers and men, and gave me orders to go to Panama and pick up an Air Force fighter squadron and take it to Scotland. And we did just that.

We left Norfolk and went to Panama and picked this P-47 fighter squadron up and took it to King George V Dock in Glasgow, where we unloaded. It was the only dock in Europe that we could get a carrier alongside of and unload the planes and tow them to an airfield to fly off, believe it or not, at that stage of the game.

Q: Why were they going to Scotland?

Adm. P.: Because it was the only place you could get from the dock to the airfield.

Q: No, but I mean the planes.

Adm. P.: Oh, they were going to Germany, but there was no place to unload anywhere in Germany, no place in Holland, no place in Denmark, no place in southern England, no place in France, no place in the Mediterranean. As a matter of fact, the U.S. Navy never got a place we could unload airplanes in the Mediterranean until we built Rota.

Q: And this in spite of all the World War II facilities!

Adm. P.: That's right. There was no place you could unload from a carrier to a dock and tow it to an airfield and fly them off, except this one.

Well, after we put the squadron off at King George V Dock and they were towed to a local airfield and flew to Germany, I spent ten days in Glasgow. I had an opportunity to go for the first time to north Scotland and see my father's birthplace at Banff. General Telfair Smollet, who was the colonel-in-chief of the Highland Light Infantry, was in residence close to Loch Lomond, where we were docked, and he called Sir George Abercrombie at Turriff, the "Lord of the Land" in the immediate vicinity of Banff, and made arrangements for me to go up. And I went up and stayed two days with Sir George and Lady Abercrombie, and went in to Banff to see my father's birthplace, and I found three elderly men who remembered my grandfather singing in the Kirk. He was the presenter, and the presenter in the Kirk runs all the service in the Presbyterian Church, except the preaching, which the preacher does. These three old men remembered him, which was very interesting, and I saw the church where he was the presenter and saw the little house where my father had been born.

It was a very interesting visit to me and I enjoyed the visit to Scotland.

As soon as I returned to Norfolk that summer I was given a full crew and sent to Guantanamo Bay for refresher training and became an active antisubmarine warfare carrier and spent the rest of that year in working in antisubmarine warfare.

Q: The full crew was 700, then?

Adm. P.: Yes. We did some exercises in the Guantanamo Bay area. I remember at that time we operated one fleet exercise in which we took dirigibles aboard and refueled them and replenished them. They were flying out of Key West and Guantanamo on like 100-hour flights, and we refueled them on the deck of the Sicily.

Q: Were they the Goodyear types?

Adm. P.: Yes, blimps.

We did another exercise up in the Greenland area and went quite far north. We did some exercises in the late summer of 1948.

Q: Were there some new techniques being employed in AS warfare?

Adm. P.: Well, we were developing. At that time we had about the same number of aircraft on board, fighters and torpedo planes, that we had used during World War II, but there were advanced methods. We were flying more at night in those days. We were flying both day and night.

Q: What complement of planes did you have on the Sicily?

Adm. P.: About nine torpedo planes and I'd say fifteen to eighteen fighters. About the same as we had in World War II.

It was a very interesting cruise. I had been in an anti-submarine carrier, the Mission Bay, during the war, so it was a real experience to me to be commanding officer and have a chance to work a crew up completely from scratch. I didn't have one man on the flight deck when I went down to Guantanamo to commence that refresher training who had ever seen a flight deck of a carrier.

Q: Refresher course!

Adm. P.: I only had one officer.

Q: This was starting from the beginning, wasn't it?

Adm. P.: We did it from the beginning. Three months' workup in Guantanamo, and we had a considerable amount of difficulty getting there but we did, including night flying.

Q: In these exercises, how successful were you in outwitting the submarines?

Adm. P.: We were quite good. I think we were advancing and getting to the point where we could handle them. Unfortunately, the sonar buoys were not as good as they should have been and it took some years for us to get first-class sonar buoys, but they're here now.

We made several interesting visits to ports in the Caribbean and Leeward Islands, Barbados, during that period, and several to our East Coast ports.

Q: Was there any contact with the Royal Navy?

Adm. P.: Not at that time.

I was ordered to the National War College again in the spring of 1949 and had my orders. I was asked to come to the Naval Academy to see Admiral Holloway, the Superintendent, in the spring, and he asked me if I would come to be Commandant of Midshipmen, and I said I had my orders to the National War College. He said, "I'll get them changed because I think it's more important that you come and be Commandant of Midshipmen."

Q: Did you agree with him?

Adm. P.: He had my orders changed. I agreed, I'd like to come as Commandant of Midshipmen. That was a very interesting, fine job. Not that I wouldn't want to go to the War College.

Q: You were a captain at that time?

Adm. P.: I was a captain, and I got to the Naval Academy in August of 1949 and took over as Commandant of Midshipmen. My predecessor, then Captain Frank Ward, had left to go to command a ship.

Needless to say, my tour of duty August 1949 to January 1952 as Commandant of Midshipmen was the most interesting and fruitful tour of duty and it was one of the greatest experiences in my life. We had at that time the maximum, about 3,600 midshipmen. Bancroft Hall was crowded and they were living under somewhat adverse conditions, but the rebuilding and extension of Bancroft Hall was being planned and some of it went forward during that period.

Q: Your term here spanned two superintendencies?

Adm. P.: Admiral Holloway was superintendent up until 1950 and Admiral Hill came in May of 1950.

Q: This is a good place to talk about the two men and their approach to the job here. How did Holloway function?

Adm. P.: He was a great believer in picking his subordinates and he had a great team when I arrived, and those that he picked subsequently. When I reported to Admiral Holloway in August of 1949 he said, "There's one thing that I want to get absolutely straight with you in the beginning, and that is that I'm Superintendent and that I run the Naval Academy, exclusive of the brigade of midshipmen, and that you run the brigade of midshipmen, and I'm not going to interfer with you. You're the boss as far as the midshipmen are concerned."

We got along famously because we did exactly that. I had several other chores outside of being commandant, such as chairman of the athletic committee, but it worked out very well. The director of athletics was my close friend Whitey Taylor and we got along very well during this period.

Q: Was there any change in the direction of the athletic program?

Adm. P.: No. We went ahead. As I already said before, it was during this period that Sauer left and Eddie Erdelatz came. By that time the director, Admiral Taylor, had gone to sea and the Director of Athletics was Howard Caldwell.

Q: What was the prevailing philosophy at that time in terms of the athletic program? How important was it considered as an integral part of the training program?

Adm. P.: I think we all recognized that the athletic program not only as a physical fitness program but as a morale program for the whole of the Naval Academy was a great thing and had to be given a great deal of emphasis.

First of all, all of the funds for the athletic program at the Naval Academy, for all sports, was raised through football. The receipts from football paid for all the varsity athletic program and for all the equipment, and the equipment that the class teams and battalion teams and company teams used. The intramural program was all furnished by hand-me-down equipment from that program. I think in subsequent years the Congress has begun to appropriate some money for the intramural program, but at that time none of it was taken care of by the Congress. It was all done by the receipts from football.

Q: And this was dependent upon having some good people?

Adm. P.: If you had poor teams you were going to have poor gates. You were going to have less money to spend on the rest of your athletic program, so it was a very important part of the program. While Admiral Holloway was vitally interested in it, Admiral Hill was violently interested in it, and he came wanting to win and was a great boon to the athletics here at the Naval Academy.

It was during this period that we established squash. We built some additional squash courts and established squash rackets as a varsity sport, and Admiral Hill took a great interest in that.

Q: You talk about athletics as being important in terms of morale. Is there a direct relationship between a successful football team and the morale that prevails at the Academy?

Adm. P.: I think there is. I've always felt that it's one of the most important - winning teams are very important to the morale of a military organization, and it's most important at the service academies because they're confined vis a vis the civilian university, where they don't live as closely together and spend as much time together as the midshipmen and cadets do. It becomes a very important morale factor.

Q: Admiral, we've been talking off tape a little about the policy of playing major teams, major universities, and all the problems that are related to that. Will you say something on tape?

Adm. P.: Well, there are a great many facets to the reasoning behind and the reasons for playing the kind of a football schedule we do. The first that comes to mind is the fact that we need the money to operate the athletic system. Receipts from football pay for the full athletic program at the Naval Academy. There are no appropriated funds which pay for any of the varsity athletic program at the Academy.

Secondly, we don't want to play second-rate, we want to play first-rate. There has been a great transition in forty years in the caliber of students at the Naval Academy or West Point or at the Air Force Academy vis a vis civilian institutions. For example, a good athlete, principally football, basketball, can go to a civilian institution and take physical education or business administration which don't require the educational qualities and capabilities that are required at the service academies. The entrance requirements to the service academies in college boards alone are much higher than they are at practically any civilian institution in the country.

However, we have accepted the fact that we must play the best teams and we have an organization working at the Naval Academy under the superintendent and the director of athletics to go out and get the best kind of athletes that we can with the educational qualifications necessary to come to the Naval Academy and compete. We have a great deal better quality of athlete today than we had five years ago and, in my opinion, in the next four or five years we will improve that much more and will again be able to win the majority of our games against major competition.

Q: That's a very promising outlook.

Adm. P.: That's the best I can say.

Q: You were telling me about Holloway before we got off on the athletic program. From what he told me, he had a very great and deep interest in the educational process and considerable knowledge of educational techniques. Was this apparent when he was here?

Adm. P.: Yes. Admiral Holloway was vitally interested in education. One of the first things that I remember after I reported -- the Eisenhower Committee was formed to look into the service academies and their methods and whether they should continue to exist. There was a great feeling in the country that they should be made into postgraduate schools and that all undergraduate education should be undertaken at civilian institutions, and Admiral Holloway had a great part in his testimony before the Eisenhower Committee in defeating this philosophy and in maintaining the service academies as such, as undergraduate institutions.

He started a teachers' forum here while he was superintendent, and I attended the first one in which we had a considerable period during the summer devoted to improving the quality of the instructors and the teaching methods. He got prominent educators to come and take part in these instruction classes and forums, and as a result of that I am sure improved greatly the quality of instruction and the quality of the instructors and professors during this period.

I remember that one of the lectures that I was most impressed with during that first forum was by the vice president of Ohio State

University, who was talking about the numbers and he related these statistics during his lecture. The indoctrination and the loyalty which is inspired in the graduate and he related that in all the history of the Naval Academy from the beginning, 85 percent of the graduates had to be forcibly separated. In other words, only 15 percent of all the graduates of the Naval Academy resigned or left voluntarily, and, conversely, the records of the American colleges and universitites are that only 15 percent of all graduates of the colleges and universities of the United States ever do what they set out to do or were educated for. That includes all lawyers, doctors, dentists, all professionals - only 15 percent. I thought that was a great statistic.

Q: A very interesting one.

Adm. P.: I don't know that it holds today, but this was in 1949 or 1950. Now, Admiral Holloway did take a great interest in educational values and did, I'm sure, a fine job in defending the Naval Academy as an undergraduate institution and improving the quality.

Q: Admiral, would you talk about the problems that are inherent in maintaining the educational standards at the Naval Academy and yet dealing with entry - boys who come in who are not qualified scholastically but they are in every other way?

Adm. P.: We had some very interesting and sad cases in those first postwar years. I remember distinctly that the first academic board that I attended we had the son of a vice admiral, naval aviator, come before that board who hadn't passed in one subject and that's a miracle of understatement. I don't think he'd made a mark as high as 2.0 in any subject. But he had been a back-seat airman fighting in the Pacific as a second class petty officer, he had a Silver Star, Distinguished Flying Cross, an Air Medal, a Purple Heart, a great many decorations, and he came before the Board not having passed one subject. It was heart-rending to listen to him tell us that he had never been in his memory to any school during his boyhood for a period of as much as one year. In other words, his parents had been moved around and he had never had a chance to get his feet on the ground educationally and he couldn't make it. Of course, we had to let him go.

Another two boys during that same period came before the Board who couldn't write a sentence. This came about by virtue of the fact that they had these objective tests in which you gave "true""or "false" and put a check mark in the box for answers, and they had never had to write a theme and no one realized that they didn't - couldn't write until they came up to their first examination in English, at which time they were discovered and we had to, of course, let them go, and they were fine upstanding boys who hadn't had an opportunity.

Q: What was the policy of the Academy in terms of special tutoring for deficiencies? Deficiencies in reading and that kind of thing?

Adm. P.: We had extra instruction pretty well established in those days, probably not as well as it was in later years and is now. But there was available extra instruction for those people, but in a good many cases I don't think there was enough extra instruction available to get some of those boys by.

Q: You had been talking about Admiral Holloway and his theories of education and his emphasis on this aspect of Academy life. Now talk about Admiral Hill, if you will, and his particular interest as to the Academy.

Adm. P.: Well, Admiral Hill having been the president of the National War College –

Q: Having set it up.

Adm. P.: – having set the National War College up, had a great interest in teaching history and teaching politics and geo-politics. In my opinion, things may have been a little too advanced for midshipmen, for undergraduates. However, he had a great interest in the other academic departments and, I'm sure, carried on well where Admiral Holloway left off. He did have this great abiding interest in athletics and in the importance of athletics to the institution and to the morale, which I think overshadowed his interest in academics.

Q: I'm told that he appeared at all sorts of practice games.

Adm. P.: He was always at practice and always at the games. I remember one instance when we played Notre Dame in Cleveland in an ice storm and when the game ended the only two people on one side of the field were Admiral Hill and I, sitting in the stands, frozen to death with ice all over! Having been roundly beaten by Notre Dame!

Q: Tell me about some of your trials and your tribulations as Commandant of Midshipmen.

Adm. P.: During my midshipmen days we had a sort of a change from a very loose and weak regime, so far as discipline was concerned, to a very tough and rigid discipline system under then Captain Sinclair Gannon and Admiral Louis Nolton, the Superintendent. My battalion officer was Ike Giffen, and they had a real tough group of duty officers. During my first class year I was a company commander - we kept our stripes the whole year at that time - and so far as discipline within Bancroft Hall was concerned, we had a tougher year as first classmen that we had as plebes.

I remember very distinctly that one of the things that they did was to stop "Frenching Out," and the way they did it was that the duty officer would come in the middle of the night and wake you up - wake me up - and say: "You go to the second and third decks of another battalion," where you couldn't get into the battalion office to find out who was absent and who was supposed to be present, "and mark all the empty beds." There was no way you could have tried to fix that but it sure did stop "Frenching."

Q: Counting bodies!

Adm. P.: Counting bodies. So when I became Commandant of Midshipmen I remembered that, and we were having a little "Frenching" trouble so I invoked the same system, and, believe me, I got a good reputation for that among the midshipmen in those days. They called me hearted Bob."

Q: They meant the reverse!

Adm. P.: They meant the reverse! But it was an interesting period. I believed in stern, stringent measures and discipline. I told the midshipmen the first time I talked to them after I became commandant that there was a great distinction between what were moral offenses and what were military offenses, and that I considered that the moral offenses, those that involved lying, cheating or stealing, were offenses for which I would recommend dismissal in any instance and that they might as well get that straight in the beginning. That there were other serious offenses, which were military offenses, for which they would be punished severely, but I thought that they could be salvaged, but that those offenses such as being late to formation or untidy in dress or not getting out of bed in the morning or not being turned in at night, such offenses as that, they were military offenses and they would be treated as such. My point being that there's no sense in having a room with four midshipmen in it and requiring one midshipman to stand in the door and say, "All out, Sir" meaning everybody's up, or "All in, Sir," meaning everybody's in bed. It's up to the authorities to find out whether they're in bed and not that midshipman. I made a distinction between what were military offenses and what were moral offenses.

Q: From time to time, as you say, policies of relative laxness have been exercised at the Academy. What is the justification for this policy?

Adm. P.: I think some officers are a little more liberal in their thinking about stern discipline than others. I think some are far too rigid. I can remember when I first got out of the Naval Academy I was in destroyers down in Guantanamo Bay, and there was one destroyer, the USS Converse, which they nicknamed the "USS Reverse," because the commanding officer made them come to meals in their dress clothes, with their collars buttoned, and you know in the wardroom in that hot weather, stand behind their chairs and he gave the order "Seats" and he had them in mess jackets two nights a week, with the stiff collars and all that business, down in Guantanamo. He was a real tough nut. So all the boys named it the "Reverse."

Some disciplinary measures are not necessary, but others are. It's necessary to be ahead of them all the time. I used to start rumors in Bancroft Hall to stir the midshipmen up. I think you've got to have them on their toes and moving all the time. It's like an anthill, and if the anthill is dormant nothing is going to happen. You know there's no building going on, you don't win any athletic contests, you sort of lie fallow. But if you keep that spirit up and they're moving all the time, you've got to get action, and I used to start rumors to be sure that we got a lot of action every day. Crazy rumors.

Q: What kind of rumors?

Adm. P.: I'd go in and tell the chief "Jimmy legs" in the rotunda of Bancroft Hall that we weren't going to have any Christmas leave this year,

Or some silly rumor like that that anybody would know was false, but it would get immediately to everybody in the brigade and I'd be visited by hordes of class officers, stripers! I think it's a matter of principle that you've got to keep an organization moving and active, and not let it get dormant.

Q: In this present time, with the anti-military attitude generally prevalent among the people, it has to be some sort of middle-of-the-road policy, does it not?

Adm. P.: Well, I'm not in favor of it, but that's neither here nor there. I just don't believe in these kind of policies. I believe that you ought to march and you ought to have to go to chapel. I don't care what kind of a chapel it is, if it's a Mohammedan chapel, but you ought to have to go. This is just licence, not doing those kind of things and I think they eventually reflect on the discipline of the individual, and the discipline of the individual is absolutely necessary in his future life in a military organization, because this is the only way he can discipline anyone else. He's got to first be able to discipline himself and do it well.

So I'm a stern disciplinarian.

In my last year as Commandant, Admiral Nolton, who was then quite old - he had been Commandant of Midshipmen before World War I and then Superintendent during my time as a midshipman - he came and sat on the porch and for two or three hours discussed the handling of midshipmen and his philosphy of how to discipline and run the brigade of midshipmen, and they were almost exactly what I had been trying to do. I think that my experience as a midshipman when we had a weak regime when I first came and we had a very strong and disciplined organization when I graduated, reflected itself in the fact that in my first class year, when that stern disciplinary system was just really taking hold, we didn't do very well in football that year, but we had the same people, the same players, who in the next year were national champions. We changed coaches, went from Osley to Bill Ingram. But the same people in the next year were national champions, and I think it was because to a great extent it was because of discipline and we had a strong attitude in Bancroft Hall of stern discipline.

Q: Admiral, under your regime as Commandant of Midshipmen, how important was the chapel and attendance at chapel, as part of the over-all program?

Adm. P.: I think compulsory attendance at chapel is a great discipline. Again, it's a discipline. Whether you're deeply religious or not is not the point. It's a matter of recognizing that it's a responsible part of an individual's life. It's like going to school. If you let all the little five-year-olds decide — or six-year-olds — decide whether they're going to go to school or not, you wouldn't get a very big participation. It's the same way with religion. If you don't get participation you have failed to discipline.

I greatly believe in Naval Academy chapel and its importance and I believed in the importance of the chaplains. During my period as Commandant we had the first Catholic chaplain come, who was Cy Rotrig, who has just retired as a rear admiral. He stayed here four years and Cy was a great influence for good with the Catholic boys who were in trouble. He understood exactly what we were trying to do and he tried to help a boy who was in difficulty, that had a broken home or had some kind of difficult problem. Cy was a terrific individual influence with Catholic boys who were in difficulties, and he was a great influence for us in Bancroft Hall with the Midshipmen and with the disciplinary system.

To go on with the chapel. I believed in running the chapel in a military fashion, and I went to the Library and found the old prayer book which is autographed by old Chaplain Clark I believe in the early part of this century, in which he has written in his own hand the reasons for using the Episcopal form of service. He was a Methodist. I strongly believed in that form of service, any formal form of service, and I'm a great believer in music. I was in the choir when I was a midshipman, and I was in charge of the choir as a first classman, so I had a great interest in that. When I became Commandant it was obvious we had about two or three times as many midshipmen who wanted to sing in the choir, were candidates for the choir, as we could seat in the main choir. So Professor Gilley and I devised the antiphonal choir, as it's known today. We put the antiphonal choir in the rear of the chapel and were thus able to accommodate two or three times as many midshipmen to sing in the choir as had previously sung there, and that little prayer "Create in me a clean heart, O God" is mine, and was put in the service while I was Commandant of Midshipmen by me, not by the chaplain or by Professor Gilley, but by me.

Q: Well, we can be doubly grateful to you now! This brings in more midshipmen that they'd have ordinarily.

Adm. P.: Also I believed in discipline among the ushers and among the midshipmen while they were in chapel. We had some very loose and horrible incidents in the chapel when I was a midshipman, and I could not stand that. I think that one of the great things about the chapel is that it's a great public relations medium, as it was run, with the midshipmen marching in and going to chapel, that part of the service. And I always felt that if we could get members of Congress, all the members, if we could get them down here, but particularly those that we're interested in on the Senate and House Armed Services committees and the Senate and House Appropriations and the Appropriations Subcommittee, we would gain everything that we needed for the Naval Academy, and that it was the greatest public relations medium that we had, not only with the Congress but with people in the country. But I attended yesterday and I get no feeling at all. I mean whatever the necessity for non compulsory attendance, I think it's been a great mistake.

Q: You overlooked one important bet, then. You concentrated on the Congress but you didn't bring in the Supreme Court!

Q: Shall we hear about the cribbing scandal at West Point and its repercussions at the Naval Academy?

Adm. P.: In the spring of 1950 the so-called cribbing scandal at West Point - it was in the summer either of 1950 or 1951 - word came to me on a Saturday morning about nine o'clock that there had been a cribbing scandal at West Point and a considerable number of cadets involved, particularly those on the football squad, and that it had not appeared in the paper that morning but would be later.

I checked with West Point immediately to find out - to verify this, and then later called Admiral Hill, who had gone on leave to Maine the day before. Before I called Admiral Hill I found that there were some reporters in the yard from newspapers in Washington and Baltimore and the news magazines making inquiries about the honor code at the Naval Academy.

I called Admiral Hill and told him that there had been such a scandal at West Point and that we had already had inquiries from the newspapers about our honor system, and that I was quite concerned about it. He informed me that I was Acting Superintendent and, with that, ceased the conversation and hung up the telephone.

Q: Big satisfaction that was to you!

Adm. P.: Yes! This left me with the responsibility for taking action, if there was any to be taken, with the press boring in on us here with regard to our honor system.

Q: Did you suspect anything at the Naval Academy?

Adm. P.: No, there was no suspicion whatever of any problems here.

I thought this over. We had one-third of the second class and all the plebe class here at the time, and I went down to the mess hall at noon and told them that if they were asked any questions by anyone, including any newspaper or news magazine reporters, that they were to say "that we were very sorry that any such a thing had happened at our sister institution," and that's all they were to say.

During that day there were numerous reporters from the news magazines and the newspaper media picked up who were trying to determine what our honor system was and particularly to determine why we wouldn't have a similar scandal to that at West Point. It hit the papers that afternoon and by Sunday afternoon I'd been called by Captain Dennison, who was then the naval aide to President Truman, and asked about our honor code and what should be said to reporters. I told him that there was a paragraph in the regulations which said: "You will not lie, you will not cheat, you will not steal, and if you are found doing any of these things you will be subject to dismissal." He said:

"Well, I may need you over here Monday morning to talk about this, because the President is considering having a commission appointed to investigate the honor system at the service academies. We're trying to do our best to get this stopped."

On Monday I went over to the White House and Dennison had some news media and magazine reporters in his office, and they asked me questions about our honor system. I told them what our honor system was, and it was quoted out of the regulations, as I have just said. They didn't have much more to ask me because that was our honor system, and they never printed a word that was said at that conference. Therefore, indicating to me that the news media weren't interested in what the facts were or what the truth was, but only in what they were trying to dig up.

Q: Only in the scandal aspect!

Adm. P.: The scandal aspect.

Q: Why would the President become so exercised by that incident at one of the academies?

Adm. P.: Well, I think it was blown up in the press, and I think he was genuinely concerned about if this could happen how could it happen and why don't we do something about it. Or someone influenced him to that belief. But eventually the services were able to prevail on him not to appoint a commission, and the Army and West Point were permitted to go ahead and take care of their own difficulties. No more about the West Point cribbing scandal.

Q: What were the duties of the Commandant of Midshipmen when the summer cruises came along?

Adm. P.: We still had two classes - the first and third class - going on regular shipboard cruises, and the second class had what they called an "aviation summer," which was devoted mostly to aviation and traveling by air to one of the major naval air facilities, or to several of them, where they were indoctrinated in naval aviation.

Our principal duty here during the summer was to indoctrinate the plebe class, to induct the new plebe class and get them started.

ready for the beginning of the academic year.

Q: Would you talk about your relations with the Board of Visitors and people of that sort who came?

Adm. P.: We had a very interesting group on the Board of Visitors during my time here. Several I remember who stayed with us in the Commandant's quarters were Father Hesburgh from Notre Dame, a great friend who I've always admired, Senator Long, of Louisiana, who was on the Board of Visitors during that period.

Q: That's Russell?

Adm. P.: Russell Long, a young senator at that time. I knew Russell Long when he was a young boy, when I was a test pilot at Anacostia from 1931 to 1933. Here he was a senator and he came down and stayed with us during the Board of Visitors time at the Naval Academy.

We had interesting times with the Board of Visitors in those days. I don't think we were put upon as much in the period as they have been during the recent ultra-liberal periods of our time.

Q: In what sense?

Adm. P.: Most of the Board of Visitors believed in the system as we were running it and in a military institution as it was being run, and we weren't questioned so much about the over-all operation of the institution as they have been during the hippie-liberal days of recent years.

Q: How vital is the Board of Visitors to the ongoing life of the Naval Academy?

Adm. P.: I think the Board of Visitors is a very important function, in that it's appointed by the President. It's the board which should advise him as to whether the Naval Academy and the other service academies are being run properly, and they have several members nominated by the Congress for the President to appoint. So that it also is a body which should reflect what the Congress believes should be done about the service academies. And it's very important in a country where it's a national institution and I think should be the most powerful.

Q: Did you have duties that pertained to the development of the budget for the Naval Academy?

Adm. P.: Yes. The Commandant of Midshipmen basically is charged with not only being in command of the brigade of midshipmen, but he had the commissary store, the mess, the midshipmen's mess, the tailors' shop, and the dairy to run and was fiscally responsible for all of them. I had to sign the audit reports and be responsible fiscally for all those departments.

Q: Did you have anything to do with public relations?

Adm. P.: Not as such. As Admiral Holloway said, I'll run the Naval Academy, you run the brigade of midshipmen, and we always divided it up that way, and so did I with Admiral Hill.

Q: What about the planning for future physical expansion at the Academy? Since you were concerned with the welfare of the midshipmen?

Adm. P.: Realizing that the principal buildings at the Naval Academy had been finished in 1907, or at that time period, our principal concern was that they were forty years old and hadn't had a face-lifting or hadn't been really overhauled was to get them modernized. We hadn't yet thought about real expansion, although Bancroft Hall obviously had to be, if we were going to keep the same number of midshipmen or increase, we had to build some more wings in order to get them out of overcrowding. This took place subsequent to my time as Commandant of Midshipmen.

The modernization plan which is now in effect, including the new engineering Michelson Hall and the Nimitz Library, none of that had been developed, nor was it considered at that time. The Field House was one of our projects which did go through and we were able to get.

Q: Was the Congress more or less sympathetic to overtures for funds for expansion?

Adm. P.: No, I don't think so. I think we always had to fight for funds for expansion at any of the service academies.

Q: Did you use the Board of Visitors?

Adm. P.: The Board of Visitors were used to the fullest extent possible, but you still had to go justify everything and got a tremendous amount of opposition from those who wanted to do away with us as an undergraduate institution.

Q: You were just telling me off tape about Captain John Perry.

Adm. P.: Immediately following the war, the first civil engineer officer of the rank of captain was ordered here to take charge of the civil engineering department. Up to that time, the head of the Public Works Department at the Naval Academy was a line officer captain called the Head of Buildings and Grounds. He made his reputation with the Superintendent on how little he spent on preventive maintenance and the modernization of buildings here, rather than how much he could spend.

Perry arrived here immediately after the war and found the buildings at the Naval Academy in horrible shape. The copper roofs were all leaking, the downcomers from the gutters were cast-iron pipe and were all beginning to leak through the walls. The electric wiring and plumbing conduits in Bancroft Hall or in any other buildings were all buried in concrete and were all leaking and causing difficulties. As a result, some millions of dollars' worth of contracts were let in that period to do emergency repairs to the wings of Bancroft Hall and to the academic buildings. It wasn't until later that any of the fineries could be done to make them into really decent and livable quarters. But these were emergency repairs which caused us to close one wing at a time and make the midshipmen double up and live in five wings, instead of six. The two wings that now front to the west on

Bancroft Hall were built in the early part of World War II and were the only modern wings that we had.

It wasn't until later that real modernization and the recognition that we had to expand and build other wings to Bancroft Hall and really modernize it took place. During my time as Commandant of Midshipmen we did a tremendous amount of modernization to the galley. When I arrived as Commandant of Midshipmen they were still cooking bread in old gas-fired brick furnaces, and meats were cooked in individual steel ovens. We finally got rotating electric ovens and modern bakery equipment, modern dishwashing equipment, and that sort of thing put into the mess hall while I was Commandant.

As I said, I had responsibility for the dairy. We had many assaults on the Naval Academy dairy by the outside milk producers who wanted to grab that plum, and we fought that off successfully all during my period and I believe to this day. The Naval Academy dairy was started in about 1910 or 1911 during a tubercular epidemic, typhoid epidemic, at the Naval Academy to provide us with pure milk. Now, what we did pricewise was this. With a dairy, while I was Commandant of Midshipmen, of around 350 Holsteins, we not only gave the midshipmen all the milk they could drink, but we saved the butter fat and during the summers saved all that butter fat and we sold them ice cream for one-fifth of the cost that we'd have had to sell it to them if we'd bought from the outside dairies. We proved this to the Congress and were able to prove it. I still think we're able to prove the fact that the Naval Academy dairy is a self-bailing unit and very essential to running of the Naval Academy.

Q: Where is it located?

Adm. P.: Gambrills, out here, five miles away.

The tailor's shop was under the same kind of assault by every tailor in the world who wanted to get the business away from Jacob Reed who'd been doing it for years. Fortunately, Jacob Reed are still doing it and still doing a fine job.

Q: Did you have relations with your counterparts in the other service academies?

Adm. P.: Yes, a very close relationship with the Commandant of Cadets and with the other people who ran these various services. At West Point they had another captain who was not a line officer, a supply type, Quartermaster Corps they called him, who ran the tailor's shop and the commissary and the rest of that business. The Commandant didn't have responsibility up there for those things.

Q: What sort of problems did you solve in common?

Adm. P.: Well, we determined what the ration cost was, what uniforms cost. We had conferences all the time as to what our general comparative costs were. I went into the mess, as to what they were feeding and what we were feeding and whether we had comparable costs.

Q: In that particular job did you have anything to do with the curriculum?

Adm. P.: We had an outfit that was back and forth to West Point at that time who did work on curriculum, but I wasn't involved in the academic part of the thing. I was only involved in what we taught in leadership and in our system for aptitude for the service. We generally got into the same pattern postwar as aptitude for the service. When I was a midshipman it didn't amount to anything. It was a popularity contest. If you were a big athlete or you were a big shot in the brigade, if you were something, why, you got a big grease mark, as we used to call it, aptitude for the service. There was no opportunity for the midshipmen, your own classmates, to mark you — if you were an under classman to be marked by the upper classmen or for the professors in the classroom to mark you, or for anybody to mark you, except this damned grease mark which you got principally from your company officer.

Well, we formalized this in the post World War II period and we got marks coming from classmates and from upper classmen and under classmen and from the professors in the classrooms. We got a good cross section of what this individual amounted to and what he was doing in aptitude for the service.

Q: A much better yardstick?

Adm. P.: A much better yardstick of how to judge. And, by the same token, we tried to get rid of misfits. We were not too successful in the beginning, but I think they have been more successful in recent years. We had a great many misfits that we couldn't get rid of.

Q: You mean emotional factors?

Adm. P.: Well, mostly people who wouldn't conform in any way to the military, who didn't want to conform. It's no use to put up with those kind of people in a military organization because obviously if he couldn't be led he wasn't going to be a leader.

Q: Did you have to contend with pressures from individual congressmen and senators in this area?

Adm. P.: On the aptitude area, very much.

Q: How did you fend them off?

Adm. P.: We weren't very successful. As I say, we tried to get a number of boys out on lack of aptitude, but were successful in only two or three cases while I was Commandant. It was very rough going. They were defended to the hilt. A misfit in this area usually has a broken home or has some kind of a misfit parent.

Q: A reflection!

Adm. P.: A reflection on the parent, so the parent goes to the congressman or to anybody he can get with influence and tries to get this stopped. In my opinion, during my time as Commandant of Midshipmen, of the hundreds of bad misfit cases we had, aptitude cases for boys who couldn't get along at the Naval Academy, almost 100 percent were due to broken homes or to drunken mothers or fathers, alcoholics or dope fiends, or one kind or another of a broken home. There was no boy ever brought up in a reasonable family atmosphere who has ever had any difficulty here.

That could be confirmed by both chaplains during all my period here. Cy Rotrig, the Catholic Reverend and Bishop, the Episcopal chaplain.

In December 1951 I was nominated by the detail office to be commanding officer of the Coral Sea. Admiral Hill, having been Commandant of the National War College, thought I should go to the National War College —

Q: You mean on the staff?

Adm. P.: No, to go as a student. I told him that since I had missed out twice going to the War College, I felt that my time was limited before I came up for selection to rear admiral and that I ought to get to sea and get a command so that I would be eligible. He said:

"Oh, you won't make rear admiral for three or four years." And I said: "Well, I'm not going to take a chance. I think I'd better go to sea in the Coral Sea."

So I went to sea in the Coral Sea in February. I was selected in June, the last man on the list, to rear admiral within six months of the time he said that.

Anyway, I did leave here in the last part of January and reported to the Coral Sea the 1st of February 1952 in the Navy Yard at Norfolk — Norfolk Shipyard.

Q: What was she undergoing?

Adm. P.: She was finishing an overhaul and Jim Russell, my classmate, was the skipper I relieved.

Pirie #4 - 205

I went to sea for a brief under way to determine that the overhaul had been properly completed, and then immediately left for Guantanamo Bay for a refresher, where I was on refresher training for three months. I was there February, March, and April, and the last of April got back to Norfolk, loaded, and immediately sailed for the Mediterranean for deployment, to relieve one of the carriers in the Mediterranean.

Q: Did you have a full complement when you were at Guantanamo?

Adm. P.: I had a full complement of officers and men. It was merely a refresher to get them ready for this next deployment to the Mediterranean.

Q: So in no way it was a repeat of the Sicily?

Adm. P.: No repeat of the Sicily disaster. I had a full crew. I had a lot of new people, a great many that had to be trained, but we had a full complement.

My exec was Jim Gray, and the air group was commanded by Larry Geis, who's now Commander, Fleet Air, Jacksonville. There were a good many young aviators who were with me then are now prominent flag officers in the Navy, including Bill Hauser, who is the present DCNO, Air. He was in one of the squadrons in the Coral Sea at that time.

It was a very interesting command for me because when I deployed to the Mediterranean my flag officer was Cat Brown, Rear Admiral C. R. Brown, of considerable fame in the Navy, and it was a most happy and amicable cruise with him to the Med that year. We had, of course, many interesting experiences in the Mediterranean both at sea and in port. We spent about half the time in port and half the time at sea.

Q: You had no designated port, did you?

Adm. P.: No designated ports. In those days they made a schedule up and you went from one to the other. The first port that we went into after getting to the Mediterranean - of course, we stopped at Gibraltar to have our relieving ceremony with the carrier we were relieving coming in, and then we had about a week of exercises and went in to Cannes which, in the late spring of the year, was a wonderful experience. One of the things I did while in Cannes was to go and make a call on the Aga Kahn, who was a most interesting and fascinating individual. It was a great experience to sit and talk to him for two hours, or three hours, which I did. He had a beautiful villa.

Q: That he made his headquarters, didn't he?

Adm. P.: Yes. He was a great man.

We went to Genoa and to Naples and to Istanbul and Athens and to Salonia, all of those normal ports that the carriers go to - Barcelona. One of the most interesting experiences that I had at that time was to go in to Split, Yugoslavia, and take Marshal Tito out on the carrier for the first time. He'd never been on an aircraft carrier. We went in there to Split and had a delightful luncheon with Tito at his villa there, then took him out on the carrier and had a two- or three-hour flight exercise, showed him the operation of the aircraft and what not, then brought him back in and anchored in Split. It was a fascinating visit and an interesting conversation with another great man.

Q: Was the State Department involved in that particular arrangement?

Adm. P.: No - but obviously our going in to Yugoslavia had to be pretty well cleared. We were the first ship that had been in there in years. I think probably since the war. It was a most interesting visit because we were looking at the difference in the people and the way they operated. For instance, there were no competitive athletic contests, none of that kind of stuff. Their only athletics was to get out in the middle of a great big stadium and take calisthenics. Hard to believe, but that was it.

We went through their naval academy and all that. Their navy didn't amount to much.

Q: You had access to the North African ports?

Adm. P.: Yes. We went in to Mers-el-Kebir in Algeria and during that period I had an opportunity to go through the countryside down to Sidi-bel-Abbas, the headquarters of the Foreign Legion.

As I said, half the time was flying and half in port. We did a considerable amount of night flying in those days, even without an angled-deck carrier. I had an absolutely solid loaded deck. I only had room for about one airplane after I got the barriers up, and so it was a tight squeeze all the time to get all these planes on and off.

Q: How many operational planes did you have on the Coral Sea?

Adm. P.: About one hundred. We had the A-1s, which were old propeller-driven planes but we had Gruman Fires and we had the Banshees, a McDonald-Douglas two-engine attack airplane. Then we had the AJs which were the predecessors of the A-3D. It was a turboprop airplane for heavy attack. We had nuclear weapons and nuclear weapons exercises.

It was a very interesting cruise and I had a great group of people with me, and great aviators, great squadrons, a very successful cruise in every way.

I was selected in June and I was the last man on the list. I didn't think I'd make it that year, but I made it. I was the last one selected for rear admiral. So they immediately give me a set of orders to detach me. I don't know when I got the orders but Jerry Wright, the admiral in London, asked for me as his chief of staff. So I got a set of orders to report to him as soon as I was detached, and I got orders to be detached in November.

We stopped in Lisbon on the way back from this cruise to the Med and had our turnover there. Then we got back to the United States and went into the Navy Yard for a short period, and Herb Riley, who was the operations Officer for Admiral McCormick, relieved me while the ship was in the Navy Yard. We went out for a short run so he could at least see the thing operating one day, and then I was detached in mid-November and I reported to Jerry Wright in London the 1st of December.

Q: Let me lap back for a moment and ask, when you were in the Med, what was the relationship of our fleet with the NATO organization?

Adm. P.: We were a part of NATO.

Q: In the Med, and were there exercises?

Adm. P.: It was just getting started, in 1952. Had Ike gone in? I know George Anderson had gone with General Eisenhower and I guess then he was detached from there and went to the FDR. He relieved me in the Med that year.

While I was there we did particularly antisubmarine with the Greeks and the French and the British participating with our submarines. We always had two submarines in the Med, and we had some joint exercises, I remember quite well, but I don't remember that we had any surface exercises at that particular time. Later, in 1956 when I had Carrier Division Six we had several exercises with the Royal Navy.

Q: There was no evidence of the Russians in the Mediterranean in 1952, was there?

Adm. P.: No. We went in to Istanbul. In the Bosporus the Turks were always involved in monitoring the Russian movements and so forth, but we didn't see anything of them in the Mediterranean at that time.

Q: You mentioned the Turks. We were instrumental in helping them build up their Navy, weren't we, at that time?

Adm. P.: Yes, we gave them a number of ships under Lend-lease and trained a good many of their crews.

Q: Well, Sir, you came back and were relieved by Herb Riley.

Adm. P.: And I had a couple of weeks' leave there in the States, and then proceeded by air to London and reported to Jerry Wright on 1 December in absentia. He was off on a trip to the Mid East. I arrived just in time for what was called the black fog. It lasted five or six days and was the worst fog in the history - modern history - of London, and was the instigator in getting the chimney pots out of London and getting it cleaned up and getting that horrible smoke and smog out of London, which they have done now. But it was violent and you couldn't see anything anywhere. We were lost for those first few days we were in London because we were afraid to even venture out of the front door of this set of quarters we'd been provided with. It was a great relief to get that over with.

My duty with Jerry Wright as his chief of staff in London was one of the happiest periods of my whole naval career. I not only had great respect and admiration for Jerry Wright, but I have great affection for him and for that period we served together.

Q: Admiral, I've heard you say several times that such and such an assignment was one of great joy. This seems to be characteristic of you yourself.

Adm. P.: Well, all of my career in the Navy was a great joy and a great period, but some better than others. I really enjoyed being with Jerry Wright and Phyllis. Bobbie and I had a great relationship with them, we enjoyed their companionship and the time we spent with them there and have since been great friends.

Q: What were your duties on his staff?

Adm. P.: I had not just normal chief of staff's duties, but he was gone a great deal of time on trips around his parish, which included the Mid East and -

Q: He was CinCNelm, wasn't he?

Adm. P.: CinCNelm, so for a month at a time he and Mrs. Wright would be gone on a trip and Bobbie and I would go out to Virginia Water and stay with their two children, Marian and Bill, and live in the house with them while they were away.

The principal event during this period was the coronation of Queen Elizabeth, which took place in June of the next year, and we had a lot of visitors and a lot of social events going on during that period, and we had a ship or some ships in the naval review that they had at Spithead. So we all had a great time.

Wentworth, the golf course on which the CinCNelm residence was located, was a great pleasure for me because I was a good golfer,- not a good golfer, but an avid golfer - and I enjoyed playing there a great deal.

I joined the American Club shortly after getting in to London and got to know a great many American businessmen and people outside of the Naval service. We had some very interesting and enjoyable people in both our Army and Navy there and in the other services, and we saw a great deal of the foreign military attachés' group. We enjoyed the theatre and the golf. All of London was very interesting and exciting to us.

Our son was in the Naval Academy at this time and our daughter went over with us and went to school for one year in one of the Air Force schools outside London, then later came back and went to school in this country.

We had many interesting conferences with our Army and Air Force commanders in Europe. Frankfurt was the headquarters for the European Command. It was eventually moved to Paris. We enjoyed going to those conferences with the Army and Air Force in Frankfurt and then in Paris, and we had many conferences with the NATO officials particularly with regard to the organization of the NATO Mediterranean Command, particularly with Lord Mountbatten who got to be a great friend, and with Field Marshal Montgomery, who was then Deputy SACEur.

Q: Did you get to be a warm friend of his?

Adm. P.: No, I wouldn't say that. I would say that he was one of the most difficult individuals we've ever had to deal with. Admiral and Lady Mountbatten became quite good friends of ours. We not only saw them on social occasions but we had the privilege of staying with them in their home a few times, and I must say I had great admiration and affection for both of them.

Q: This was at - I was about to say the height of the Cold War - but certainly the Cold War was very much in evidence at that time. Did it make for more complicated duties?

Adm. P.: Well, we began to feel the Russian ascendancy in the things that they were doing. I suppose during that period they became more evident, but not to a great degree.

One other interesting event took place in 1954 before I came back. They had a huge earthquake in the Greek Islands, just to the west of Greece, which wiped out a couple of those islands. We sent the Sixth Fleet in there with supplies and medical people, furnished them with tents and food, and all the necessary emergency equipment, because the houses were just flattened on two of these islands. I would guess that the population amounted to between 10,000 and 15,000 on each of these islands. They were absolutely devastated. On one island the only thing that I could see standing was a church steeple that was built of steel.

It became fairly evident after two or three days with the Sixth Fleet in there that if we didn't pull them out the Greeks would like to have them stay there forever. So Jerry Wright said, "You get in an airplane and go down and check this out. I've checked it out with Washington. You go down and tell the ambassador that I sent you down and tell him that the Sixth Fleet's got to pull out in such and such a length of time and that they'd better get organized to take this thing over because we can't stay in there. We'll leave the supplies and things that we've put in there, but we can't stay."

So I did just that. I went down and got hold of the Ambassador and we went over to see the Prime Minister. Eventually we got out in two or three days. It was an interesting experience. I went in to the islands in a helicopter with some nurses and saw this terrific devastation. I couldn't believe that the place would be absolutely flat, but it was. But we got out and somebody else took over.

Q: Admiral, how did our naval unit in the Persian Gulf figure in the total picture? What was its purpose?

Adm. P.: We had a unit in the Persian Gulf post war, I think principally, to look out for our oil interests and other commercial interests we had in that area.

Q: What was it, a cruiser?

Adm. P.: No, it was a small converted seaplane tender. We had several in that class built and they were a little more than a destroyer. I think they were probably about 3,500 to 4,000 tons, and they painted them white and had air-conditioning systems put in them so that they could stand that terrific heat down there. They went from one area of our interest to another in the Persian Gulf and were our link with our commercial interests there. We, of course, had a great interest in our oil companies at Dhahran in Saudi Arabia and in Bahrein and in

Qatar and all of those places. And then they went down the coast to visit Haile Selassie and those ports along the African coast.

It was a very interesting cruise for the people who had an opportunity to make it and to see that part of the world.

During the latter part of my time in London Admiral Wright sent me down with Slim Beecher, a class ahead of me at the Naval Academy, who was going to take the Persian Gulf command. I rode down in the plane with him and Mrs. Beecher and had an opportunity in four or five days to visit most of the principal cities in the area. I had a chance to see Basra, Iraq, Kuwait, Bahrein, Dhahran, Cairo, and to see what our oil interests were in that area.

One of the most interesting calls that I made was on the Sheik of Bahrein. I'd been warned before we went to beware of the horrible concoctions that they gave you for tea, and they lived up to every expectation. You could smell them for a mile and they were full of perfume. You could hardly get them to your lips. So when these cups were served in quick succession, I think in about a 20-minute visit we had about ten different varieties, and one of these huge eunuchs would come around and grab the cup out of your hand and throw the contents on a beautiful Persian rug, what was left, and this distressed me greatly because I hated to see the Persian rug ruined!

I'd been warned to beware of the rose water. They had an atomiser which was about the size of a gallon can that this fellow brought around and squirted rose water on your hands afterwards. I was told to be sure and hold them out far enough because if he got it on your clothes you'd never get it out. I thought I had my hands out far enough, but he apparently got me pretty good because I had to throw the uniform away eventually that had this attar of roses on it and I couldn't get rid of it.

Q: The use of that was in lieu of water?

Adm. P.: Yes, no water.

Q: Did we have concern for the Suez Canal in 1952?

Adm. P.: No, nothing had developed at that stage of the game at all. The real problems with the Suez Canal came up later and I'll have something to say about that when I get to my Carrier Division Six command.

Q: All right, Sir.

Adm. P.: The Queen's coronation was a most interesting event from our standpoint. Not only the social parts of it, but to see the great ceremonial events connected with the Queen's coronation and with the naval review at Spithead. The weather was very bad and the whole coronation parade took place in the rain but it didn't daunt the participants.

In connection with the Queen's coronation they had a huge naval review at Spithead, at Portsmouth.

Q: That is a part of the tradition, too, isn't it?

Adm. P.: Part of the tradition, and in connection with that Admiral Wright appointed me to be his representative to go to the conferences with the officials at Portsmouth with regard to the naval review and with regard to our participation. We had one of our cruisers - my memory is that one of our cruisers participated. All of the European countries participated and included was the first Sverdlov cruisers. On the night before the review at Spithead the British commander, Admiral Sir George Creasy, had a dinner on the flagship, which included the heads of each one of these ships, or the head of the naval delegation coming to the naval review. It was obvious that the Russian was pretty stuffy and that the Royal Navy admiral didn't think much of this and was pretty outspoken.

Admiral and Mrs. Wright and my wife and I stayed at the Keppel's Head Inn, which was a rowdy place in the middle of Portsmouth, made famous by Lord Nelson's having used it during his days, and I must say that I don't think a thing had been done to modernize it since Lord Nelson had been there! The Wrights and ourselves couldn't have been happier to escape.

Q: It was service people who reviewed the fleet, not the political representatives?

Adm. P.: No, it was all just Navy and the Queen was on the royal yacht Britania and passed through the line and got the salutes from each ship.

In the late spring of 1954 Admiral Wright was relieved by

Admiral John Cassidy and he left to take command of SACLant and Commander-in-Chief of the Atlantic and Atlantic Fleet. I remained on with Admiral Cassidy until August when I was detached and went back to take overeas Deputy Chief of Staff to Admiral Wright and later his Chief of Staff.

Q: Had that been prearranged? I mean when Wright was called back?

Adm. P.: Yes, he told me he was going to get me back.

During the period when Admiral Cassidy took over from Admiral Wright, we had one interesting trip to the continent with the Cassidys, when we went to Holland for four or five days and had the opportunity to see Prince Bernhard and the Queen and we had a very interesting visit there.

Q: What was the purpose of that trip? To get acquainted with the Dutch?

Adm. P.: Yes, just to become acquainted and speak to the Dutch Navy.

Q: How strong with the Dutch Navy as a unit in NATO?

Adm. P.: I think very strong for the number of ships they had. They're very good at sea and they had very good ships, and could give a good account of themselves. They, of course, had to have a fairly strong navy out in the Far East while they had the East Indies. They're good seamen and they had fine ships.

Q: What sort of impression did Bernhard make on you?

Adm. P.: I liked Prince Bernhard. I saw him two or three times afterwards. As a matter of fact, I had him in one of my carriers when I had a carrier division at Norfolk - I think the _Forrestal_ - and he had never been in one of our large carriers before and was very much interested in the whole operation. It was very interesting. I've seen him some since and I have a great admiration for Bernhard as an individual and in his military knowledge.

Interview No. 5 with Vice Admiral Robert Burns Pirie, U.S. Navy (Retired)
Place: The U. S. Naval Institute, Annapolis, Maryland
Date: Wednesday morning, 17 October 1973
Subject: Biography
By: John T. Mason, Jr.

Q: All right, Sir. I'm looking forward to this chapter, the resumption of this most interesting and amusing story.

Adm. P.: When I was detached as Chief of Staff to CinCNelm we had three weeks of leave and we took two weeks and went to Scotland with a driver and visited a good many of our naval friends — Royal Navy friends — at Edinburgh and Arbroath, then went up to Banff and spent a couple of days with Sir George and Lady Abercrombie. Then we went up to Thurso, on the north coast, where we had a day's fishing with Bill Blackett.

Q: Salmon fishing?

Adm. P.: Salmon fishing, and then drove down through the middle of north Scotland, which is as desolate as any part of the world you'll ever see. You go miles and miles and never see anything except a shepherd with some sheep. And we ended up in Turnberry and visited Loch Lomond and the Burns country. We came back to London and flew from London to Naples, where we spent a week with Jim Gray and Peggy, his wife. Jim had been my executive officer in the Coral Sea. We spent a week on a yacht they had at Capri. That was one of the finest vacations I've ever had.

Q: An ideal way to have a vacation.

Adm. P.: It was great. Then we got into the S.S. Independence with the Grays and came back to New York. I proceeded to Norfolk and reported in immediately to Admiral Wright as his Deputy Chief of Staff.

It was a great pleasure to be with him again, and I had another very pleasant tour of duty with him.

Q: What were you specific duties as Deputy?

Adm. P.: The command at Norfolk held by Admiral Wright had three hats - SACLant, Supreme Allied Commander, Atlantic; CinCLant, which is the commander of the Atlantic area under the Joint Chiefs; and CinCLantFlt, which is the naval command under the CNO.

I was Chief of Staff to CinCLant/CinCLantFlt area, and there was a great deal of work with the unified commands as well as with command of the Atlantic Fleet itself. The Chief of Staff at the time I reported was Slim Ingersoll, and he stayed on for some five or six months before I relieved him as Chief of Staff.

One of the important duties that I had was coordinator of the nuclear warfare, which was just in its infancy - the organization was just in its infancy, and I went to a good many meetings with the Air Force, SAC (the Strategic Air Command), and our Pacific Fleet commander on coordination of delivery of nuclear weapons.

Q: What nuclear weapons were available at that time? This was before Polaris.

Adm. P.: We had a good many nuclear weapons in the carriers, the original ones, and had delivery aircraft. The exact numbers I can't remember and it would be classified information anyway. But we had nuclear weapons that could be carried by carrier aircraft of two or three types.

I continued that duty as the senior U.S. Navy coordinator for three or four years and had meetings, as I said, with the Strategic Air Command and Air Force people in Omaha, Paris, and London.

Q: This was in the period when they were pushing the Jupiter - the Army was, and there was some talk - well, there was an effort to get the Navy to cooperate with the Army and develop one missile.

Adm. P.: Yes. Everyone was trying to get into the act at that time, and there was a great deal of bickering and argument about who should have complete control over the delivery of all weapons - whether the Air Force should have complete control over the delivery of all weapons, or whether the Army or Navy were going to have any part in it. This was before the Air Force had developed any large missile, before the Atlas, and their delivery system was completely in the aircraft. The development of Atlas and Minuteman and the subsequent missile system, Polaris, came along later.

It was interesting that Admiral Raborn, who had the job of developing Polaris, was a captain at the time I was Chief of Staff to Admiral Wright at CinCLantFlt and was the Operations Officer on the CinCLantFlt staff. And he was ordered from that staff to Washington to start the Polaris project.

Q: That was in 1955 when he went to Washington.

Adm. P.: Right. When I reported to CinCLantFlt staff, Admiral Ingersoll was Chief of Staff and he asked me if I would go down to the operations center and take a look and see what I thought of it. I went down and took a look. There wasn't much there. There were no communication facilities, no electronic displays of any kind. They had some maps on the wall and one telephone that went to either Key West or San Juan, I can't remember which. That's the only communication system they had, other than regular radio communications. No telephones, no fast communication system.

So I was back up in Ingersoll's office in about ten minutes and he said: "I thought you were going down to take a look at the OpCon center."

I said, "I've looked at it."

He said, "Oh, you're a smart so and so."

"Well," I said, "it didn't take long to look at what is down there. I never saw anything that reminded me so much of a morgue, except I didn't see any 'stiffs' lying around."

"Oh, you smart so and so," he said, "if you're so damned smart, you tell us what we need as an OpCon center."

As a result of that I sat down and wrote in longhand what I considered the Commander-in-Chief, Atlantic Fleet, should have as an operations control center. And that basically consisted of an instant communications system with all units, all subcommanders, and the ability to see on a television screen any segment of the Atlantic Ocean or the command that he wanted to see from full-scale down to an area fifty miles on a side showing all surface ships, aircraft and submarines in the area.

The Navy has worked fairly hard to achieve that goal and I have to report that some twenty years after I wrote that, it is finally coming to fruition and they're going to have that system down in the Atlantic Fleet headquarters in 1974 - twenty years after I wrote it. Progress comes very slowly and very hard.

Q: Yes, but foresight is necessary.

Adm. P.: The second interesting thing was that I asked the individual I relieved as Deputy Chief of Staff where they kept the plot or record of what ships they had to fit into the war plans in case of emergency. War plans are quite carefully drawn and in some considerable detail, but I wasn't able to see where they had any kind of plot or display of what ships you had to fit into -

Q: The availability.

Adm. P.: - the availability of the ships to fill the plan. They told me that there was a book kept by the CinCLantFlt duty officer. I went down, and there was a loose-leaf binder with a lot of sheets in it with the basic plans, and they had filled the ships' names in in pencil and it was all lop-eared and had been erased. It wasn't up to date and it was a pretty sad situation.

So immediately when I took over I got a room and put the war plans in white letters on a black wall and then had that kept up to date and photographs taken of it every week and sent to each of the commanders so that they would know what forces they had available in case they had to implement a war plan. That was available so that you could go down and take a look and you knew instantly what ships you had available to fullfil the plans and what you couldn't fullfil - that is, ships that were in Navy yards or off on some extraneous duty. I think Admiral Raborn, then Captain Raborn, got the idea for - the original idea and concept for his PERT system from that plot that we had for fulfilling our war plans.

Q: That certainly was a major step forward. Were you inspired in any way by the British system, which was a thorough-going one? You remember their Pink List and Red List and so forth?

Adm. P.: I don't know that I'd ever seen their system, but really basically a great many people are involved in fullfilling these plans and it's very important that they be displayed and have immediate availability to as many key officers on the staff as is necessary.

Q: Well, they're somewhat useless as plans without implementation. Let me ask you, in terms of plans for various contingencies, how many plans would be in being at a given time? How many contingencies did you anticipate?

Adm. P.: Oh, there are dozens and dozens of contingency plans based on who the possible enemy is, and the implementation of a war plan has a good many facets and they're in some complete detail. This room that I spoke about was on the order of 40 feet by 20 feet and the walls were covered solid with the organization to implement these plans, and they also told you what ships were in the Navy yards and where every active ship that you had was in being at the time and what you could get your hands on - ships and aircraft, including submarines, of course.

Q: There must have been some crossing of lines with the existence of a strike force plan as to the availability of U.S. ships, wasn't there?

Adm. P.: Well, we had NATO plans and by the same token NATO and SACLant had the same sort of a system and a scheme for implementation in case of a NATO conflict, and that included all the forces that he had, our U.S. Strike Fleet plus the British and the Dutch and the French, all the nations that contributed something to the NATO war plans.

    I afterwards had command of the Second Fleet and command of the Strike Fleet, and had one large exercise which I'll have something to say about later.

Q: I suppose that's part of the wisdom of having CinCLant serve as well?

Adm. P.: Yes. He had a separate staff and his chief of staff on the SACLant side was Page Smith.

During this period we had a large naval review in connection with the Jamestown Anniversary and had not only all of our naval units but naval units from all of the Atlantic nations took part in this, including a couple of very beautiful sailing vessels - training vessels for a couple of the navies, the Spanish and I believe the Danes. It was quite an occation and there were a good many social events.

Q: Did President Eisenhower come to this?

Adm. P.: I don't think he came to the naval review, but we did in my next assignment as Commander, Carrier Division Six take the President out in the Saratoga from Jacksonville. It was the first time he had been on a carrier and I'll talk about that a little later.

Q: Admiral Radford was Chairman of the Joint Chiefs at this time?

Adm. P.: Not at that time, was he? I guess he was. This was 1954 or 1955.

Q: Yes. Radford was Chairman of the Joint Chiefs and Burke was CNO.

Adm. P.: He became CNO during this period. He relieved Admiral Carney during the time that I was at Norfolk.

Q: Talk about your educational program for VIPs and that kind of thing.

Adm. P.: We had a good many VIP cruises in those days. The Secretary of the Navy sponsored taking as many distinguished Americans as we could out in ships of the fleet for orientation cruises. We also had our own Naval War College, National War College, and Industrial College, Armed Forces Staff College orientation cruises.

Q: They came as a body, did they?

Adm. P.: Yes, whole group. We'd take them on a carrier for one or two days.

Q: Did you have a specific role in that?

Adm. P.: No, just organizational. After I got command of the carrier division I had several groups of Secretary of the Navy guests and advanced National War College and Armed Forces Staff College on board carriers.

Q: At that time your role was merely organizational?

Adm. P.: Just planning and organization.

Q: Admiral, off tape you were telling me several experiences you had on CinCLantFlt staff with weapons that became available but there were no trained people to operate them. I think that's a very interesting story and I wish you'd put it on the tape.

Adm. P.: During the time that I was Chief of Staff, CinCLantFlt, the first atomic depth charge was delivered at Yorktown, the mine depot in Yorktown, and much to our chagrin we found that there had been no facilities built at any of the places where we intended to deploy the atomic depth charges and operate it with patrol aircraft -

Q: I take it it wasn't within the province of Research and Development to do this?

Adm. P.: No, the weapon had been built, researched and was ready to go without the logistics having been either planned or, if they had been planned, followed up to see that they were available at the time that the weapon system was available.

There were no enlisted personnel trained to operate the weapon nor had there been a training program set up, with simulators or any means of training personnel. So, in effect, it was about three years from the time that that weapon was delivered before we were able to deploy it and make it useful.

Q: This became the project of CinCLant then?

Adm. P.: Well, this immediately came to our attention because we were the ones who had to operate it, had to make it operational, and it wasn't possible to make it operational because the tools hadn't been provided.

Almost the same thing happened with Regulus I, which was ready to operate and was delivered, and no facilities or training had been provided. In going into the plans for development and inducting Regulus I into the fleet, the plans were adequate but they had broken down because of budget problems in the various segments of the Navy in Washington, and there was no coordinator and no one to follow up to see that the facilities and the personnel and the training were all coordinated with the development of the weapon itself and, when the weapon was available, that the training and the facilities were all adequate to make it operational in the fleet.

Q: I understand that when the weapon was available and the other aspects of the program were not, you took it upon yourself to pursue this?

Adm. P.: Well, it was my job, and I went to Washington and worked with the various offices and called this to their attention and got them started correcting the deficiency in logistics and personnel.

As a result of this, when I later became DCNO, Air, I had firmly implanted in my mind the fact that all the pieces of the puzzle when you start the development of a new weapon - you have got to have the plan for all of the logistics, training, and personnel coordinated with it as it is developed in order that it will be operational at the time that it's ready.

Q: Tell me about your conversation with the various people who came in and said "but it's too early to do this."

Adm. P.: When I got to be DCNO, Air, my subordinates broke out the plan and they said, "We don't have to have personnel or supply people for another year on the particular airplane," and I said, "Oh, yes, you do. You've got to have them right now." And they said:

"Here's the plan and it says we don't have to have them for a year yet."

And I said, "Well, whoever made the plan didn't understand modern weapons systems. It wasn't very difficult in the day when you only had a machine gun and a bomb rack on an airplane, not even a bomb sight. You looked through a telescope to deliver dive bombing. But now you've got complicated aircraft that are full of electronics and they have complicated weapon delivery systems, and you've got missiles that have got to be fitted and coordinated, and all of this requires that you back up all your logistic requirements and all your personnel and training requirements and they've got to take place early in the development of the aircraft."

As a result of this, we did start ordering officers and men who were going to operate the vehicles earlier in the development cycle. Also we backed up the "provisioning," the logistics, the spare parts and supply business, so that when we got the airplane through test and ready to be inducted into the fleet, we had adequate personnel and we had adequate spare parts and systems to operate the aircraft. This was particularly so in connection with the F-4 McDonald fighter and the A-6 and the A-5. I will discuss this in some more detail when I get to DCNO, Air.

Q: Did BuPers come around to your point of view then?

Adm. P.: They have always resisted putting enough effort, enough money, and enough time into the training of enlisted men particularly, but also officers. We had an adequate enlisted training system at Memphis which was developed during World War II and is a necessity in the air game because it's life and death. You can't have a man half-trained when he is taking care of an airplane in which the pilot's life is at stake. We had an adequate training system, which was a World War II development. We tried our best to influence the surface Navy to take similar systems in connection with training personnel on weapon systems and torpedoes, guns, missiles.

A classis example of how inadequate their training system was was the Talos, the Terrier, and the Tartar, which, in my opinion, aren't even adequately operational today. But they wouldn't put adequate effort on it. Until Admiral Zumwalt got to Washington there hadn't been adequate emphasis on training the rest of the Navy, outside of aviation and submarines.

Admiral Zumwalt has organized a training command, which is now at Pensacola under Admiral Cagle, which takes all of the Navy, submarines, air, and surface, and he, Admiral Cagle, has the responsibility for training and education in the Navy. It's now all coordinated and they are now spending adequate amounts of money in all departments of the Navy to see that we have decent training.

Q: In that earlier period, did you have any problem with the budget people or with the congressional committees?

Adm. P.: You always have great difficulty in the budget with funds for training and personnel. You have to fight it every step of the way because there's great competition for funds in every area. There's great competition for funds in research and development, great competition for operational funds, there's great competition for an adequate ship program and an adequate aircraft procurement program. By the same token, there's great competition for funds for personnel and great competition for funds for training.

One of the things that we learned during the war was that we needed simulators and training devices to use to take the place of actual operating weapons systems, which is quite expensive, and you can build simulators or training devices which are relatively inexpensive which will teach the individual the same thing. In other words, in a complicated aircraft we teach a pilot in a simulator, in which he sits in a cockpit in a trainer and we have operators who operate the simulator and he goes through the same processes and actions that he would in an actual aircraft. But it is infinitely less expensive to teach him on the ground, and then when he gets in an airplane he's familiar with where everything is and what's going to happen to him in case of emergencies and that sort of thing.

This was a World War II project, and Rear Admiral Luis de Florez was the head of training devices.

Q: That was his great contribution!

Adm. P.: Great contribution, during the war. As a result of this we have a training device center which is now in Orlando, where we give these types of training, and we have operational trainers at each of the large centers to teach these techniques to both actual pilots or operators, officers and men, and then the same sort of training takes place in submarines, where they also have to bear in mind that safety is paramount, particularly in the nuclear submarine business, where this schooling and training is so important.

Q: Admiral, how long in advance generally does the operational fleet have knowledge of a weapon like Regulus I coming on?

Adm. P.: They know about plans for weapons. The Commander-in-Chief, Atlantic, and Commander-in-Chief, Pacific Fleet, are asked for recommendations on new weapons. They can make a recommendation themselves as to new weapon systems, but if a weapon system is invented, thought up, or developed in Washington or at one of our laboratories, the Commander-in-Chief of the fleet is asked to comment, and has an opportunity to comment before the development plan is implemented. So, they know in every instance what is being developed and have a chance to comment and kibitz during the development.

Q: Admiral, was there wisdom then, since the development of this whole area depended on the attitude of BUPers and its cooperation, in naming the head of BuPers as CinCLant? Did this give it impetus?

Adm. P.: Well, I think the development of the weapon itself and the personnel, training, and logistics are all equally important, and are all part of the development plan in each case. It's most important that they be carefully coordinated and that everything come out at the proper time to put the weapon system into operation.

During this period that I was Chief of Staff the Forrestal and Saratoga, new carriers, the Forrestal being the first of the class were commissioned.

Q: And they joined the Atlantic Fleet?

Adm. P.: They joined the Atlantic Fleet. When I left CinCLantFlt as Chief of Staff in early 1956, my flagship in Carrier Division Six was designated as the Coral Sea, but I had an exercise off the East Coast and I flew my flag in the Forrestal as an operational commander, and I was the first flag officer to fly his flag in the Forrestal. I had the Forrestal and the Saratoga in a fleet operation off the coast. This was before I went on the Mediterranean deployment in the summer of 1956.

Q: Maybe this is the place to talk about the improvement in the Forrestal over the Coral Sea?

Adm. P.: The great operational improvement was in handling the aircraft, the flight deck, and catapults, and in handling facilities for aircraft, the size of the hangars and the elevators - all were a great improvement over the earlier carriers. The one area where I noted immediately no improvement, and if anything a retrogression, was in the CIC

The CIC was still not segmented. It was not modular. There was too much confusion. They were not prepared to take on all the warfare tasks. The only thing that they really could do was mon craft and do air defense, and they were mixed up even in that area by having the individual in the CIC monitoring fuel state, which is very important in the case of jet aircraft and emergencies, instead of being in air plot where he belonged. There was great confusion caused by the operators of the individual radars and this individual fuel monitoring in emergencies.

As a result of seeing that CIC had not developed and progressed the way it should, I immediately sat down and drew up in rough the modular CIC that we now have in the carriers, where whoever is in charge of the CIC, if it's a flag officer, sits with his staff and sees the display of all of the information in each area of warfare, air defense, air attack, the air offensive capability, whatever they had, electronic warfare, surface warfare - surface plot, just to navigate and avoid collisions - antisubmarine warfare, all the facets of warfare have got to be displayed on the four walls of this room without having operators of equipment, PPIs and so forth, in the room. In other words, whoever is going to be the commander in the center - and it should be called a command center, not a combat information center - is not being diverted by either sight or sound, he can see displayed on a real-time basis everything that he needs to know.

Now, the operators are in the back, back of those display boards in each instance, but isolated, as I say, by sight and sound. You have a door, if you want to go into the air defense operator's room. You can open the door and walk in and see what he's doing, but he provides for you on the display the necessary information to operate.

I got the idea, as I say, while I was deployed in the Forrestal for the first time after I got Carrier Division Six, and during that time that I had the carrier division, or subsequently when I had the Second Fleet, I was able to go to Washington to a joint meeting of the Ships' Characteristics Board and the CIC Division section of the Bureau of Ships and convince them that this was the type of combat information center we needed in order to give the commander adequate tools to do his job.

So I take great pride in saying, not being at all egotistical, but the modular CIC is the Pirie Concept and I put it over single-handed by going to Washington and convincing them in rather violent fashion –

Q: Was there much opposition?

Adm. P.: Oh, yes, all kinds of opposition. People who didn't know what the problem was – ignorance. The problem was they had a lot of people working in BuShips and in the CNO's office and Ships' Characteristics who had never had to operate and were ignorant of what the problems are connected with operating. For instance, after I took Carrier Division Six – this is also germane to the problem – I had a fine staff. My chief of staff was Dan Smith, affectionately known as "Dog," who had been with me during the war. He was a captain. And I had Wally Clark as operations officer, who'd been in Fighting 5 with me in the Yorktown and was a great flyer, and I had several other fine lieutenant commanders, one of whom was Charlie Smith, who has now gotten out of the Navy. But Charlie had just finished aeronautical engineering PG at Princeton and while he was taking the aeronautical degree at Princeton he also studied and passed the bar exam and became a lawyer while he was taking the aeronautical PG. He was a very smart and fine officer.

Well, I went on the bridge the first time at sea with the staff and here's Charlie Smith as the duty officer, my duty officer, with a task force around me -- two or three carriers, two battleships, and a couple of cruisers, and fifteen destroyers in a circular formation. The carriers are flying. He's the only one up there, and he's responsible to give the orders for changing the formation, to get into the wind, to launch and recover aircraft. Any emergencies that took place or any replacements in the plan that we had for the particular flight that was going on, he had to do. Submarines were attacking us and he's responsible for submarine attack. Everything. And I said if they just put a broom up his rear end he could also sweep the deck!

Anyway, I was furious that he was the one individual up there with all this responsibility -- the possibility of collision, I mean just to avoid that kind of thing. So I called Dan Smith right away, my chief of staff, and told him that I wanted one officer up there responsible for a change in the air plan, for example, if there were an emergency or anything that had to be done in connection with changing operation plans, it was not going to be that duty officer. He was responsible for operating the formation and to avoid collision. He had to have somebody that was responsible for antisubmarine warfare and had to have one that was responsible for the attack plan in the offensive warfare that we were doing - we had a room designated down below for that.

Smith said, "We've only got fourteen officers on the staff. There aren't enough." And I said:

"I don't give a damn if they have to stand watch and watch. You get one officer on watch in each of these functions, and that's the way we're going to operate."

Well, this came as a great surprise to my staff. But we had a man responsible for each one of those things to protect my watch officer up there operating the task group. He was responsible only for that, and he didn't have any of these other functions that were going to divert or distract him.

As a result, we had a collision at sea in which a destroyer tried to run through the Wisconsin in bad weather. It turned out in the investigation that there was an argument going on between the division commander and the commanding officer of the ship. Anyway, they had a very bad collision in the fog. I was an interested party, of course, as the operational commander, and one of the things that the court wanted to know right away was what was my organization. And I had gotten this organization in which my watch officer was responsible for this only.

Q: Did he take the rap, then?

Adm. P.: No, the skipper of the ship took the rap because he was responsible. It was a change of course and a change of formation and he forgot to look at his CIC and ran right straight into the Wisconsin, which was a very bad thing to hit with a destroyer.

Q: Admiral, in the birth of this idea, the modular CIC, it would seem from the earlier accounts you've given me that there was a certain amount of fermentation taking place within you, which suddenly developed on the Forrestal. This seems to be part of your genius.

Adm. P.: Well, I'd gotten the idea during World War II, when I was with Bogan, and I've related before to you that there was so much confusion in the CIC with people that were operating the individual scopes, you know, and so forth, the fighter director or the CIC officer there was so much noise by sight and sound confusion that it's a wonder we ever got anything done. Anyway, Bogan, my boss, said to me: "I can't get any accurate information through the telephones, with an enlisted man and an officer on each end. You go down to the CIC and you tell me what I have to know up here."

So I went to the CIC and I spent most of my time, when I was his chief of staff, down in the CIC. Well, the confusion that reigned in that place, you just can't imagine. It's a damned wonder to me we ever did as well as we did to knock down Jap airplanes and to direct our fighter aircraft onto incoming attacks. I had the idea then that the flag officer's representative, the captain's representative - he's got a big stake in this, too - the gunnery officer, who was responsible for the antiaircraft in the world war, and the navigator, each should have a representative looking at the plot and seeing what is going on that's being brought in by radar, and be in soundproof booths looking down at this plot. That idea germinated in my head and I tried to convince the CIC people in King's staff at the end of the war. So the idea had always been in my head that you needed something that sanitized you from the confusion of sight and sound but gave you all the necessary information on which to take action.

All you want to do in air defense, for example, is to see when a bogey shows up on the screen, and it's very simple - you have a circular plot and a red dot, or whatever they use to designate the bogey, shows up out here at 100 miles or 120 miles. Then you know where your fighter aircraft are. You can see the plot and you see what is taking place in the air defense, who's going after that bogey, how big the bogey is, how many airplanes do you need. Do you need to launch another dozen fighters to take care of it, if there are fifteen or twenty attacking? All this sort of thing is displayed right on that board.

The same thing with submarines. The minute you get a submarine contact, you've got the board right there and you know right where that submarine is and you know what action is being taken, what destroyer or submarine you've got going after him, what airplane have you got going after him. The same thing takes place with the surface plot. You can look and see all of your ships right here and what they're doing. You can see if a guy's moving in the wrong direction or if there's confusion or a chance of collision.

The same now is most important in electronic warfare. We're now in the era of the Styx missile, the Russian-developed missile which can be launched by aircraft, by surface ship, or by submarine. It is most important that a commander have displayed immediately in front of him the situation with regard to when they know that that kind of a missile is launched. You know that by the radio frequency. He has to have turned on a frequency for guidance. So you get the information on his having launched a missile before you can see it or before you detect it by any other means by monitoring the frequency and knowing that he's launched something.

All communication with regard to what actions you're going to take now all has to take place not by voice, which was the fastest communication system we had, but data link, which in real time tells you exactly what's going on all the time in each of the areas which you need to know. And that information's all got to be displayed for this commander so that he can take action, so he can turn off radars or communication circuits, any electronic emission, be able to take such action as he wants to, if he wants to choose what he wants to turn off and what he wants to leave on. Maybe he wants to leave one gun out there, a destroyer, as the goat and let the bomb hit him. Leave his turned on and everybody else turned off. Or put up a decoy. Whatever action he's going to take has got to be taken instantaneously and by data link.

You can understand that if you had all of these operators, or people who are gathering this information for you, in the same room with you, what a terrible amount of confusion takes place. So you've got to have these things displayed without confusion, out of sight or sound. The modular CIC becomes more and more important every day in modern warfare.

Q: And the use of a kind of a staff system to accomplish this?

Adm. P.: That's right. The people who are doing the work for you are out of sight. You're sitting in the room seeing all this. Now the same thing, the combat control center, for the commander-in-chief on shore. There's one at Norfolk, one in Hawaii, and one in Rota, I think, or somewhere in Europe, where the fellow who's operating the whole fleet gets the same kind of picture and information. In other words, he wants to know where every submarine is. He wants to know where every enemy submarine is. He wants to know where all of his own are. He wants to know where every surface ship is, including all of the merchant shipping, and he wants to know what airplanes are in the air over the Atlantic or over the Pacific. And this is quite a job, and it all has to be done, as I say, not by antiquated communications methods, but by data link.

Q: And that, combined with the immediate knowledge of the availability of units of the fleet, makes the perfect picture.

Adm. P.: So you know what you've got to work with and what's actually happening.

Q: About the data link, you said that it had developed from the program of the astronauts?

Adm. P.: Well, all of this communication is instantaneous, all the way to the moon and back. You hear them talking on the moon, and it's done by data link. They know exactly what's going on, not only voice but all of the instruments that they monitor. For example, in Houston, in one of these space vehicles as far away as the moon, they're monitoring dozens of different systems and they can see what the astronaut is seeing on his instrument board, they see by the system known as data link. Real-time, instantaneous transmission of the information on that man's instruments, or oxygen, or whatever, any system.

Q: Admiral, would you say a little about the fact that when you were with CinCLantFlt coming on stream were a lot of new developments, a lot of new ideas out of research and development and out of the experience of World War II, which in total made it a new era in warfare which was dawning when you were with CinCLantFlt? Would you comment on that?

Adm. P.: There were a great many new weapons systems. I guess a good many of them came from World War II experiences, but a good many both defensive and offensive weapons systems came into being during this period.

Atomic weapons, both small atomic bombs carried in aircraft and large ones carried in aircraft and a missile system such as Minuteman for the Air Force and Polaris for the Navy came along at this time. We also had a transition in air-to-air missiles in the Sidewinder and the Sparrow. Sidewinder came into being because of the heat-seeking capabilities and that came as a result of jet aircraft predominance and the ability to see the infrared device on the nose of the Sidewinder.

the tailpipe of a jet and be able to seek it and hit it. The Sparrow, which was electronically guided. The air-to-ground missiles came along at this period, and the tactics necessarily had to be modified to take care of all of these things.

The surface-to-air missiles, the Terrier, Talos, Tartar, and modern weapons systems in antisubmarine warfare were under development and coming into being.

Q: What was the nature of the impact all of this made upon the fleet commander?

Adm. P.: Almost all of them were fairly complicated systems and required greater knowledge, a greater amount of training both of officers and men, and it required a good deal more expertise in the knowledge that a commander had to have to make decisions - operational decisions. A commander today has got to have a considerable knowledge of these weapons systems in order to be a commander. He can't depend on having an expert in each one of these fields sitting near him to tell him what to do. He's got to know himself what's important, what to do, and how to do it.

This is very important in the air warfare game and it's very important in the antisubmarine warfare game that we have knowledgeable people in command. You just can't dredge somebody up who's wearing a suit and say that he can be an effective commander. He's got to know. Our educational systems have had to be greatly expanded and modified to take care of modern weapons systems. The understanding of electronics and electronic warfare is vitally important to us today. Everything is computerized and run with computers. A modern aircraft, for example - people wonder why aircraft cost 10 million dollars a piece. The reason they cost 10 million dollars a piece is that you've got pieces of equipment in the aircraft that are all tremendously expensive. There's a computer in every one of these airplanes today which is quite expensive. Everything that you have costs a great deal of money. In the modern airplane the airframe itself costs about one-fourth of the total cost of the aircraft. One-fourth of the total cost is in the power plants, one-fourth of it is in electronic equipment, and one-fourth in weapons equipment, weaponry.

As an interesting comparison, the aircraft that I flew in 1929 and 1930 from the first Lexington was a Boeing F3-B. The total cost of that airplane, power plant, bomb racks, guns, gun sights, was $36,000 in inventory. Now, a fighter airplane on a modern carrier is up to $10,000,000.

Q: Tell me, Sir, how did a fleet commander like Admiral Wright, how did you, prepare yourselves for the transitional era with the new equipment? How did you gain the additional knowledge that hadn't been yours in earlier training?

Adm. P.: Well, we kept ourselves up to date by going to the site and learning what the system was. As a matter of fact, updating the education of the individual goes on continuously throughout his career and when you are about to take command of a ship or command of a group of ships, a division, or go into any command, they have a training period, a transition period, before you go in and you are brought up to date by going to school, so to speak, en route to your new assignment. And this is most important, that the individual be brought up to date and know what all of the modern weapon systems are.

Q: Admiral, during this period with the fleet in the Atlantic, I believe the treaty was arranged with Spain where we got a base at Rota. Do you want to talk about that as it related to your job?

Adm. P.: The importance of having a base somewhere in the European area where you could put a carrier alongside of a dock and offload aircraft to a field and vice versa we found to be one of great importance to us, and it wasn't until we made the Spanish base deal that we were able to get an adequate area where we could dock a carrier and resupply. It was also desirable that it not be in the Mediterranean because we could defend and protect it better if it were outside.

Rota was a natural for us because of its protected harbor. We did have to do some considerable dredging to get a large carrier into the dock at Rota, and it fell to my lot later on, when I was DCNO, Air, to have to appear before Mr. Vinson of the Armed Forces Committee to get the last 10 million dollars of authorization to do that dredging. A great many congressmen at that time didn't want to give us the money and wanted to cancel the project, and I explained to them that the only purpose of having the base at Rota, as far as aviation was concerned, was to be able to get a carrier alongside of a dock. If they weren't going to do the additional dredging to get the carrier alongside the dock, we might as well abandon the base.

Q: What was the opposition? Was it largely the fact that –

Adm. P.: Lack of knowledge mostly. When you explained to them what the purpose was, to offload and onload, resupply, and be able to get airplanes on and airplanes off, we didn't have any great difficulty. I spent a good deal of time going around to individual congressmen before we had that vote on that 10 million dollars, getting them knowledgeable so that they would be for the project.

Of course, Rota's being used for a great many other things subsequent to its development. The Polaris submarine, for example, change their gold and blue crews there. That's where a certain number of them change, and they fly them from the States over to Rota and the command and put them right on and the crew that comes off gets right in an airplane and flies back home.

Q: What sort of facilities were at Rota when we took over?

Adm. P.: There was nothing there. It's Cadiz, Spain, a small Spanish base there that didn't amount to very much.

Q: It necessitated the building of some rather ingenious underwater breakwaters, did it not? What do they call them – tetrahedrons or something?

Adm. P.: It was the first time I'd ever seen a tetrahedron, large concrete blocks in the shape of a tetrahedron were used to build the base for the docks and breakwaters. They had to build a huge breakwater to protect it because it's fairly open, you know, particularly from the south.

Rota has proved very effective for us and we've used it very well since it came into being for a number of purposes.

Q: We have to pay a fairly high tariff, do we not, for its use?

Adm. P.: Yes, I think we do. Of course, the Air Force had three quite extensive bases in Spain that are still in existence. At least one of them is still in existence and they still use Rota.

Interview No. 6 with Vice Admiral Robert Burns Pirie, U.S. Navy (Retired)

Place: The U. S. Naval Institute, Annapolis, Maryland

Date: Thursday morning, 18 October 1973

Subject: Biography

By: John T. Mason, Jr.

Q: Well, Admiral, today we're going to hear about your command of Carrier Division Six. You took over in March of 1956 and continued in command until July of 1957, and there were several exciting events happening during that time. Do you want to tell me, Sir?

Adm. P.: I relieved Swede Ekstrom in command of Carrier Division Six, and the staff was shore-based at Oceana at the time I relieved him, but we shortly had an exercise off the East Coast with the Forrestal and Saratoga taking part in a combined exercise for the first time.

Q: How many carriers did you have in it?

Adm. P.: We had three. We had the Coral Sea and Forrestal and Saratoga in that exercise. It was most interesting in that we got into some fairly rough weather and the water over the flight deck on the Coral Sea was such that we had to cease operations, but the Forrestal and Saratoga both continued to fly throughout this, which showed us that they were better operating in heavy weather than any carriers that we had had previously. They were a good deal more stable longitudinally fore and aft. They didn't pitch as much and, consequently, didn't get as much green water over the deck.

Q: What contributed to this?

Adm. P.: The hull form. A great deal of it was hull form and I afterwards had an opportunity in fairly rough weather to operate in both the Saratoga and the Forrestal and found that you could fly in almost any kind of weather without being bothered by the motion of the ship or by heavy swells, heavy seas. Of course, you're limited somewhat by the amount of wind over the deck because the flight deck crews can't stand up in real strong winds and it's necessary to cease operations to protect them.

Q: The human element entered into it!

Adm. P.: The human element, yes.

This was a very interesting time with those two new ships and it was the first time that they'd operated together. We also were getting some of the newer jet aircraft, Grumman fighters. We had the AJs turboprop aircraft for the heavy attack mission and it was during this period that we got the first A-3Ds to replace the AJs in the heavy attack wing.

I was ordered to deploy to the Mediterranean to relieve the

carrier division commander about the 1st of May, and the Coral Sea, which was my flagship, had some stripped reduction gears and had to go to the Navy yard so it was necessary for myself and staff to fly over to the Mediterranean, and we flew from Norfolk to Heracleum in Crete. I joined the Randolph there and relieved Rear Admiral Dale Harris en route back to the Western Mediterranean.

Q: Why the speed in getting to the Mediterranean?

Adm. P.: Well, we relieved as a unit the division commander who had tactical command of the carrier task group in the Med which consisted of carriers and cruisers and destroyers. We relieved as a unit so it was necessary for me to get over there to be with the unit.

When we went into the Gulf of Palma, the southwest corner of Sardinia, for the relieving ceremony, Admiral Felt was the commander of the Sixth Fleet and he had the relieving conference on the Randolph. At the end of the conference he told me that we were going to have a posed sortie exercise on Monday morning - this was a Saturday that we had the conference - and that the two U.S. submarines that we had with the Sixth Fleet would be the opposition and that he was sure they were going to get me on the way out. I took exception to that, of course, good-naturedly -

Q: You offered to bet, did you not?

Adm. P.: Yes, I said how much do you bet, and Admiral Felt said he wasn't a bettor, so we let it go at that. Anyway, I thought about what to do about this, so I wrote up a sortie order to sortie at five o'clock in the morning and saw that it got a lot of dissemination so that everyone would get a look at it, particularly the two submarine skippers.

When I got back on Sunday from a stroll along the beach I put out an order to all the ships in the task group to come up on Nancy gear, which was an infrared signaling device, and on Sunday evening, about nine or ten o'clock, I put out a signal declaring radio and radar silence, turn off all radios and radars and all lights, darken ship. Then at eleven p.m. I sent a signal out on the Nancy gear to get under way and follow me out in the Randolph. The other carrier was the Intrepid.

As a result, we had no radars, no transmissions of any kind, electronic transmissions, and no lights, and I was about forty miles to the west going at high speed when the two submarine skippers found out that I'd gotten out of the harbor without their knowing it.

Q: Is the gulf a pretty wide one?

Adm. P.: It had a long reach of about fifteen miles and it had a fairly easy channel to get out. We could go at fairly high speed right after getting under way.

This was one of my first efforts at deception, which I will have some more to say about while I was commander of Carrier Division Six and later of the Second Fleet. I believe deception is one of the great tools of command and should be used a lot more. We have picked deception up as a tool now and use it to a considerable extent.

Q: How did you happen to develop this idea?

Adm. P.: I always felt that deception was a good tool in that there are easier ways to win an engagement than a frontal attack, if you can do it by deception and outsmarting the enemy.

When we got to Cannes shortly after that the two submarine skippers accosted me on shore and said that I sure had given them a bad time and that they weren't going to let it happen again. I said, "Well, you'd better watch out."

We went into another Sardinian port on the southeast coast that had two channels going out, the exits being about twenty miles apart, and we had another one of these opposed sorties coming out of there and I tricked them into getting on the wrong channel and got out again without their catching me. That was the second effort at deception which worked.

Q: Did you have comment from Admiral Felt as a result?

Adm. P.: No, I never did get a comment from him. Later, Admiral Felt was relieved by Admiral Cat Brown and we had an exercise later in the summer in which they put the carriers inside of a square, sixty miles on a side, with five submarines - two U.S., two British, and one French. I decided that my deception in this case was going to be to run around the periphery, the outside of this square, at high speed and hope that they would take my bait which I put out in an op order with some positions and points in the middle of this sixty-mile square.

This exercise lasted for some four or five days and

never did get to me until I had to stop to fuel after about three days, and they never did discover that I was running around the outside of this square at high speed. But when I had to stop to fuel, we were sitting ducks and they fired. They thought they were firing at the carriers. They were firing at some other ship. One U.S. submarine commander had discovered through my transmissions what I was doing and he figured out that we were on the outside of this, and as a result of that I then changed the method of signaling so that it wouldn't be possible for anyone to find out by reading my radio transmissions what I was doing.

At the end of that cruise I had another exercise in which we were up north of Corsica, between Corsica and the mainland, late in the afternoon, steaming to the northwest at sundown, and the air attack was mounted from the beach to attack us, and our job was to protect ourselves air defensewise from these attacks after dark. Well, immediately it got dark I split the two carriers. I sent one up to the coast, the mainland coast to the north, to hug the coast about two or three miles offshore and head back to the southwest, and I went around the Corsican coast, hugging the coast, and down through the Bonafacio Strait. So they never found either one of us. In the critique the opposition claimed that I was unfair, that I shouldn't have broken up the carrier task group, and I said anything is fair in war and there had been no specifications as to how I was to be formed up or do my job.

Q: Were you sustained by the commander-in-chief?

Adm. P.: Well, yes. It was an exercise to protect yourself.

Q: Admiral, is there any danger — were there any examples — of your deception boomeranging? When you issue op orders and then do something quite different, is there any possibility of deceiving your own unit?

Adm. P.: There would be if I didn't tell them. I fortunately forewarned all my units that I'm going to do something different and to be ready to respond to it, that we're not going to follow the op order to the letter so far as geographical reference points and operational plans that we say are going to be carried out. I may change those by dispatch, so be ready, and watch out for it.

There is a danger in deception if your own forces aren't wide awake and don't know that you're going to be doing something of that character. I'll have something to say about another exercise in deception during Strike Back, the exercise we had in the Norwegian Sea when I had the Second Fleet.

Q: Does this technique of yours carry over into your bridge game?

Adm. P.: Well, no, I use what's called the Pirie version of the Gorham system, and I wouldn't say that I'm the best bridge player in the world. My wife is continually discouraged with my bidding particularly. Deception in a card game is beyond my capability.

During my deployment to the Mediterranean, the commanding officer of the Randolph, Eddie O'Neil, had a heart attack and had to be detached, and I recommended that the command be given to my chief of staff, Dan Smith. That went through and Dan took command of the Randolph for the rest of the cruise. I later transferred to the Intrepid and finished the deployment in that ship.

In June or July Admiral Felt was relieved by Admiral Cat Brown at Venice and we attended the change-of-command ceremonies.

Q: Do you want to tell me that delightful story of Admiral Brown?

Adm. P.: I think I'd better leave that one out!

I enjoyed very much working for Admiral Brown as Commander, Sixth Fleet, because he'd been my division commander when I had the Coral Sea and we had the same philosophy of operations and command, so he was a delight to work for.

Q: You liked him much better than Felt didn't you?

Adm. P.: Yes —

During this period we did a good deal of night re-fueling, which hadn't been done to any extent up to that time. It was quite exciting, particularly when we had to launch aircraft or take aircraft on at the time you were fueling.

Q: I expect your experience in the Pacific had some bearing on this, did it not?

Adm. P.: Well, we did a lot of day fueling during the Pacific war but not much had been done at night, particularly with putting a carrier, a large combatant ship, alongside a tanker. A technically perfect navigator is almost essential in night re-fueling particularly, because you've got to know what your distance is from the ship when you're a couple of thousand yards astern in order to make a decent approach.

We didn't have as good lighting and as good equipment for getting the hoses over, getting hooked up, and performing the re-fueling operation and the re-supply operation as they have now. The art has been developed greatly in the last fifteen or twenty years, and they now have excellent equipment and lighting for night work.

Q: Were the NATO forces in the Mediterranean with whom you worked on occasion, were they proficient in these techniques?

Adm. P.: Yes. The Royal Navy ships had all perfected this technique. I can't remember operating with any French surface vessels. We did have one Dutch cruiser operating with us that was very good operationally and had excellent electronic equipment.

Q: What was that, the Tromp?

Adm. P.: It seems to me it was, but I can't remember the name. It was an excellent Dutch group.

During this deployment to the Mediterranean the Suez crisis took place. About a month prior to the actual outbreak of hostilities in this case a Royal Navy task force commanded by Vice Admiral Manley Power, affectionately known as "Lofty," came to the Med and we jointly made the plan for taking the Suez Canal.

Q: Was this after Nasser had nationalized it?

Adm. P.: Yes.

Q: Which he did, I believe, in July.

Adm. P.: I don't remember whether the action took place before or after that, but we drew up this plan with Admiral Brown and unfortunately when the action took place the United States backed out of it and left the British and French sort of high and dry.

Q: In the planning, what sort of role was our fleet to take?

Adm. P.: Well, the carrier task force was to support our amphibious force. We were the only ones that had an amphibious force in being in the Mediterranean and we were to give them the support they needed in order to take the key points.

Q: How large an operation did you anticipate in your planning?

Adm. P.: Well, of course, we only had a battalion of - a reinforced battalion embarked in our amphibious ships, but it was the only one in being in the Mediterranean at the time, and it could have given a considerable account of itself particularly with the kind of air cover our carriers and the Royal Navy carriers could provide. We didn't anticipate any difficulty in carrying out the mission of sanitizing and taking the canal.

Q: You included the French in your planning?

Adm. P.: We had the French in it?

Q: What were they to do?

Adm. P.: They provided some, if my memory is correct, some surface Navy ships. I'm not sure whether they had a small carrier in that operation or not. My memory is that they did not have a carrier, that they just provided some surface ships.

Q: Did they cooperate in the planning rather readily?

Adm. P.: Yes. It was a joint venture.

Q: Was Israel taken into consideration? Was she to play any role in this?

Adm. P.: No. As far as I know they weren't to play any role in this particular action. It's all history now, but it was interesting that we did that planning and I got to know Lofty Power quite well. He afterwards was commander of the British component of the Strike Fleet I had at Strike Back in the Norwegian Sea. Lofty Power had been Admiral Cunningham's operations officer in the Mediterranean during the war as captain and was a very fine naval officer.

Q: Well, Admiral, the Suez crisis came to an actual shooting episode at the end of October 1956 and you were there in command of Carrier Division Six. What did you do at that time?

Adm. P.: I'd left by that time. In late September or early October

I came back to the United States, having been relieved by Rear Admiral Frank Ward of Carrier Division Two or Four, and so was not in the Mediterranean during the actual crisis. We got back in the fall and I spent most of the fall and winter with my staff on shore at Oceana. Shortly after the first of the year 1957 I was given the job with my staff of drawing up the plans for the carrier task force operation in Strike Back, which involved coordination with the Royal Navy's section of the striking fleet and coordination with the Norwegian shore bases which we would have to use in emergency.

Q: This was to be under the aegis of SACLant?

Adm. P.: Strike Back was a NATO exercise under SACLant, but I was the carrier task force commander and had to write that part of the plans and orders that had to do with the carrier operations. I made a trip with my staff to the United Kingdom to confer with Admiral Power and then to the Norwegian capital, Oslo, to see the Defense Minister, and made visits to all of the air bases along the Norwegian coast which we might have to use in case of emergency.

Q: What was the objective of Strike Back? What were you trying to prove in this operation?

Adm. P.: We had plans in the NATO community, in SACLant's - Supreme Allied Commander, Atlantic, plans to have a large-scale naval exercise which would involve all of the NATO navies once every three years. They had had the first one in 1954 - no, 1952 - and the next one had been deferred for some reason. Strike Back was planned for and took place in 1957.

Q: It being the second one, then?

Adm. P.: Yes, and it involved all of the NATO countries, their contributions to the forces involved varied considerably, but the largest contribution was being made by the United States and the United Kingdom.

Q: On occasion, in later years, I believe the Scandinavian countries, Norway and Denmark, didn't participate too enthusiastically in some of these operations. What was their attitude at this point?

Adm. P.: They were cooperative in every way, but the cost of taking part in one of these operations was considerable and the defense budget in those small countries couldn't stand large participation, and that principally is the reason for them not having greater participation. It was financial.

Q: It wasn't a latent fear of antagonizing the Russians?

Adm. P.: No, I don't think they really had any such fear.

Q: Tell me about the planning.

Adm. P.: I worked closely with Vice Admiral Charles Wellborn, who had the Second Fleet at that time. I had the privilege of relieving him as Commander, Second Fleet, in June and commanded the Second Fleet during the Strike Back exercise, which I had made plans for as carr division commander.

Q: Well, it was obviously anticipated that you would take over the Second Fleet, and that was the reason you took part in the planning?

Adm. P.: I'm not so sure of that. I was quite surprised when I found in the late spring that Admiral Wright was going to recommend me to take the Second Fleet. There was a very interesting episode during the month of April or May. I was ordered to plan for and execute an operation to take President Eisenhower out on the Saratoga from Mayport, Florida. He had never seen an active carrier operation and this was to be a two-day operation to demonstrate what the aircraft carrier could do in carrier warfare.

Q: Why was this set up?

Adm. P.: It was set up through the Secretary of the Navy in Washington.

Q: As an educational cruise for the President?

Adm. P.: Educational for him, and I think Pete Aurand, who was then President Eisnehower's aide, had a great deal to do with it. Eisenhower had great respect for and confidence in Pete and he talked about it and it was just a matter of getting the time and place that was convenient.

Well, we had the Saratoga available and I was an available division commander, so we organized and planned this exercise in which we not only had a demonstration of the carrier, but a demons

Pirie #6 - 264

the weapons systems on the cruiser, the Terrier, and some antisubmarine warfare aspects, as well as carrier operations.

The Saratoga was alongisde at Mayport, and the President and his party flew down and boarded us at Mayport. He had in his party Mr. Dulles, the Secretary of State, Mr. Humphrey, the Secretary of the Treasury, Mr. Wilson, the Secretary of Defense, all of his own immediate staff. Louis Strauss, who was on the Atomic Energy Commission. We had Mr. Tom Gates, the Secretary of the Navy, Admiral Burke, the CNO, and Admiral Wright, who was Commander-in-Chief of the Atlantic Fleet.

Q: Heavy with brass!

Adm. P.: Yes. We fired a couple of planes off the catapult at the dock just as they were boarding to demonstrate that we could do this operation without going at high speed through the water.

We went out and had demonstrations in the afternoon, such as showing them shooting a target down with Sidewinder, which you could view from the deck, a Sparrow firing demonstration. The cruiser demonstrated firing Terrier. We had bombing and machine gun strafing demonstrations and a demonstration of all the weapon systems we had.

They were all very much interested in the atomic capability and we took them through the nuclear storage and showed everyone. Practically none of these people had seen at that stage of the game an atom bomb, which amazed me. But they were all very much interested in the atomic weapons and their capabilities.

Q: Did you have to deliver lectures on all these things?

Adm. P.: I was along but I had my various people in the ship and staff to do the lecturing and the talking.

We had night flying that night and we had an aircraft in the carrier suite at that time which was having some considerable difficulty with engine stoppage due to ice ingestion at high altitude. Unfortunately, that night two of these aircraft went through some precipitation at high altitude and had engine stoppages and the two pilots parachuted. One was a squadron commander and the other an ensign in the squadron, one of the new pilots. They landed, of course, in the open ocean in their parachutes and my job, immediately we had an emergency of that character, particularly with this caliber of VIP on board, was to do something in a hurry.

Fortunately, I had planned for this kind of an emergency and I'd written an op order to take care of just such a situation, and Rear Admiral Bill Miller, a classmate of mine, who had the antisubmarine warfare carrier that was along with us, was my designated commander for such an emergency operation. I executed that within seconds after we found out that these boys had ejected from their aircraft.

We had a surface search all during the night and found them in the morning. Unfortunately, the ensign had drowned in his boat but we picked up the squadron commander. During the night the President was greatly concerned by this and he had Pete Aurand, his naval aide, and Hagerty, his press aide, coming to me constantly during the night to get current reports on what we were doing and how things were going.

It was an unfortunate incident in that we lost this one boy's life, but it was part of the rub of the green at that time with an engine we were having difficulty with. As a result of this, we finally took some drastic action to correct the icing of this particular airplane and solve the problem.

In the morning, at breakfast, after we had finished this rescue operation, we were going back into port, and the President sent word that he wanted me to come to breakfast in the admiral's cabin where they were eating. I came in and he and all of his cabinet members were sitting round the table, and he had me sit on his right, and when breakfast was almost finished he said:

"I have a very pleasant duty to perform. Admiral, I've just signed your commission as a vice admiral in the United States Navy and now would like to announce to you and to all of those present that you are going to take command of the Second Fleet. Here's your commission," and he handed it to me.

Q: How wonderful!

Adm. P.: A ceremony at breakfast in the Saratoga, which was a great surprise to me. I'm sure that Pete Aurand had used his fine "Italian" hand in this. Admiral Wright and Admiral Burke, of course, knew about it, but it came as a surprise to me, and a very pleasant surprise.

Q: Did the President demonstrate knowledge of the value of the carrier during this cruise?

Adm. P.: Oh, yes. I think they all recognized, you know, what our capabilities were. That's what we were trying to show them. We showed them both offensive and defensive exercises to demonstrate to them how we would protect a carrier, as well as our offensive capability.

They were all very interested in it, and it was a real highlight in my period as a carrier division commander.

Shortly after that, in June or July, I took command of the Second Fleet.

Q: In July. Admiral, going back to the planning for Strike Back, was there any attempt to carry over from the first NATO exercise in 1952? Were there any loose ends from that exercise that were taken up in the one in 1957?

Adm. P.: The one in 1952 did not include atomic weaponry. While we had the atom bomb, we hadn't had any joint exercises, and I don't believe it included any atomic weaponry. They had very bad luck with weather in that exercise. It was very rough during the whole of the exercise. All the ships were somewhat damaged in the Norwegian Sea, and they did very little flying during the whole of the exercise on account of this weather.

Q: Why was the locale of the Norwegian Sea and the Arctic area chosen at the site of the operation?

Adm. P.: Well, we already had the Sixth Fleet in the Mediterranean. That was already in being and they held many exercises down there. The Mediterranean command was not yet organized in 1952. You see, we did that afterwards. I was in several conferences with Admiral Wright with SACEur and Admiral Mountbatten in the Med getting the Mediterranean command set up. We afterwards had NATO exercises in the Mediterranean with the Sixth Fleet, on sort of a continuing basis. But the large-scale exercise in the Atlantic -- the only logical place to have this exercise was in the area north of the United Kingdom, or in the area around the United Kingdom, the North Sea, the Norwegian Sea, and to the west of it in the Atlantic.

Q: It was the logical place, given that the potential enemy was Russia?

Adm. P.: Yes. Well, it meant that you had to get within range, and to get within range you've got to go in to that area. You have to get into the Norwegian Sea to get within aircraft striking distance.

Q: So it was taken for granted that the opponent was Russia?

Adm. P.: Yes. In making plans for the Strike Back operation in 1957, we then had atomic-weapon delivery plans and had the capability of flying at low level, doing toss bombing, and we had to plan for this kind of simulated nuclear-weapon delivery, not only in the United Kingdom and Scotland - England and Scotland - but down into France and the Low Countries. That required some coordination with the civil authorities in those countries so that we wouldn't be endangering any lives with civil aviation.

Q: This was all a part of the planning?

Adm. P.: Part of the planning.

Q: Did you meet with the utmost cooperation on the part of the civil authorities?

Adm. P.: Yes, I don't remember that we had any great difficulty with them, but it, of course, had to be left to the military authorities in those countries to deal with the civil authorities. We, as the U.S. military, didn't have any direct contact.

Q: Did Admiral Wright have any role in the planning?

Adm. P.: Well, as SAC Lant, it was his exercise. He ordered the exercise and then we planned and executed it.

Q: Well, Sir, you assumed command of the Second Fleet under very auspicious circumstances, a rare thing, for the President to hand your commission to you. Tell me about the Second Fleet.

Adm. P.: I relieved Admiral Wellborn in early July 1957 in Norfolk in the flagship, the Northampton, and the Strike Back exercise took place shortly thereafter. We proceeded with the U.S. elements of the striking fleet, which consisted of the Forrestal, Saratoga, and one antisubmarine warfare carrier, an Essex-class, and proceeded to the Clyde, Scotland, where we joined up with the Royal Navy and other NATO country elements.

The Royal Navy were the largest contributors, having three carriers and several cruisers and destroyers, or frigates. The Dutch cruiser which had a great capability in electronics joined us there.

Q: The same one that had been in the Mediterranean?

Adm. P.: Yes.

We sailed from the Clyde in rather blustery weather and had another one of these opposed sorties, with quite a large number of U.S. and Royal Navy submarines opposing us, but we were quite fortunate in getting out without being attacked by them.

Q: Any deceptions?

Adm. P.: I hadn't used any up to that point, but I did use deception then. I changed the geographical reference points after I got to sea and caused a certain amount of confusion. The Nautilus, our first nuclear submarine, was operating in opposition to us and it was the first time we had a nuclear submarine opposing us. He fortunately took the geographical points in the operation to heart and got himself confused for about five or six days. The only ship that he finally attacked was the antisubmarine warfare carrier.

Elements of the attack carriers, both U.S. and British, were never attacked by any submarine during the period of the exercise.

Q: May I interrupt? You mentioned confusion. Was there any preliminary kind of an exercise when you launch forth on a joint exercise of this sort? Was there any preliminary one to more or less indoctrinate the extraneous units from the various foreign fleets doing it?

Adm. P.: No. We had them divided. We didn't operate as one task group. We divided up the task groups. There were the U.S. carrier task group and the Royal Navy carrier task group, operating in coordination, as we did during World War II. Much the same thing took place when we had four large carrier task groups, we weren't all assembled in one formation. We had three or four circular formations and operated in coordination with each other. We did that at Strike Back, so they were already more or less prepared. I believe I put the Dutch cruiser with Lofty Power.

Q: Were there Danish ships of any kind?

Adm. P.: I don't remember any naval units other than the Dutch cruiser and the Royal Navy in that exercise. We might have had submarines from some of the other NATO countries in that exercise. Most of them were our U.S. submarines and Royal Navy submarines.

Q: Was the Iberlant Command drawn into this?

Adm. P.: No, it hadn't been formed yet. Iberlant came later.

We had excellent weather, so to speak. It was almost calm for most of the period that we operated during Strike Back, which was a ten-day exercise. The only thing that really bothered us was the aurora borealis. It was so strong at this period that we had very little, if any, radio communication. We weren't even able to communicate with the Norwegian bases on the beach, and it interfered greatly with our voice radio transmissions and it interfered greatly with our radar.

Q: Had this been anticipated?

Adm. P.: Not in the strength that it developed. We expected to have the normal summer northern lights, but nothing like we actually experienced.

This had a great effect on our air defense capability and it was one of the great disappointments of the exercise that we did very poorly in air defense. We couldn't get any kind of a message traffic off through our normal communications systems, and one of the most embarrassing parts of this was that we had a good many U.S. press correspondents, the most prominent of whom was Hanson Baldwin of <u>The New York Times</u> and he wasn't able to get his story of Strike Back off daily and he made some rather strong complaints to Admiral Wright about this. Admiral Wright, by the same token, made a complaint to me about communications, and we did everything we could. We looked into it thoroughly but there was nothing much we could do about this interference of the aurora borealis.

I think probably in this day and age we'd have gotten on better with ultra high frequency and ultra low frequency. We've found ways and means of getting through this great interference, but at that time we didn't have anything that would break it.

Q: Along with your newspaper reporters and so forth, did you carry any scientists as observers?

Pirie #6 - 273

Adm. P.: No, I don't believe we had anyone other than the press as observers during that period.

Q: I would have thought that might have been wise to do.

Adm. P.: Well, I don't remember that there was anyone that had to do with the aurora borealis, with the strong northern lights.

Q: Were you accompanied also by Russian trawler observers?

Adm. P.: Yes, we had a good many Russian trawlers fooling around during this exercise, particularly as we sortied from the Clyde. I don't remember there being so many after we got up in the Arctic circle.

Q: Why would they concentrate at the mouth of the Clyde?

Adm. P.: They wanted to see what was coming out, what we were doing, I guess, and find out something about our tactics in sortie probably. They didn't bother us too much after we got up there.

Q: How far north did you go?

Adm. P.: We were north of the Arctic circle most of the time during this tne-day period.

Q: Did you encounter other difficulties?

Adm. P.: No. There was no ice, of course, at that time of the year. As you know, there's a considerable amount in the Davis Strait, over to the west of Greenland. When I had the Sicily we had an operation up there in the Davis Strait and there was a considerable amount of ice during the summer, but in the open Norwegian Sea there's none at that time of the year.

Well, air defense was quite a disappointment and, later, on the wayback from the U.K. to the United States, I ran some quite extensive exercises and experiments to try to improve our capability. One of the big difficulties is the human element in the communication chain. It came as a great surprise to me, on running some considerable tests day after day, how little information that comes into a man's ears is really transmitted accurately from his mouth into a microphone to go out. I found I was getting less maybe than 10 percent of the information through accurately, so I started using captains and commanders on my staff on the circuit and found I could improve it to about 50 percent, but never much more than that, which shows the fallibility of the human being in a communication chain where you're transmitting and retransmitting information several times.

This was the principal reason for our development of data link - accurate, real-time information transmission.

Q: Was the time element a considerable factor in this?

Adm. P.: Yes, it takes time when you put two or three humans on a communication chain, and again it takes time or loss of time, but I think the aurora borealis affected us more than anything else.

Q: What were the pluses to the operation?

Adm. P.: Well, I think we had a good antisubmarine exercise, and we, of course, had the opportunity to work with each other, the various NATO elements, which is basically the reason for having such a large-scale exercise, to be sure we're coordinated and understand each other's methods so that we can operate together.

Q: What is your actual feeling about a joint operation involving units of foreign navies where language might be a barrier?

Adm. P.: I think the language is possibly a problem but all you need are good interpreters. You have the same problem in commercial aircraft operations throughout the world, which requires that you have good interpreters to be able to understand and translate orders and messages.

Q: But, where you have a fleet of component parts from foreign navies, what about the nautical background of the men themselves? It isn't always uniform, is it?

Adm. P.: Well, they operated a little bit differently in some cases, but in the last fifteen years we've had a unit in the NATO command in the Atlantic of six or seven nationalities put together and operating on a somewhat continuing basis, so that they do get used to each other and used to each other's operational methods and tactics. They had this unit formed subsequent to this Strike Back exercise, but it has frigates and destroyers from several NATO nations together quite often to do just what you're pointing out - to get used to each other's tactics and methods.

Q: Earlier you spoke about the cost of participating in an operation like this. How great was the cost, say, for the Royal Navy?

Adm. P.: It's a considerable cost and you find the Royal Navy down to one carrier now, if they have any, because of cost. This was the last large exercise they ever took part in with these numbers of ships because the cost is quite considerable to operate for any extended period of time in a large exercise of that character. Operational costs are -

Q: In terms of fuel?

Adm. P.: Fuel, and other logistics. All kinds of supplies. Everything that you use. In the case of carrier operations and ship operations, principally fuel.

Q: Well, where a navy is maintained by a nation, could an operation like this not be considered a part of their normal training?

Adm. P.: Yes, it would, but they don't operate very much. Most of those navies spend 90 percent of their time in port - or a large percentage of their time in port, and I can remember the day when we did. When I first got out of the Naval Academy in 1926, we didn't have any bed of roses so far as operating was concerned. In other words, the number of rounds of ammunition you could shoot in gunnery practice was quite limited, and the amount of fuel that you could consume was somewhat limited, by comparison with the immediate prewar, World War II, and postwar days. And post World War II we got into the same thing that the operational cost was so great that we'd spend a lot of time in port.

Q: This changeover then signals our different role in international affairs?

Adm. P.: The largest contribution to the NATO command in the Atlantic is by the United States in ships and men.

At the end of Strike Back we came down through the North Sea and went in to Portsmouth for a critique, and spent a week or so reviewing the exercise, the good and bad things about it.

Q: Was Admiral Wright convinced at this time of the difficulties with the aurora borealis?

Adm. P.: Oh, yes, I'm sure he realized the difficulty we had in communications, and it was one of the problems we tackled as a lesson that we learned. That communication problem was one of the lessons learned and the air defense problem that I spoke about was another serious lesson, and then antisubmarine warfare is a continuing problem and the submarines weren't very successful in being able to attack us on a continuing basis. In other words, it was a standoff as far as we were concerned. I believe that with the advent of the nuclear submarines in large numbers they've got a somewhat more difficult problem, but it isn't one that's insurmountable. It's a matter of training and working to contain them.

Q: You cite at the post mortem the fact that communications was a real problem in the exercise. Where did you take it from there?

Adm. P.: Well, it got back in to the Chief of Naval Operations and they took it to Research and Development people to improve the quality of communications so that they'd be able to get through that heavy interference.

Q: You imply that something has been accomplished?

Adm. P.: Yes, I'm sure we can now.

Q: In the light of this operation, what are the prospects for the defense of that northern area in actual warfare?

Adm. P.: Sea defense has a great many elements to it and there are a great many developments in the last twenty years to try to contain the submarine and to get intelligence on the submarine, know where he is, and be able to do something about him. That's the most important naval task in the Atlantic. The business of naval forces being of any value in land assault or in support of land forces is somewhat questionable, particularly in view of the large number of days of bad weather in that area.

It was the famous Murmansk run during World War II that was a horror story of the first order for most of the forces involved.

Q: But we learned something from it, didn't we?

Adm. P.: We learned that there's bad weather! And that it's a good thing to stay out of it if you can.

However, the protection of shipping and convoying has been updated and has to be updated more. It's going to involve the use of large numbers of helicopters or vertical rising aircraft to try to sanitize areas around merchant shipping. I would hope that we wouldn't have to do much of it.

Q: How does the helicopter perform in the Arctic area?

Adm. P.: Well, the helicopter is somewhat limited by wind, and in very high winds he can't operate. There's a limit to what anybody can operate, and you're frankly out of commission in all ships in real bad weather, but the helicopter is embarrassed in real high wind and gusty wind, particularly getting on and off the ship.

Well, on the way back from Portsmouth to the United States we held several days of intensive air defense exercises to try to improve our capability and learn where our weaknesses lay. As a result, we did improve ourselves considerably and I believe that some of the large air defense exercises held by the Second Fleet after my time on the East Coast were quite successful.

Q: What other operations did you conduct as commander of the Second Fleet? Was there anything involving the Caribbean area?

Adm. P.: No, I didn't have any exercise down in the Caribbean. I took the relieving Sixth Fleet forces over in early 1958 and we had a conference with Admiral Brown on his flagship at Majorca. That was really the only other major operation I was involved in until I was detached in May.

Q: That's an unusual thing, isn't it, for the commander-in-chief of the

Second Fleet to take units that are going to relieve in the Mediterranean?

Adm. P.: No, not necessarily. It's part of the job.

Q: They are your units, as Second Fleet units?

Adm. P.: Yes, turning them over to Sixth Fleet, and we wanted to have a coordinated conference with Commander, Sixth Fleet. There were a lot of operational and planning matters, so it was an ideal time to do it.

Q: Would you talk about the Striking Fleet a little bit?

Adm. P.: The Strike Fleet consists of elements of the NATO Atlantic force which are involved in strike operations, particularly carrier strike operations, and they consist of the carriers, cruisers, and destroyers in each of these navies which make a contribution to the Strike Fleet.

Q: Is it emergency in nature?

Adm. P.: No, it's organized on a continuing basis but ready to carry out contingency plans, if called on. The principal contributors to that striking fleet had been the United States and the United Kingdom, Canada to a certain extent, but the only ones who during this period had any real carrier strike capability were the United States and the United Kingdom.

Q: It's in a sense a fleet within a fleet, isn't it?

Adm. P.: Well, the Striking Fleet is a part of the NATO naval command. There are other parts, such as the submarines, and escort for convoy forces, and other forces that he might organize separate from the Striking Fleet. Striking Fleet means something that has an offensive capability and offensive capability basically lies in the carriers.

Q: Was there any question raised during your term there about a British over-all command for some operations? Did they ever indicate a desire to be in command?

Adm. P.: Well, I think it depends on the contribution probably to the forces. That's decided on the basis that if we're going to contribute the most - the majority of the forces to the Striking Fleet, then the Striking Fleet commander should be of the nationality that contributes the most forces.

Q: Is this accepted without question?

Adm. P.: I don't think so. I think a lot of people go on the theory that they know better how to operate forces than the next individual, but I think command by the major contributor has sort of become a principle that can't be denied because if we contributed three-quarters of the forces and some one of the other nations said I've got to command these forces because I know how to do it better than you do, he's not going to get very far with the United States command.

Q: Admiral, accepting the fact that predominance of force is the governing factor in the over-all command, the nature of that command, did the

U.S. Navy take any measures to assuage the feelings of the Royal Navy people and the French and so forth in this situation?

Adm. P.: My experience was that we got along very well with the Royal Navy by not trying to press them and telling them how to run a carrier task group operation. I tried to leave it up to them to operate their own carrier task group, and we'd operate ours in coordination with them, and we got along very well and mutually supported each other. We landed a few of the Royal Navy airplanes on our carriers and had a few of ours go over to their carriers, just for the purpose of being sure that we could operate from each other's. We have a little bit different equipment. We've tried to standardize it through the years so that we would be able to operate in support of each other and I believe we have.

Q: I suppose the MAAG program helped in that area, didn't it?

Adm. P.: Yes.

I knew a great many officers of the French Navy and the Italian Navy, the Greek Navy, but we never had any great contribution of forces to any of our exercises from any other than the Royal Navy.

Q: How does the U.S. Navy look upon this whole effort at international naval cooperation?

Adm. P.: I think it welcomes any allies who are going to help you and have the capability to help you, rather than carrying all the load yourself. But here again we run into money, finance, and I believe that a great many people in this country believe that we're carrying too much of the load. It's not difficult to come by that if you read the comments of our senators and congressmen on the subject. They think we're carrying too much of the load, that some of the other countries should shoulder more of it, and this means carrying more of the financial burden. We've given away a great deal of our national wealth since World War II in keeping large forces in being and also in giving them actually cash contributions so that they can keep forces in being. I believe that a certain amount of that criticism is justified. There comes a limit to how much of the world's problems we can shoulder, and it seems to me we're getting to the turning point in how much of our national wealth we can contribute to the defense of the world.

Interview No. 7 with Vice Admiral Robert Burns Pirie, U.S. Navy
(Retired)

Place: The Naval Institute, Annapolis, Maryland

Date: Tuesday morning 12 March 1974

Subject: Biography

By: John T. Mason, Jr.

Q: It's always a delight to see you, Sir. You do something for one's spirits!

Today, we're going to begin that very significant period in your naval career when you became Deputy Chief of Naval Operations for Air, and that was in May 1958. Do you want to take up the story at that point, Sir?

Adm. P.: I reported to the Chief of Naval Operations in early May 1958 to assume my duties as Deputy Chief of Naval Operations, Air. My predecessor, Vice Admiral William B. Davis, had been detached before I arrived, and I actually took over from my assistant who, at that time, was Rear Admiral F. N. "Knappy" Kivette.

Q: Who late became commander of the Seventh Fleet?

Adm. P.: He was ordered from that job to command the Seventh Fleet.

When I reported to Admiral Burke, he told me that there were two things - very important things - he wanted me to accomplish during my tenure as Deputy Chief of Naval Operations, Air.

Q: Incidentally, what was the normal tenure for that job?

Adm. P.: It varied all the way from less than a year to five years. I think I broke the record at the time. I was there over four and a half years, and the only one who had held the job for anything like that length of time was Tom Connolly, who retired last year.

Q: He told you there were two things he wanted you to concentrate on?

Adm. P.: Yes. The first was it was very important that we get an aircraft carrier authorized, so he considered that one of my prime jobs, to manage the business of getting a carrier authorized.

Q: A nuclear carrier?

Adm. P.: No. Another carrier. At that time, a nuclear-powered carrier hadn't been proposed. A conventional carrier - to get another one authorized. Secondly, he said: "I want you to know more about the budget than anyone else here - any of the other deputies or anyone in the CNO's office."

I believe, looking back on the events that took place during my term, that what he had in mind in saying that to me was that just months prior to our arriving they had changed the budget system which had an expenditure ceiling, and they lost a considerable amount of appropriated funds in that year, and I think the secretaries and possibly the CNO considered that my predecessor and the then Chief of the Bureau of Auronautics, Bob Dickson, were responsible for this.

My opinion is that they were not responsible for it, but it was a change in the budgeting system which was responsible. As a result we lost about 500 million dollars in that period for the procurement of aircraft.

That's what Admiral Burke had in mind in telling me that he wanted me to know more about the budget than anyone else.

As a result of these two things that he told me he wanted me to pay particular attention to, during my period as the DCNO we had two aircraft carriers authorized to be built, one of them was a nuclear carrier. No, I'll take that back. The Enterprise had been authorized before I got there, the nuclear carrier. We had two additional conventional carriers authorized during my term with CNO, and I did make a very thorough study of the budget. I worked hard at it and I believe I did know as much or more about the budget than any of my contemporaries there at the time.

Q: May I ask a question about the first point that Admiral Burke made, that you should see that authorization was made for a new carrier. Was there a great problem in getting carriers at that point? Was there great controversy?

Adm. P.: The aircraft carrier always was under heavy criticism from opponents who have always thought that the aircraft carrier is very vulnerable to attack and to place this much of your money in a vulnerable weapon system was not sound. We aviators didn't agree with that. Nevertheless there were great opponents to the aircraft carrier from the very beginning, and after World War II they were even stronger in their opposition because of new weapon systems that were coming into being and they thought that we couldn't defend the aircraft carrier.

Q: I take it a lot of this opposition was in the Congress itself?

Adm. P.: Yes, so that it was necessary to work hard in the Congress to be sure that you had a majority who were for it - for the appropriation to build an additional carrier, and that was the job I had and which I had as a continuing project all during my term.

Q: There was emphasis being placed upon your ability to deal with people, which is an obvious ability?

Adm. P.: Well, I got to know all the members of the House Armed Services and Senate Armed Services Committees and the appropriations subcommittee for the armed services, later known as the Defense Appropriations Subcommittee of both the House and the Senate. I had to appear before them to support not only my aircraft budget, procurement, maintenance, training, and research and development, but also to support the aircraft carrier.

Q: You became a sort of a principal lobbyist for the Navy itself?

Adm. P.: In this respect.

With regard to the budget, the organization and framework which Admiral Burke set up revolved around the CAB, the CNO's advisory board, and the CNO's advisory board was headed by the Vice Chief of Naval Operations and the members were the deputies. We met regularly to frame the budget in each year, and after getting our directions and working on getting it approved by the Chief of Naval Operations, we then had to present it to the Secretary before it went to the Secretary of Defense. Then, once approved by him and by the Bureau of the Budget, the White House had to approve it and put it in the annual budget. From there we took it to the Congress and had to appear in defense.

My part of the budget in those days amounted to about five billion dollars, authorized funds. In the budget cycle we had many meetings with the Assistant Secretaries, the Under Secretary, and the Secretary of the Navy, and with the Defense Assistant Secretaries and Secretary.

Q: Do you want to say a word about them? Gates was Secretary?

Adm. P.: The Secretary of the Navy at the time was Thomas Gates and the Under Secretary was Bill Franke.

So much for those two questions that Burke raised.

When I reported, there was some considerable actions going on which I inherited, one of which was the closing of a number of bases, aircraft establishments. My memory is that there were about twelve or fifteen being closed in various parts of the country -

Q: This in the interests of economy?

Adm. P.: Economy and not supported by the local congressmen. So we had almost continuous meetings in the Secretary's office with regard to these closings, with the individual local congressmen trying to save the naval establishment in his particular area.

Q: Did they all have a similar cut-off date?

Adm. P.: They were all to be done within this fiscal year after I reported. Some of these meetings were quite volatile, but they made all of these closings stick and it wasn't too happy a situation to go through these meetings in the Secretary's office.

Q: Was this a policy at the behest of the President himself?

Adm. P.: Yes, a general cut-back in all of the armed services, and this was our share - the Navy's share - of base closings at that time.

Q: What arguments did the congressmen use to retain these bases?

Adm. P.: Every local congressman is beholden to his constituents, and to keep a base open in his district, even though he might in his own heart believe it's a good thing to close it, knows that there had to be some retrenchment from defense expenditures and that this was a part of it. But he's still got to fight to save it with his constituents. So it's a very unpleasant business to go through.

The other thing that was very much in the forefront at that time was the nuclear seaplane. The P-6M was the jet-powered seaplane.

Q: Known as the Seamaster, wasn't it?

Adm. P.: The Seamaster, P-6M, and it was in a stage of development at the Martin plant in Baltimore, where they'd lost one of the airplanes and they had at least two flying at the time and making tests. I can't remember whether the second one was lost after I got there or whether it was just before. Anyway, these tests were going on and there was a great deal of question about whether the program should be continued.

We had a large base under construction down in North Carolina -

Q: Seaplane base?

Adm. P.: - seaplane base, to accommodate them because it couldn't be done at any one of the existing bases.

Q: Where was this? At Elizabeth City?

Adm. P.: Hertford, I think. It's near Elizabeth City, in that Pamlico part of North Carolina.

I went over very shortly after I took over and made a personal visit to Martin's plant and witnessed a couple of flights, and I went into the problems that they were having with the Chief of the Bureau of Aeronautics. One of the great problems that they were having was what they called a "catastrophic instability on the water." At high speed on the water, it began to porpoise or get out of control, and this was a real worry beside the fact that they had lost two in the air from what turned out to be a stability problem in which the plane got out of control in the air and, in the first case, lost the tail section. The second loss was a structural failure of the same order.

So it was under a cloud and the question of whether the thing should be continued or not was a real problem.

At my first conference with Mr. Gates on this subject, he asked me what I thought of it and I told him my opinion at that stage was that it should be cancelled. He was very disappointed at this and he asked me why I hadn't said something about it before. I said I'd never been asked before, that I'd just taken over, and no one had asked me my opinion of the whole concept or my opinion of the aircraft as it existed, and my thinking was that not only it wasn't a good aircraft at the time, but I didn't think so much of the concept.

He got very angry with me over my making this statement because he'd been a party to having this aircraft produced.

Eventually, what happened was that we decided we'd continue the program on a limited basis to try to salvage the seven or eight airplanes that they had left in the program, and possibly operate them to try to prove out the concept of a jet seaplane of this character.

Q: The Navy had a contract with Martin for a certain number?

Adm. P.: A certain number at a certain price.

Q: And the price was high, I take it?

Adm. P.: Yes. I've forgotten the exact figures, but it was hundreds of millions of dollars.

Q: What was your basic objection? Did you feel that the seaplane was obsolete as a concept?

Adm. P.: Well, I thought that this type of aircraft - a supersonic seaplane, that is that had a higher speed than the speed of sound, there were so many difficulties with the logistics and you had to have a terrific amount of water and fairly calm water in which to operate, and there weren't that many places around the world. So the concept really didn't make much sense, vis à vis multi-engined land planes.

Q: Which were capable of performing the same duties?

Adm. P.: Yes. And it was a more expensive weapon system.

Q: That has come to be the prevailing attitude of the Navy, has it not?

Adm. P.: Well, we've cancelled all seaplanes, the P-5M being the last to go out because landplane operation is much more feasible and much sounder.

Q: Then I would guess that the compromise you arrived at at that time with that particular plane, the Seamaster, was a compromise based on the objections of Gates himself? He wanted to salvage something from it.

Adm. P.: Yes. What I was getting at is we had a final meeting on the subject in which Mr. Gates wanted to try to let the Martin Company down easy - if you can use that word - and not cancel the thing out completely with the loss that they might sustain. So he made a proposal to Mr. George Bunker, then head of the Martin Company, that he pay them a certain amount in the cancellation of this contract and that we would have the aircraft that were left to do with them as we saw fit.

Bunker didn't buy this and, at a meeting in Mr. Gates' office, he told the Secretary that if it wasn't a good project for the United States and the United States Navy, it wasn't good for the Martin Company and the whole project was cancelled.

Q: Loss or not?

Adm. P.: Loss or no loss. He wouldn't take the money. So the project was cancelled and we broke up and salvaged the planes that had been built and we closed down the base in North Carolina. That was the last of the supersonic seaplane.

That was not a very happy episode, but one that had to be dealt with.

Q: 1958, in terms of naval affairs, has often been called a transition year, when the Navy was turning from guns to missiles, going into the realm of nuclear power, and it was going from subsonic to supersonic speeds in the air. Do you want to comment on that whole concept?

Adm. P.: Weapon system development was growing very rapidly at that stage of the game, getting into supersonic speeds and the operation of supersonic aircraft and missiles. A number of new and fascinating developments and also at that time the Polaris missile system was under full development. All of these had a great effect on our budget considerations and on what types of aircraft, missiles and ships we were going to buy.

The nuclear submarine program, which was in its infancy at that time with the commissioning of the Nautilus imminent, also had a great bearing on weapon system development.

A great many new and interesting aircraft developments were taking place at the time. Shortly after I took over, we had to make a decision as to what fighter we were going to buy, whether it was going to be the F-4 — now known as the F-4, it was then known as the F-4H — or whether we were going to buy the F8-U3, a product of the Chance-Vought Aircraft Corporation, now LTV. The F8-U3 was a single-engine fighter which in performance and handling characteristics actually was a little bit better than than the F-4H, at the time, according to the preliminary evaluations of the pilots, the test pilots, but one of the basic reasons for our taking the F-4H was that it had two engines. My philosophy was that two engines in every combatant aircraft were better than one, because you always had an opportunity of getting back with one engine. With an engine failure in a single-engine supersonic jet you are almost called on, if you can't get the engine started, to eject and the plane is lost, whereas in a twin-engine you can make a successful landing and save the aircraft and the crew, if necessary.

Well, the cost of these modern weapon systems and supersonic aircraft had gotten to be so great that this seemed to me to be a primary consideration, and it was, in making our final decision. We chose the F-4, and it's been a very successful aircraft not only in our own Navy but throughout the world.

Q: Roughly, what is the cost of an F-4?

Adm. P.: At the time we bought them, it was in the area of two million. I would say they're over four million with more modern electronic systems. I doubt if the production cost could be less than that. The production costs on some of our aircraft - modern supersonic aircraft - are in the order of ten million dollars. I'll deal with some of those in a while.

Q: So money certainly was a factor to bolster your argument?

Adm. P.: Right. That decision had to be made and was made shortly after I took over, and the F-4 then got into production. We had a number of other aircraft coming along, the A-6, which has been a very successful attack airplane; newer and better versions of the A-4; the RA5 reconnaissance aircraft; the EA-6 electronics countermeasures aircraft; the E-2, the airborne early warning aircraft; several versions of helicopters, the modern Sikorsky which has been so successful; the Boeing helicopter. All of these were very expensive projects and we had to work hard to save them.

Q: You told me, off tape, that there was a very interesting story connected with the RA-5C. It was originally a bomber design, I believe, that became a reconnaissance plane. Do you want to tell me that story?

Adm. P.: The RA-5 was the successor to the A-3. The A-3 was our twin-engine carrier-borne attack aircraft which was capable of carrying a large atomic weapon, and the successor to that was a design by Douglas - no, by North American - and we couldn't sell it as the successor to the heavy attack aircraft, but we did sell it as a reconnaissance aircraft. We had a great need in the Navy at the time for this type of reconnaissance aircraft which could do the whole spectrum of reconnaissance chores, had the capability to carry the equipment required to do this, either internally or in pods, and then the capability which we later built into the carriers to read out the results of reconnaissance flights on a very real-time basis in order that the commander have within an hour or so after a flight landed the complete information which had been gathered, rather than sending it back to some base within the continental United States and getting the information back twenty-four to forty-eight hours late.

Q: That meant photograph interpretation and all the rest?

Adm. P.: Photographic, radar, side-looking radar, infrared, all coordinated, and all the sounds of the electronic reconnaissance coordinated with the photographic and IR and side-looking radar. It was quite an expensive aircraft but the then Commander Bill Holcomb in the Bureau of Aeronautics and I sort of bulled this whole project through and got approval for it, and started the whole program and the training of the people and the necessary read-out organization and equipment on the carriers, in addition to developing the airplane.

We had a nefarious scheme between us to get the J-58 engine, which was under fire and being cancelled at the time, into this airplane out at Columbus, and we were just about to accomplish it when President Kennedy was elected and Secretary McNamara came along and some of his people found out about this and stopped it. So we would have had an airplane that would go at very high speeds and would have operated at an altitude around 90,000 feet, but we never did quite accomplish this. But we did get it with the engine that it now has and it's been a very successful reconnaissance aircraft.

Q: And the attack capabilities were read out?

Adm. P.: Yes. Heavy attack basically was taken over by the A-6.

The aircraft nuclear-propulsion program was one of the most interesting and controversial when I took over in 1958. We had an office in my establishment looking to the development of the aircraft nuclear-propulsion plant to go in a large seaplane. We had two companies developing aircraft nuclear-propulsion plants, that is, to produce the energy to run an engine and drive a propeller or a jet to power the aircraft, and the aircraft we had in mind at the time was without building a complete new development of a large aircraft were three Princess flying boats which the British had in mothballs, I think on the Isle of Wight, in good condition and they were large enough to be able to handle the weight which we would require in an aircraft nuclear-propulsion system. The reason that the weight had to be so great was to shield the power plant, the engine, from the crew so that it wouldn't effect them. That required a sizeable aircraft.

I appeared before the Congress, particularly the Joint Atomic Energy Committee, to try to get authorization to continue the development of these aircraft nuclear-propulsion systems with the possibility of leasing or buying these Princess boats from the British. This program was not supported by Admiral Rickover, and as a result of his opposition, in my opinion - prinicpally his opposition, the program died.

Q: What was his opposition?

Adm. P.: Well, it was not invented by him. I've told him that to his face, so I'm not saying anything out of school. In my opinion, had they let us continue this development at what I considered a reasonable cost at the time, we could have had an aircraft nuclear airplane flying, oh, ten years ago or twelve years ago. However, the program was discontinued and has long since been abandoned.

Q: That would have been a seaplane, then?

Adm. P.: A seaplane. The Air Force had a similar program, which also died aborning, to power a large landplane bomber with aircraft nuclear propulsion.

Q: Admiral, why were the Princess flying boats in mothballs? Why had the British abandoned them?

Adm. P.: They were costly. In my opinion, even their value as anti-submarine warfare vehicles, when compared to the cost, wasn't viable. In other words, it cost too much to operate for what you got out of such a weapon system and you could do it cheaper in another way. Therefore, they abandoned the Princess, much the same as we abandoned the supersonic seaplane and also lighter-than-air.

Q: What was your relationship with the research and development people in Defense?

Adm. P.: The office of Research and Development within the CNO, OP-07, with a deputy to head it, was not in being at the time that I reported. It came into being in my term, I think in the first or second year after I reported.

Q: Was Jim Wakelin the first one to hold that job?

Adm. P.: I believe he was, and Chick Hayward was the first deputy CNO for R & D.

Q: Admiral, in this period, as always, there were brush fires occurring in various parts of the world involving our military forces and particularly the Navy. What repercussions did this have on the Navy's budget?

Adm. P.: These so-called brush-fire wars, and these were particularly in the Mediterranean at the time, the larger-scale ones had taken place in the Far East —

Q: There was Taiwan and the Taiwanese Strait always.

Adm. P.: Right. The use of naval forces entails considerable expenditure in two parts of the appropriation and personnel and in maintenance and operation, and somewhat in aircraft and ships, but much smaller amounts. The large amounts of money expended are in personnel, because you've got to augment personnel, and pay and training enter into it, but O and M principally in the expenditure of monies to operate the forces on an accelerated basis.

In each one of these instances we expended a great deal more money than had been appropriated, so it was necessary for the Navy, and similarly the Air Force and the Army, but to a greater extent the Navy.

to go to the Congress to recover these monies. If you didn't recover the money expended in the personnel and in operations and maintenance, it would have to come out of procurement funds, the only place that you could recover money, and we were violently opposed, as officers trying to operate the Navy, to taking away from procurement of aircraft and ships, which we already considered inadequate.

Consequently, in appearing before the Deficiency Appropriation Subcommittees of the House and Senate, we had some very interesting and trying periods to recover this money. While I didn't have a large stake in the actual deficiency appropriation, if we didn't win the battle for the funds, to get additional appropriations to cover these expenditures, it meant that we were going to lose aircraft out of procurement. Therefore, I was vitally interested. I used to work not only within the committee at the hearings, but I worked on the individual members of the committee at appropriate times outside. I think we were quite successful in getting most of those deficiency appropriations.

During that period, I made some great friends among the members of these deficiency appropriations committees. The principal one in the House was Albert Thomas, from Texas, who was the chairman of the Deficiency Appropriations Subcommittee, and he became a great friend of mine. And I made two or three very close friends in the Senate. The Deficiency Appropriations Subcommittee was handled by Senator Chavez, and he had as senior Republican Senator Dvorshak, of Idaho.

Also, at this time, Senator Styles Bridges, of New Hampshire

Q: He was the minority leader, wasn't he?

Adm. P.: He was the minority leader, but on the Appropriations Committee he helped me greatly in trying to solve some of these problems.

Q: How knowledgeable were some of these men about naval affairs, naval problems?

Adm. P.: Almost all of those committee members that I had to deal with were very knowledgeable and spent a great deal of time in traveling and studying and getting to know what and how the Navy operated. I looked on individuals on the Appropriations Subcommittee like George Mahon and Harry Shepherd and Bob Sykes, and, on the Republican side, Jerry Ford and Mel Laird - in my opinion they were all very knowledgeable. Those on the Armed Services Committee, like Mr. Vinson, Les Arends, Mendel Rivers, and Eddie Hebert, all very knowledgeable.

Pirie #8 - 303

Interview No. 8 with Vice Admiral Robert Burns Pirie, U.S. Navy
(Retired)

Place: The U.S. Naval Institute, Annapolis, Maryland

Date: Friday morning, 3 May 1974

Subject: Biography

By: John T. Mason, Jr.

Q: It's great to see you this spring morning looking so trim and full of vigor, Sir. You're going to talk first about the development of aircraft and the people involved during the time that you were DCNO.

Adm. P.: In my previous interview we discussed several of the individual airplanes that were selected and developed during my tour as Deputy Chief of Naval Operations, Air. I'd like to go back a little in history and talk about the development of the naval aircraft suit that we've had in the last two decades, how the development came about, who the people were that were the most responsible, in my opinion, for this development, because I believe firmly that the U.S. Navy has the best military aircraft for the purpose intended in the world. They're all designed specifically to do the jobs,

I'll have a little bit to say about that. Also the aircraft engines which we developed. In the earlier days the Navy were the principal developers, and in the last fifteen to twenty years the Air Force and the Navy together have developed a fine suit of aircraft engines.

Well, to go back to the aircraft development, post World War II three of the chiefs of the Bureau of Aeronautics who I believe were significant - four really - in the development of these aircraft and engines were Mel Pride, who retired as a vice admiral and had a great deal of World War II experience; Apollo Soucek of record-breaking fame in his early days and who had quite a World War II record; Jim Russell, who I think is the principal and most significant individual in the development of aircraft for the U.S. Navy; and his successor, Bob Dixon. Jim Russell and Bob Dixon spent a great deal of time in the Bureau of Aeronautics during their careers and I believe they're the principal contributors particularly to the carrier aircraft development that has been so successful.

I might name two or three individuals who passed through the flight test section of the Navy and had a great deal to do with the quality of aircraft that the Navy had. First, Fred Trapnell who I was in the test section with, back in 1931 and 1932 and who I believe personally is the best pilot I've ever been associated with, and I think he probably was the best test pilot. His successor was Bill Davis - William V. Davis - and they together contributed a tremendous amount to the development of naval aircraft through the test and evaluation program. They set up those programs at Patuxent pre-war, during the war, and subsequent to the war and Tom Connolly, who was a protege of Trapnell and was the first head of the flight test school at Patuxent. They all had a significant part in the development.

Another individual who had a great part in the engine development was Bill Schoech. Bill had his postgraduate training at CalTec in engines and he, I think, probably as much as anyone is responsible for the fine engine development, particularly through the Pratt and Whitney Company and United Aircraft.

Now that I have mentioned these particular individuals, I'll say something about the aircraft.

The development of aircraft with turbojet engines, which permitted us to have a significant increase in aircraft performance, took place post World War II and, under the guidance of these individuals I have mentioned. Most of the fighter aircraft were developed by three companies, Grumman, McDonald Douglas (McDonald at that time), St. Louis, and North American under Dutch Kindelberger.

The fighter aircraft that's probably the most successful up to the present time is the F-4, which is the McDonald and I have previously discussed that. The F-14 which is now in production at Grumman, and I was told just this last week that the 72nd operational aircraft has been delivered and induction into the fleet is now taking place and the first squadron will be fully operational and deployed in September of this year.

Q: And what's the prognosis for it?

Adm. P.: I believe that it's the finest fighter airplane in the world today. It is by far the most sophisticated in every respect, in its ability to deliver weapons systems in any mode. By this I mean it can deliver stand-off missiles of great capability, it can dog fight with cannon or with short-range missiles. It is very maneuverable, and, to show you a comparison, it can come aboard a carrier 25 knots slower than the F-4. Low-speed handling characteristics are extremely pleasing and it's a great tribute to the people who have been in the development and to the Grumman Corporation and the engineers who are responsible for it.

Q: Have they attempted to focus on that aspect of a plane's development in the past?

Adm P.: We've tried very hard to keep low speed within reason because of the great difficulty in the material aspects of getting a plane on board a carrier. By that I mean not only very-high-speed landings require great strengthening of the aircraft, its landing gear and the tail-hook assembly for arresting, but also the arresting gear and the cables and the arresting engines themselves. And the lower we can get the speed, the less the requirements in strength and weight for arrested landings. It's far easier for the pilot to get aboard under all conditions with the speed down at some reasonable level. These advances have taken place over a period of the last ten years that permit us to get lower landing speeds. I think the same probably applies to the SA-3, the new antisubmarine jet, but I'm not as familiar with that at the present moment as I am with

F-14.

In the attack plane field we have two or three great airplanes today, the A-6, which was developed specifically for accurate weapon delivery by the Grumman Corporation, and the A-7 which is the Vought aircraft development that is a very significant airplane in our suit today, very successful. In the antisubmarine plane field Lockheed is building the new SA-3 jet -- twin-engine jet -- for carrier operations, and it I think is probably the finest airplane in its field today. The patrol plane that we're using, the P-3, is a splendid long-range antisubmarine warfare craft and the systems that go with it I think make it the finest antisubmarine weapon that there is in the world today.

Q: What is that plane's range?

Adm. P.: Oh, easily 3,000, but it depends on how much load you're trying to carry, but it has almost unlimited range. I think it can fly 10,000 miles if you want to put fuel in it vis-à-vis weapon systems. That record is held by this airplane now and it's quite a long distance. The development of the electronic systems for each of these aircraft kept pace with the actual airframe and engine development, and in antisubmarine warfare the systems that are used for searching out and finding the submarine as well as holding contact with him until you can destroy him are extremely effective and the destructive systems are extremely effective. I believe that the aircraft system is a better system than any surface or subsurface system in existence today for the same purpose. And I think that the SA-3 has an equally effective system in a smaller airplane that can fly off the carriers.

In the field of fighter aircraft we have new aiming systems that are developed around laser beams that are most effective and can pinpoint not only hitting another aircraft but hitting a ground target, and they are being used in our attack aircraft for pinpoint accuracy.

All of these developments came from a very responsible early education system. Most of these officers that I have mentioned had postgraduate training in aeronautical engineering and had the real background knowledge and foundation to become experts in the field.

Q: Let me ask you, Admiral, say, take the SA-3. What time process is involved from the beginning when this weapon is conceived until it goes through the various phases of development and finally reaches the fleet?

Adm. P.: I'd say on the order of five years. That's a ball park figure. It may be a little longer than that from the concept, but from the time that they decide on the development until they actually get the things flying in the fleet it's roughly about five years.

The expense of our aircraft weapons systems has come in for a great deal of criticism in the last few years, and I think with some justification. However, everything has become tremendously more expensive - automobiles, farm machinery, televisions, kitchen equipment, and what have you, all cost a great deal more. Any mechanical electronic equipment. However, in our effort to give the pilot and the crew of each of our combatant aircraft the most significant and best systems we can give him to do his job, you get a great many research and development and engineering personnel working on the development and manufacture of these systems and by the time you get them into operation they are very expensive. The only way you can cut the cost is to take away from the aircraft a significant system for fighting, which I don't think is justified, either in the offensive weapon systems or in defensive systems for protecting the flight crews in the performance of their mission. All these things have got to be taken into consideration in modern warfare.

I believe that the devastating destructive power of these modern weapon systems showed up in the recent Israeli-Arab conflict in which large numbers not only of aircraft but of tanks and missiles were destroyed in the shortest period of time ever recorded in history, and I think it's that kind of accuracy of both the offensive and defensive systems that is going to rule the next conflict that we see.

Q: Admiral, what is the comparable unit in the Navy to the Ships' Characteristics Board - the unit that governs the characteristics of planes?

Adm. P.: Basically, it's the Air Board. It's headed by the Deputy Chief of Naval Operations, Air, and he has both the ComNavLant and ComNavAir Pac and the head of the training command and the Chief of the Naval Air Systems Command, and they combine to sort of set policy and then the Naval Air Systems Command has his own organization for determining the aircraft systems and development. He's now a vice admiral, the head of the Naval Air Systems Command, which indicates the importance the Navy attaches to this particular function.

Q: You talk about the gradual buildup of a group of very skilled officers and technicians who develop these weapons systems. This implies the need to have a constant feed-in of new weapons systems being conceived and developed, does it not, in order to keep these teams intact?

Adm. P.: I haven't yet talked about our system of training, which I will briefly, but new developments in all weapons systems associated with aircraft is a continuing process and is going on all the time. We have some real expert military and civilian people in this field.

Q: Just as a way of a footnote or comparison or what have you, do the Russians have planes that are comparable to some of our new types?

Adm. P.: Yes, they have excellent performance characteristics and I think that they have given a good account of themselves in the actions in the Arab-Israeli War. There are all sort of arguments as to which one is really better, but I think that the actual losses from air combat, discounting those destroyed by ground-air missiles, is very much in favor of the Israelis.

The training system that we use for pilot and air crew training, I think, is most significant in naval aviation and has been from the beginning. An excellent flight training from the real inception of naval aviation, starting in World War I, and then in the interim period between World War I and World War II when the carrier came into being and became a significant weapon system we had to develop techniques for carrier operations, and the training kept pace with it and I think that as proof of our system - and I will discuss this later - we had a significant number of the astronauts chosen from among naval aviators and naval aviators who were test pilot graduates.

The training of flight crews and the training of ground crews we found in the early stages of our naval aviation that it was most important that we devote a lot of time and effort to training programs vis à vis just training under operational conditions and the technical training programs which we developed and had been started at Memphis have really paid off. I think we have the finest kind of aircraft crews and the finest kind of ground support personnel.

I can remember when I was DCNO, Air, trying to convince the Chief of Personnel that they should do the same for the surface Navy, particularly I was interested in the field of missiles, firing surface-to-air missiles, and that they should adopt our methods. He always said, well, our methods cost two or three times as much as their methods of training and they couldn't afford it. I said, yes, but our people are trained.

Q: That was your rationale?

Adm. P.: Yes, and it's significant that in both aircraft and submarine craft training it's a matter of survival. If you have poor ground crews or poor air crews you're going to lose lives and airplanes, and the same thing happens on a submarine. Therefore, we've had to have good training in the aircraft business and in submarines. The surface people never quite got around to that because they weren't faced with survival just from operations in peace or war.

Q: Were they relying too heavily on the normal educational background of the recruits?

Adm. P.: Not particularly that, but they did most of their training on the job, instead of having significant training at a technical training center. I think they've got around to it now. The concepts that have been put into effect in the last two or three years, where all training is now headed up by one training command, and that's now headed up by Chris Cagle at Pensacola, but he has surface, submarine, and air training within his aegis, including the Naval Academy, and including officers' training.

I also think that our postgraduate training is excellent. It's done professionally and at some considerable expense in the sense of taking officers out of operational assignments for two or three years in order to do it. But it's significant that we do, I believe, have the finest personnel, the finest aircraft, and the finest ancillary equipment required for these aircraft for both offensive and defensive operations that there is in the world.

Q: You had a great deal to do with the Memphis setup, did you not?

Adm. P.: Not significantly. I worked with Fitzhugh Lee on several improvements while I was DCNO, Air. Fitzhugh Lee was there on the ground and he made some very significant advances. The one contribution that I was able to make was in getting personnel to the aircraft in the development stage earlier so that they had an opportunity to learn, maintenance personnel particularly, to learn a good deal about the airplane before it got into service. I backed up the time of getting these people trained by about two years.

Q: And naturally that's an expense!

Adm. P.: It was more expensive and cost us, but we had great success in the induction of these aircraft to the fleet.

Q: I think Fitzhugh discovered in his own experience there that he couldn't count too heavily on assuming that these young men coming in had an adequate educational background either from the public educational system, so he had to supplement it and augment it in many ways.

Adm. P.: Right. I think we had good testing to determine what educational qualifications the individuals had and we then proceeded to bring them up to a standard that we thought was required to do the job.

Q: Why was Memphis chosen as the site?

Adm. P.: Well, it started in World War II. That's where we had most of it stationed. We had the equipment and we had buildings. It was a good site and it just naturally grew, and we developed a technical training center there. We moved what technical training we had in other places into one center just because of the economies involved.

There were a good many arguments and battles over numbers of pilots and flight crews to be trained, and I had an opportunity to work with the Air Force in arguing with Defense Department officials about the numbers of pilots to be trained. I remember distinctly that in the early part of the Kennedy administration Mr. McNamara and his crew thought we should reduce the pilot training rate, and I worked very closely with General Rosey O'Donnell, who was then the Deputy of the Air Force for Personnel, and we argued against real significant cuts with the thought that it is very difficult to regenerate and start up a training program and it's far more expensive to get into a conflict and start up a training program than it is to have a continuing program of significant numbers. And this actually proved to be the case.

Q: There's a difference in the quality, too, isn't there?

Adm. P.: Yes. They made the cuts, arbitrary cuts. They cut the Air Force far worse than they did the Navy and Marines, but they made some arbitrary cuts and cut our training rate down, and, lo and behold, a year or two later along came the Vietnam conflict and it all had to be turned up again and started, and the costs were significantly greater than had they continued. The thing that we fought for was to train larger numbers than you need and hold the ones that leave the service as Reserves in readiness to be called back. That's cheaper than it is - well, say, if your training rate is 300 a month and you only need 150, you put the 150 that you trained every year on the shelf, and they're your reserves. That's a cheaper system than it is to go back to 150 with a smaller training establishment and jack it up to a higher number when you get into a conflict.

Q: But you couldn't sell that!

Adm. P.: This is a hard concept to sell at the moment.

Q: But once you disperse the training personnel, they're not needed -

Adm. P.: Gone!

Q: And then it's impossible to re-assemble them, isn't it?

Adm. P.: Well, also you've got to get the pilots and the ground crews and the aircraft that are necessary to train these people, and to try to accelerate takes a significant length of time. So, if you get into a conflict it's two years before you get the first product of an accelerated program. Suppose you're at 150 a year pilot training rate and you have to go to 500, well, you stay at that 150 that's always coming off the end of the line for the first two years. It's two years before you get anything more, if you're lucky - if you can get the aircraft and the necessary pilot-training and crew-training personnel.

This was always a big argument and O'Donnell and I got thrown out of two or three offices more than once, arguing this case. But the proof was in the pudding when the Vietnam War came along and they had to build it back up again. It proved that our philosophy was right and theirs not.

Q: Well, will that be a lesson learned in future years?

Adm. P.: We hope. I think it's very important that you have a significant reserve of trained personnel and I think that in the interest of economy and of national defense it is better to train a larger number and put them in the Reserves for a number of years than it is to go to a low pilot-training rate and crew-training rate and then try to accelerate in case of emergency. It's a very dangerous concept not to have a significant reserve.

Q: Especially in the light of modern warfare. There's no time for this kind of thing.

Adm. P.: Yes, you lose so many in such a short length of time. For example, in the Israeli-Arab War the tank casualties were staggering. In that short little time there were 1,500 tanks destroyed. That used to be enough to do a whole five-year war on! And aircraft losses were significant. And you lose people, by the same token you're losing all those trained people when that guided weapon hits a tank and destroys it. If you don't have a trained reserve that you can call up to replace those people, you're going to have one hell of a time. This is one of the points about Russia. They're devoting a tremendous amount of their national wealth and gross national product to military equipment and people, and they have a very significant training background.

One other aspect that I haven't discussed is that it's very important in the operation of any of these sophisticated systems in aircraft today that we have adequate spares, and the provisioning and finding out what the use of each part of the plane's equipment amounts to so that you can buy intelligently is quite a job, and it's necessary to deploy what we call "provisioning teams" with the aircraft during its development much earlier than we did three or four years ago in order to find out what that usage rate is and not buy too many of a part that we don't need, and buy a significant number of those that have high usage. In these expensive systems today this becomes one of the most important aspects of keeping your systems operating and doing it at a reasonable cost.

For example, you can postulate that I'm just going to go out and buy 50 percent of everything, every piece of electronic equipment, every piece of gun-sight equipment, every piece of the armament, the gun, the missile, every piece of the engine - you're going to buy 50 percent of everything. Well, in a good many of these things you would never use that in the whole lifetime of the aircraft, 5 percent might be right, maybe 1 percent. But in some things you do need 50 percent. It's finding out what the percentage usage is right from the very beginning. What we do is take the provisioning team and put it with the aircraft while it's still in development, while it's goi through test and evaluation, so that the people who are going to do that understand fully what the exact usage rate is.

For example, in a hydraulic system, what kind of seals and pumps and so forth, and everything that has to do with the raising and lowering of landing gear and all that sort of business. How much electronic equipment burns out and has to be replaced. They find that out.

Q: That's where Patuxent looms large in the scheme of things, isn't it?

Adm. P.: They loom very large and then the bureau of Supplies and Accounts has a good record in the supply system of what we need in the way of spares and we try to buy those significant numbers as the aircraft is being manufactured. As I said, the F-14 now had 72 aircraft delivered and operating in the fleet. We have had two or three years of experience in determing what parts are going to wear out the fastest so we can keep them operating. It's very important that you don't have a $7-million aircraft sitting waiting for a 25-cent part.

The same thing applies in the automobile industry today. The same thing applies in the manufacture of almost all sophisticated equipment. I'm on the board of a couple of companies today where we're manufacturing $100,000 frequency change or a piece of electronic equipment and it's sitting there waiting for a $10 part and we can't deliver for six months. Well, $100,000 worth of equipment undelivered for six months you've got to then finance that. You can't get the money out of the guy you're going to deliver to till you deliver it. So you're paying for money at 10 percent. Now, relate that to aircraft development today. You've got a $10 million aircraft with a crew sitting on the ground. He can't fly. It's a terrific waste of money, a loss to the government, and we can't afford that. Therefore, we have to have these sophisticated systems to find out how to keep them in operation.

All this has been accelerated greatly in the last ten years.

Q: Yes, and you were there at the time when it was accelerating very rapidly.

Adm. P.: High-performance aircraft, sophisticated electronics, and all sorts of systems that we'd never heard of. For example, the laser or the electronic aiming delivery systems. And defensive systems. For example, defense against the Sidewinder missile, a heat-seeker, and how do you do it. Defense against an electronically guided missile being shot at you, how do you keep that thing from hitting you, maneuvering. It's only partially effective in those things, and we have to have sophisticated electronic systems to do it.

Q: Admiral, do the sophisticated defensive systems develop more readily when the original development is in the hands of a potential enemy, rather than in our own hands? Are we challenged more readily to develop a defense against a weapon system.

Adm. P.: Defense against a particular weapon system takes place based on your knowledge of what the problem is. If a significant offensive weapon system was developed, that you could know about, by an enemy, you've got a real problem defending against it because of the development time required to develop the defensive system, and it could become a dog-eat-dog -

Q: So your answer is that it's much more effective when we develop the offensive system and then a defense against it?

Adm. P.: Right. You assume, as Thucydides did, that your enemy - you must assume that he is as smart or bright as you are. If you think that you're working against a dumb enemy and that you're a lot better than he is, you're going to come a cropper, because he'll have a system that'll get you. So it's a matter of constant work to develop new systems that are effective.

I believe I've covered aircraft development and the training at Memphis, the provisioning of aircraft, and the personnel training, fairly well.

Q: Do you want to speak a little about the training of pilots, say at Patuxent?

Adm. P.: Test-pilot training started in the post World War II period when Admiral Trapnell was there, and I'm pretty sure that Tom Connolly, then a commander, was the first head of the test pilot school.

Q: Weren't they being trained at Anacostia before?

Adm. P.: Well, it was training on the job again. I was in the test section. We learned while we were doing it. It was not a school. Well, it became very evident that an equivalent of a postgraduate course is required for test pilots, so we had to put into effect a postgraduate course to train test pilots adequately. And that's exactly what they did. It went into all of the same basics that you have at the postgraduate school for bringing the mathematical and scientific education up to the point required by the individual, and that's what we did at the test-pilot training school. We gave him a basic education that he needed, mathematics, scientific, to understand the problems that he was going to face in whatever phase of training he took part in.

They started the school and were very successful in it and, I may say, that when we chose the astronauts the success of our personnel and the comparison between them and the Air Force pilots was quite significant. I believe we had an earlier start than the Air Force did in this particular field, and our people showed up very well in the program.

I might at this time go into that.

Q: The astronauts?

Adm. P.: The choosing of the astronauts.

One day in the early stages of NASA – I can't remember the exact date – but I was sitting in my office, (DCNO, Air), and the Secretary came in and said Dr. Hugh Dryden, the Deputy Director of NASA, was in the office to see me. I went out and welcomed Hugh. He was an old friend. I had been on the NACA and I knew him and had worked with him. He came in and said he'd just been to see Admiral Burke about the choosing of the first astronauts and that Admiral Burke said to come down and see me.

So I asked him what the problem was, what did he want, and he said that they had determined that they wanted to screen 50 graduates of the Navy test pilot school and 50 graduates of the Air Force test pilot school, all trained test pilots, as prospective astronauts. Now, they had some parameters of size, weight, age, and so forth, that they gave us initially and we screened the records and, after getting volunteers, gave them the names of 50 people each from the Navy and Air Force.

Q: First, you called for volunteers?

Adm. P.: They all had to be volunteers, they all had to be test pilot graduates, and then add these certain physical requirements, the height, weight business, and so forth. It was significant to me that within this 50 that we got we had several commanders who had four or five children who were volunteers, all gung-ho, ready to go.

Q: Off to the moon!

Adm. P.: Yes. Well, out of the 50 they eliminated, say 25 or 30 before they went into any extensive training program by interviews and other means. Then, I'd say about twenty of our Navy and Marines and twenty of the Air Force were put through some extensive training, and they eliminated finally down to the first seven astronauts chosen. The ones that came from the Navy were Alan Shepherd, Wally Shirra, Carpenter, and John Glenn, and when they were finally chosen they came to my office and we gave them their orders to go to NASA from the Navy, and I made one comment to them. I congratulated them and said I knew they were going to have a fantastic experience and that it was going to be a very productive one for the country, but for them not to forget where they got their original training and original opportunity to get into this program. And I must say that in my talks with them since they do remember.

Q: They're still Navy men!

Adm. P.: They're still Navy and they still talk about it. I don't have to go into their accomplishments and tell you how great they were. Then the subsequent ones were nominated and chosen in the same way. They all had to have the test pilot qualifications.

Q: That was basic.

Adm. P.: The basic fundamental.

Q: You might talk about the forming of NASA because you have that on your list.

Adm. P.: When I first arrived in Washington in May 1958 the old NACA was still in existence, and the committee had a Navy and Air Force and Army member - this was the National Advisory Committee for Aeronautics and it had several significant members from college and university and other fields. Two or three individuals I remember most significantly at that time were Leonard Carmichael, head of the Smithsonian Institution, who was a member, Jimmy Doolittle, Hugh Dryden, and Jerry Hunsaker.

When the National Aeronautics and Space Act came into being, they initially had a committee similar to the NACA, which had frequent meetings, with the Air Force, the Navy, and the Army being represented, but in the first year they did away with that military representation and only had a liaison officer because of the organization which was set up by Keith Glennan in NASA. In the old NACA we had frequent meetings to talk over national developments and problems, and when NASA was formed this was the principal livelihood and the coordinating committee was not required and the committee system disappeared.

Q: This was an interesting development, the formation of a separate agency to handle this whole program, was it not?

Adm. P.: The space program.

Q: Yes. Had the Navy not had a portion of the program as it developed before this?

Adm. P.: We had in my office an officer in charge of our program that had to do with space and the applications which we thought we could use in the Navy. For example, communications systems or navigational systems, and so forth. The Air Force had a similar office that was working on these kind of programs. But there hadn't been a significant amount of money spent in the field. Let's say that the development of large rockets, that is the development of a rocket to lift a significant weight into space, had not come about until this particular time. So this was the evolution of the rocket and the rocket engine and being able to lift large weights to get into space that really precipitated the forming of an agency to handle it and to handle what we were going to do in the exploration of space.

Q: Did the Navy have any fear at that point that its own particular interests would be submerged in a large program?

Adm. P.: Yes, I think we felt that perhaps in certain areas we could visualize like reconnaissance areas and navigational and communications, let's say, we wanted to protect our interest. We didn't want anyone to dictate what we could have. We wanted to have a say as to what our systems would be. For example, what frequencies we would be able to use and so forth that might impinge on other parts of our operations. So we did have some fear that our military problems wouldn't be taken care of, but the Defense Department had a good liaison staff with NASA and our interests were never submerged.

We still have a good deal of give and take in the communications and navigation problems today. It's a matter of constant liaison.

Q: We had developed the Vanguard satellite, had we not? Before NASA came into being?

Adm. P.: Yes, and we also had the navigation satellite. I've forgotten the code name for it. It was being developed at APL at the time NASA came into being. It was one of the first ones put out.

Next, lighter-than-air. I don't like to be known as the undertaker who drove the last nail in the coffin.

Q: But you were!

Adm. P.: It fell to my lot, and not too pleasantly, to evaluate and decide what to do about lighter-than-air. It was a costly operation and, for value received, we had to make a careful analysis of what lighter-than-air could contribute vis à vis heavier-than-air to our national defense. We did make such studies and found that —

Q: Was this in 1958, 1959?

Adm. P.: Yes, I started as soon as I arrived. It was going on, I guess, at the time I arrived. And whether to continue it or whether to use up what we had, whether there was any significant contribution that they could make. The final conclusion was that it should be eliminated as a system because it wasn't effective as compared with heavier-than-air. And so the program was cut significantly and finally put to bed during my term as DCNO, Air.

Q: Would you say that this is an irrevocable decision?

Adm. P.: No, I don't think it's irrevocable if someone can figure out a use for them. In the scheme of things, perhaps in anti-submarine warfare. The actual record of blimps in antisubmarines warfare during World War II was that they didn't sink one German submarine and that one lighter-than-air craft was destroyed by a German submarine. That was their total record. They flew a lot of hours and if you want to postulate that they did by negative search keep the German submarines down who might otherwise have wanted to come to the surface, they might have been valuable in the coastal areas.

Q: That's where they operated, near the coast?

Adm. P.: That's one of the places they operated. They're of no value in bad weather. I operated them once, from the Sicily. When I had command of the Sicily in experimenting with making landings and flying the blimps from the ship off the East Coast we had quite an extensive exercise down off Vieques for five or six days and operated them continuously away from any other base. We fueled them and provisioned them down on the decks. That was in calm weather. I think there's a limit as to what kind of weather you can operate them in. One of the primary reasons for recommending their discontinuation was the accidents that we had and signficant losses due to the weather. I think that's what destroyed the original Akron and Macon. So it was very difficult to see what their value, even of coastal patrol, was compared with the large aircraft for the same amount of area and effectiveness.

Q: Did the Coast Guard use them at all?

Adm. P.: The Coast Guard I don't think ever used them. Their sea rescue aircraft, of course, were amphibians most of them. They had some seaplanes.

Q: Then they began to use helicopters.

Adm. P.: They're using helicopters now.

Q: Has the helicopter in a sense replaced the blimp?

Adm. P.: Yes, in effect, in some significant ways. I believe coastwise that the helicopter could be of some significant value.

Of course, we have today effective radar systems which can detect a periscope, which we didn't have in World War II. Then the detection of a submarine was by eyesight. Now there are significant other means of detection which give you the same information capability. For example, underwater electronic detection is very sophisticated and gives you position and you can then get an aircraft out much faster than you could a ship to a point to destroy the enemy when you discover him. The reaction time is much faster, significantly faster.

They're making some allegations today for LTA on lift, lifting significant weights. The lifting of a large weight, particularly under adverse weather conditions, to move it a distance is going to require a little bit of doing on anybody's part. It requires quite a bit of doing with a helicopter under good weather conditions.

The next subject. The Federal Aeronautics Agency was another development that came into being in the Federal Aviation Act. The establishment of the Federal Aeronautic Agency took place during my tenure and it replaced the old CAA. The first FAA administrator was Pete Quesada, retired lieutenant general, Air Force. I had known Pete and he was a good friend of mine. We had a fine relationship.

The rapid increase in numbers of commercial and private aircraft post World War II made it mandatory that we have better, more effective control systems. This also applied, of course, to any control system of airspace which required that the Air Force and the Navy be controlled much in the same fashion. But military aircraft, by virtue of their missions, have got to be permitted restricted areas and corridors in which they can operate while cooperating with the commercial and private aircraft.

Q: They very rarely use commercial airports, do they?

Adm. P.: We seldom use any commercial fields. As a matter of fact, we're prohibited from using them except for dropping VIP passengers, flying them in and out of commercial fields. Military aircraft are kept away from large commercial fields entirely, but the cooperation required in air space must be a full cooperation between the military and the private fliers, commercial fliers.

Q: But there can only be in existence one system?

Adm. P.: You've got to have one system. There was a significant effort made to limit military aircraft operations which we could put up with. It was done by what I call little people with little knowledge of what the problems were, and a lot of pressure put on by private fliers who didn't want to be told where they couldn't fly. The civilian who has enough money to buy a $50,000 airplane wants to tell you and he wants to go where he wants to go without - he says "get that military airplane on the ground so I can fly through his area." Well, we didn't feel that way about it because we were charged with the defense of our country. The Strategic Air Force was a specific case in point. When they wanted to go they went, and they had to have an area and areas that they could get in and out of their fields and get into the air in areas where they could operate without reference to the commercial and private airplanes' desires.

We didn't have significant problems with commercial aircraft, but we did have some significant problems with private aircraft, because they came on in great profusion. When Kennedy was inaugurated he appointed Najeeb Halaby as Pete Quesada's successor, and Najeeb had some pretty radical ideas in the area of air control which the Air Force and the Navy couldn't put up with.

Q: What were some of these ideas?

Adm. P.: Well, with reference to our operating areas, limiting our operating areas and telling us when we could fly and when we couldn't fly, getting in and out of fields, and letting private aircraft fly through our restricted areas. It had to do most with that field of bombing and gunnery areas. We had some quite significant arguments.

Doc Strother, lieutenant general, Air Force, was the Air Force deputy for operations and he and I went to several conferences. Finally, we had a very significant long conference on a Saturday, I remember, in the office of Joe Imiry, the Assistant Secretary of the Air Force, in which we had quite a hair-pulling contest, but we let Halaby know in no uncertain terms that we were not going to be embarrassed in military operations and if he wanted to have a real fight on his hands that any insistence on the rule of the private flyer being able to keep us from performing our missions was out of the question and we'd take it to the Congress.

Q: I take it your problems were increased with a civilian head of FAA in preference to a retired general?

Adm. P.: Actually, Halaby had been in the Navy and was a Navy test pilot school graduate. I think he was put upon by some of the minions in the organization, which grew too fast. Private fliers are a very difficult outfit to get along with. I got to know some of them later when I was in the National Aeronautics Association, and they want to dictate to everybody how they'll operate and what they'll do.

Q: You inferred they're wealthy sportsman types.

Adm. P.: The whole of the air space is taken up today. For example, in the state of Florida the whole air space is taken up. There isn't any place you can just go fly. You've got to be controlled. All the air above Florida is controlled air space. That's not true all over the whole United States, but it's significant all around large urban communities. For example, the air space between Washington and New York, that whole corridor is all controlled. It has to be, and any private flyer who wants to get near it has got to have the equipment and know how he's doing to get in and out of these fields and to obey the rules.

In the case of the Navy, FAA has worked the restricted areas and gunnery areas over pretty thoroughly, and you see articles in the paper continuously about how they're trying to cut out military rights.

Another significant thing that came along was supersonic drag waves on the ground. For example, to accelerate a high-speed flier took a considerable length of time and if he was 30,000 to 40,000 feet the sonic boom became a significant thing because it could be heard and was quite a loud explosion that scared people and they claimed it did a lot of physical damage in actually dragging the sonic waves. The drag wave behind an airplane as it's speeding at supersonic speeds has done some damage so it got to be quite a problem, and when we actually set up for test purposes the boys at Patuxent had to go out off the Atlantic coast and have an area 400 or 500 miles in length in order just to test high-speed airplanes and that sort of thing.

Cutting short the development of a supersonic transport to a large extent hinged on the sound wave and the damage that it would probably do in crossing the country,

All of these problems we had to deal with, with the FAA and we got them all fairly well resolved.

Aircraft safety also was one of my principal jobs and, as the head of naval aviation, I was very cognizant of aircraft safety not only for the preservation of life but to cut down the accident rate also became quite significant in saving money in having fewer accidents with these very expensive aircraft. As an example, in my last year, to show you the comparative rates of aircraft accidents in military and commercial and private flying, the number of casualties - this is deaths - in the Navy, Marine Corps, and the Air Force was about the same. The Navy and Marine Corps had about 250 and the Air Force had about 250, and in that particular year in commercial aviation accidents had been about 250 deaths, and in that same year in private aviation there were 6,000 killed. Very few people realize there is a significantly greater death rate in private aviation because of compulsion of getting from one place to another -

Q: He is an amateur!

Adm. P.: Well, they're not trained to take orders or be ordered. It's the same attitude as saying "I want the air space." When you tell him he shouldn't go to New York because the weather is marginal, he says "to hell with that, I can handle myself in marginal weather." and he gets in trouble, so the death rate is significantly higher, and from lack of discipline in most cases - getting into bad weather areas when he shouldn't be in the air. That still, I'm sure, holds today.

We had a large safety organization and we worked hard at trying to get our accident rate down. Pilot error is a significant part of this and one of the things that I found was that you let a pilot for morale and publicity reasons make a crosscountry flight, maybe to his home town or on a weekend, and there's nothing wrong with that. He's recruiting or trying to help bring favorable publicity to us, but he makes this date and arrangement and then at the prescribed time the weather at his terminal is bad. But he's got a girl there or a wife there or a mother and father there and people waiting for him and he says, "I've got to get there." So he takes chances that otherwise he wouldn't take. We try to control that on the ground. If it's bad they won't give him a clearance, but if the weather gets bad en route and it becomes his decision, somebody's got to then tell him "you get the hell on the ground or come on back." We have such a system today throughout the country - the FAA - good weather reporting and a good system to follow and they can tell these flights when they should land or when they should turn back, but we did have a great deal of difficulty with people trying to get to places on personal compunction, rather than a military mission and that caused us a lot of casualties and a lot of headaches.

We tried to get control of that and our safety center worked hard in this area. In fact, we did make a significant contribution during the period.

Q: Admiral, the control tower operator is a very important cog in the whole system, is he not?

Adm. P.: Right, very. They're very important and they have to be well trained and they can't stay there too long. That's a very enervating job. They have to be rotated every hour or two. You can't just sit there for 8 or 10 hours at a time. They've got to be watched very carefully. This whole system throughout the country is a significant business because aircraft have to be controlled all the time. You've got to know what's in the air space. Control around these fields is a tough job even in good weather, but in bad weather it becomes absolutely essential.

Q: I understand that during World War II we did use WAVEs in control towers, especially in Florida I believe.

Adm. P.: I think we do now.

Q: I was about to ask how effective they are.

Adm. P.: Very good. I think they make just as good operators as the males for this purpose because it's a detailed job, looking at radarscopes and keeping track –

Q: A woman has more aptitude for detail.

Adm. P.: The work is computerized now and the female is notoriously better than the male at detailed computer work.

Q: Let's start with the TFX story.

Adm. P.: The TFX evolved from an association in conferences between

John Stack of NACA and NASA laboratory at Langley Field and General Hank Everest in command of the Tactical Air Command at Langley. The NACA and later NASA had done some wind-tunnel work and experimental work on the swept-wing aircraft concept, to sweep the wings at high speed in a 90° to the axis position for landing and take-off but at low-speed operations so that the necessary spoilers and flaps could be operated to control speed levels for landing and take-off. Then sweep the wing at high speed to cut down the drag and get to a higher speed than would be possible with a fixed-wing aircraft.

This all took place in the 1950s, so there had been a significant amount of work and a significant consideration given to this by both the Air Force and the Navy in Washington before President Kennedy was inaugurated and Mr. McNamara came on the scene. I think a great many people think this was something that was dreamed up by the McNamara regime, and that's not so at all. We had had many meeting and many studies made before Mr. McNamara's time as Secretary of Defense.

Q: Was the idea being toyed with abroad too? Did the Russians have this concept?

Adm. P.: I don't know that they did have before we did. I don't think that they did have at that time. I think theirs was an outgrowth of ours.

We had study groups working in cooperation between the Navy and the Air Force on the development of a swept-wing fighter at the time McNamara came in, but McNamara and systems analyst Alain Enthoven grabbed onto this as something that they could take as a significant development of their regime, and so accelerated the studies and development. There was established under the Chief of Staff of the Air Force, the Air Staff, which consisted of the Vice Chief and the Air Force Deputies, a committee to go into the TFX development, which had three Navy members, and I was the senior Navy member. The Navy Deputy for Research and Development and the head of the Air Systems Command were the other two.

There was competition between the Boeing Company and General Dynamics at Fort Worth. They were given competitive study contracts for development of a swept-wing fighter, and after getting their studies, there were significant meetings of this committee, which I attended, to determine which of the two systems was the best and recommend which one should be chosen to go ahead with the development.

The Air Force ran the study group under an Air Force colonel who was qualified in this area, and we had Navy members of that team. They reported their findings finally and we chose the Boeing Company's development study and their submission to go ahead with the development.

Q: Was this thing intended by McNamara and his people as a dual-purpose one? Was it to serve for the Navy and the Air Force?

Adm. P.: This was a dual-purpose. There would have to be some variations for carrier operation, but the basic airplane was to be the same.

Pirie #8 - 338

Q: Were the committee members happy with this concept?

Adm. P.: The concept was thoroughly understood and those of us in the Army and Navy - I mean the Air Force and the Navy - were satisfied that an aircraft of this character could be built, but that there had to be some variations for carrier operations. There would have to be an Air Force and a Navy version.

We in the Navy were not entirely satisfied that we shouldn't have a separate development on account of this compatability with the carriers, because there's a significant difference between the concept of fighter roles. Their great belief in an intrusion-type warfare rather than pinpointing attack. On the other hand, we felt that we had to have an aircraft that could carry a high-speed air-to-air missile for the purpose of destroying high-speed targets approaching an area that we wanted to defend, that is, a significant fleet area. This is where we had a great deal of concern in the Navy because to put this missile on that high-speed aircraft was not compatible with the Air Force's concept of having a very-high-speed aircraft for attack.

Q: Do you imply that this meant different characteristics?

Adm. P.: Yes. One of the stumbling blocks that we had was that they had a requirement - the Air Force had a requirement - to go at a speed of Mach 1.2 on the deck - this is higher than the speed of sound - for a distance of 200 miles. This required significant weight increase to the aircraft in order to take care of gust loading at high speeds, due to the bumpiness of the air at low altitudes. This meant that the aircraft had to be heavier, that it was a lot faster on landing and take-off than we could stand, and this is basically where we parted company with the Air Force on concept, because of that one requirement.

However, we thought that if this was going to be "rammed down our throats" we were willing to go ahead and try to get a Navy version, and the committee decided to recommend to the Chief of Staff of the Air Force and to the CNO that Boeing was the best design concept and that they should be chosen. We put this in writing, and the CNO and the Chief of Staff of the Air Force then took it to the Secretary of the Navy and the Secretary of the Air Force to the Secretary of Defense and we had some meetings with the Defense Department Systems Analysis and INL people, together with our Secretaries. They were not satisfied that it was the right design –

Q: Who was not satisfied that it was the right design?

Adm. P.: The Defense Department, and I think the Secretary of the Air Force and the Secretary of the Navy were beholden to the Secretary of Defense. So they decided to turn it back to us and do some more studies. We did some additional studies and again recommended Boeing.

Q: You imply that all along the line pressure was constant on the committee members. Was it?

Adm. P.: Yes. Well, they weren't dictating to us, but they were trying to imply that the other design was acceptable but we never did.

We stuck to the Boeing. In the Congressional Record on the investigation by Mr. McClelland's committee on the TFX business you find all of this a matter of record, and that right up to the end the military, that is the Air Force military, concluding with the CNO's recommendation and General LeMay, the Chief of Staff of the Air Force, recommendation to the Secretary of the Navy and the Secretary of the Air Force, and hence to the Secretary of Defense, was the Boeing design.

Eventually, the military were cut out of all these committee meetings and the civilians made the decision to choose General Dynamics, with Grumman as a subcontractor to do the Navy part of the thing. We were dead set against this, but it's what we were told to do.

It was significant that the Kennedy administration had what I call a fixer, a representative in the Department of Defense whose name was Ron Linton, who had a subordinate in each of the offices of the Assistant Secretary of the Navy, Air Force, and Army INL. I have since learned that they went to the White House every night and got from O'Brien and O'Donnell their instructions. I learned on a trip to Eglin Field to see a show for President Kennedy by Curtis LeMay, when Mr. Linton sat next to me and told me about a number of government contracts that were going to be let, including the TFX, before the decision had ever been made, that it was going to go to General Dynamics. So I went to these meetings armed with the knowledge that the Kennedy administration had already decided that the TFX was going to go to General Dynamics.

Q: On what basis? Why have a so-called fixer?

Adm. P.: He was dictating where contracts were to go. He told me about two or three other minor ones that I was party to, and they were spreading business around where it was going to be the most effective politically, instead of choosing the best contractor. This was no secret, as far as I know.

Q: So it came out of the White House rather than the SecDef?

Adm. P.: Yes, actually where the contracts were going to go and who were going to get them.

It turned out that the weight requirements for the TFX were unsatisfactory for the Navy and it never could be an acceptable aircraft for us. We got into some signficant problems with the hinge joint for the wing and, while that subsequently was solved, it was two or three years before it was and the Air Force lost some airplanes on account of it.

I think for the Air Force purposes that probably, at least as a fast interdiction aircraft, it turned out to be something that the Air Force could use satisfactorily. I don't think as a fighter aircraft that it's ever been proven satisfactory.

Q: It was used in Vietnam, wasn't it?

Adm. P.: Oh, yes, it was used to a considerable extent, but mostly for interdiction. Again, for attack and not as fighter aircraft. And this eventually now has led to two aircraft developments, one for the

Navy, the F-14, and one for the Air Force, the F-15.

Q: When you were studying the two different designs, the one presented by General Dynamics and the one presented by Boeing, what were the significant differences between the two designs?

Adm. P.: Well, the air intakes to the engines, which are very significant in a high-speed military aircraft, in supersonic aircraft, in the design presented by General Dynamics we didn't think were as good as the Boeing design. The performance characteristics were better in the Boeing, and the equipment installation we thought was better. This was all done in the greatest of detail by a big team, and aerodynamically it looked like a better airplane. Our civilian aerodynamicist from the then Bureau of Naval Weapons was George Spangenberg, who has recently retired, was a part of that team and I think is probably the foremost aerodynamicist certainly in the Western World, and he was strong for the Boeing design.

So it was a well-thought-out and well-engineered recommendation.

Q: It seems to be fraught with problems even today, though, does it not?

Adm. P.: I don't think it's a good enough airplane for the purpose for which it's designed, but they are using it as an attack airplane.

Q: And it's so fabulously expensive that to lose one is quite a casualty?

Adm. P.: Yes. I think the F-14 and the F-15 are significantly expensive and it costs a lot at reduced numbers in production. Large production numbers will get that cost down significantly.

Q: Now, they are the result of this experience with the F-111, are they?

Adm. P.: Yes.

Q: Is it possible that if the F-111 had not been produced at that time, these two planes would have come on stream?

Adm. P.: I think if they'd let the Air Force and the Navy each develop their own airplane we would have gotten a better airplane, but I don't think we could possibly have got as good an airplane as we have in the F-14 and F-15 today. They're a signficant development, significant increases in the air dynamics field, and in knowledge of building. As I noted to you, the air speed on the F-14 is about 25 knots slower than the F-4, and I suspect that the TFX, or the F-111, was higher than the F-4.

Q: How useful was WSEG in the development of these things?

Adm. P.: WSEG is the melting pot for all development recommendations, and they tried to make weapon systems compatible where each service wanted one of the same thing, and therefore they contributed a lot towards compatibility. In this particular area, I don't think they did much for us.

Q: You were talking off-tape about gust loading and your lack of experience in this area when jets first came on. Would you develop it again for me?

Adm. P.: In the early stages of jet aircraft development most of the flying at high speeds was done at high altitude, where the air is smooth and the effect of bumpiness didn't really come to light until we started to do low-altitude run-ins for toss bombing to get away from radar detection. In other words, the delivery of a weapon by coming in at high altitude and diving down and letting a weapon go posed a significant danger to the aircraft coming in, because it could be detected by aircraft and knocked down either by another aircraft or a missile.

So we developed a system in the Navy of low-altitude approach to a target.

Q: Skimming the waves?

Adm. P.: Yes. Well, going inland we did this for many years before anybody ever discovered that we were doing it. We were flying at 500 feet, particularly from the East Coast to Chicago or Detroit, and nobody ever knew it. The FAA didn't know it, the CAA didn't know it. Nobody ever knew that we were flying at 500 feet all over the country.

Jim Gray when he was my exec in Coral Sea used to fly up through the middle of France, all over hell, and never got reported once - at 500 feet.

Q: There aren't many Eiffel Towers!

Adm. P.: No. Well, you have to know where they are.

Anyway, the radar development which shows you what's ahead of you and the ability to fly low and then when you got to the target do a toss-bombing, and again an escape after you've tossed the bomb at low altitude, but in doing this low-altitude work we got into very bumpy air. And as the speed of the aircraft got higher, the strength of the wings became a significant factor for the wing and the airplane because of what we called gust loading. The bumpy air puts a very strong load, which we call gust loading, on the aircraft, and as you get close to supersonic speeds it becomes very significant so that the aircraft wing and the aircraft have to be strengthened greatly to stand this gust loading. We found that in the aircraft that we had up to that time almost all of them had to be reworked to do this low-altitude approach business, and the only aircraft company we had that really had done a good job on gust loading in the aircraft was the Grumman Corporation. They all had to be reworked, but Grumman's not to a significant degree.

So, in the TFX this became quite a consideration when the Air Force insisted on Mach 1.2 on the deck, which is supersonic. It requires a significant increase in weight to strengthen the wings and the air frames to stand the bumpiness of the air at low altitude.

Q: I'm curious about the term _gust loading_.

Adm. P.: That's a bump which will cause a gust.

Q: That's the derivation?

Adm. P.: Yes. If you've got bumpy air. You've been in aircraft in bumpy air. Well, at low altitude, it's very much worse in bad weather. It's there all the time, actually, because of changes in terrain. If you got across a river or across a bay, change from heavy vegetation to reflection from the water, there's a significant gust in effect. Constant bumping at low altitude causes the difficulty.

Q: And it's lacking in thin air?

Adm. P.: Right. In still, thin air you don't get it. Or if you postulate in a vacuum you get nothing. But when you have air currents, you're bound to have bumps. This is the one thing at high altitude. Every once in a while you read about a big jet with a lot of people in it has hit a big bump and caused injuries to the crew and to the passengers.

Q: That's why the seat belts!

Adm. P.: Well, there's significant turbulence, clear air turbulence, they call it, and these big boys now have a detection system so they can detect this, and when you hear that captain saying "Fasten your seat belts, we're about to go through - he'll always say 'moderate,' he never says 'heavy' - he says 'moderate turbulence!'" then all of a sudden, bang. Well, if you try to go through the jet stream, that's when you really get a kick. If you're up high enough to get into the jet stream and try to cross, going from out of the jet stream, through the jet stream, you get a significant kick, and that's what most of these accidents that you read about in the paper come from.

But the knowledge of how to build adequate strength into these aircraft to stand that came about in the last twenty years.

Q: Of necessity!

Adm. P.: Of necessity.

Q: Do you want to talk about the "whizz kids" and your relationship with them?

Adm. P.: It became very evident shortly after the Kennedy administration was inaugurated and Mr. McNamara came in as Secretary of Defense and appointed Alain Enthoven as the head of a new section within the controller's office to do systems analysis - it became evident that they were going to what I vulgarly like to call "mess around in my playground."

Q: Well, it's graphic, anyway!

Adm. P.: They started wanting detailed analysis of why we picked certain aircraft, and tried to tell us how to design and develop the next generation of aircraft, so we had many real confrontations with them on aircraft systems. My particular dislike for them and for their approach to the problem was that none of them had had any significant experience. Most of them were 30-year-old PhDs who'd never been in the military, never had any military experience, never had any experience with aircraft or aircraft engines, or anything to do with them. And just because they'd been hired by the Rand Corporation or some other "think tank" before they got to the systems analysis group, didn't qualify them to try to tell us how to do our business. I used to particularly express my views in pretty strong terms that experience and a lifetime in this business should be given some consideration in the design of future naval weapon systems.

Q: Did you succeed in putting across your point of view?

Adm. P.: We succeeded partially in getting our viewpoint across. It's significant that now almost all - each service has its own "think tank" and the business of evaluating weapon systems is now done within each service before it gets to the Defense Department.

I'm not sure that it's entirely effective. I prefer to have experienced people in the field make the recommendations, rather than have a lot of highly educated bookworms. Also, I have the same feeling toward super education. For example, wanting to make PhDs out of all the graduates of the Naval Academy. I have the theory that what you want to try to do is build fighting men, and the degree of education, while important in some areas of research and development - it's necessary to have a significant number of these people, but I would prefer to have a man who has a lesser education but is a willing fighter, what Admiral Jimmy Holloway used to call "cannon fodder!"

Q: Perhaps it was an unfortunate experience dealing with young men, highly educated young men, who were not knowledgable in your area and yet who wanted some authority in that area. There seems to be a conflict of interests.

Adm. P.: Oh, I think there was a great deal of conflict in those days.

Q: Did you observe that they learned as they went along?

Adm. P.: Yes, I think they learned. In time, they're bound to learn a good deal about what are significant developments in all forms of weapon systems. I disagree with a good many of the weapon system developments taking place in the Navy today, and if I was there I would be vocal about them. I think that trying to second guess the next major conflict in the world is something that is beyond the capacity of humans and, as Thucydides said, you want to reckon that the enemy's capability and intelligence are much the same as your own and you want to be prepared for any eventuality. The strong courageous men who are willing to keep their convictions and do their job are more important than a useless storage of knowledge - the storage of useless knowledge.

Q: Admiral, you retired in November of 1962 but you've been active ever since.

Adm. P.: I went with the Aerojet General Corporation for two or three years and then decided to do consulting, and I did a considerable amount of consulting for some large firms, Aerojet General, Grumman, Westinghouse, some for General Electric, some for Electro-Optical Systems, which is a subsidiary of Xerox, some for Computer Sciences Corporation, all related mostly to naval weapon systems and naval warfare.

I've given up consulting. Today I have several other major interests that I have kept up with. I'm President of the Naval Academy Foundation, and we've raised a considerable amount of money and have helped quite a few deserving boys who never would have gotten to the Naval Academy without financial help. In the last two years the number that we've helped is about 75 a year.

I'm very much interested in the Naval Air Museum at Pensacola. Admiral Radford was the Chairman and I was one of the officers, but when Admiral Radford died last year I succeeded him as the Chairman. We are now building the first increment of the Naval Air Museum at Pensacola. It will be completed this October and fully funded for the first $1.6 million. We have hopes to build the same-sized annex to it so that we can house more of our aircraft and memorabilia. We have twice as many aircraft now as we can get in the new auditorium, which is about 300 feet on the side, cantilever construction with no internal bracing, and in the middle of the floor will be the NC-4 surrounded by other significant aircraft.

Q: The sacred cow!

Adm. P.: Right.

I'm also very much interested in the Marine Military Academy at Harlington, Texas, which was started about ten years ago by a group of Marines headed by General "Howling Mad" Smith. It's a very great program tory school, privately run, privately financed. They've raised a lot of money and they have --

Q: How did you happen to get interested in that?

Adm. P.: Well, through the Naval Academy Foundation and two or three Marines I knew. They asked me to be on their advisory committee initially and then on their board. They have about 200 students, and I have a grandson who is completing his sophomore year there. It's a splendid school and he's benefited greatly by it.

Q: Is he Robert Burns III?

Adm. P.: No, this is John Abel, my daughter's son, who is a grandson of Walter Abel, the actor.

Those kind of interests keep me very busy. Also in Florida, I'm the President of my golf club, which is another non-paying client that keeps me very busy.

Q: How many boards do you sit on?

Adm. P.: And I'm on two other boards up here, Airtronics Incorporated and Baltimore Business Forms in Baltimore.

I'm trying to divest myself of as many of these things as possible, but I've been kept plenty busy. I heard someone say the other day that an admiral who'd just recently retired had too much time on his hands, he didn't know what to do with himself, and I said "I wish I could get to that happy state."

Q: It's not inherent in your nature to get to that state!

   I do thank you very much, Sir.

Adm. P.: I think that about does it. There may be some refinement on this thing.

INDEX

for

Series of Interviews with

Vice Admiral Robert Burns Pirie

U. S. Navy (Ret.)

AERIAL ILLUMINATION: Japanese use of, p 119; p 123-4.

AGA KAHN: Pirie calls on him in Cannes, p 206.

AIRCRAFT CARRIERS: role as conceived in period 1931-3; p 46; ADM Burke's request to Pirie that he get authorization for another carrier - difficulties involved, p 286-7.

AIRCRAFT SCOUTING FORCE: The big flying boats, p 51-2; the first flight to Hawaii, p 52.

AIRPLANE TYPES - development: Pirie as DCNO involved with decisions on a number of plane types, p 294-6; the RA-5, p 296-7; summary of plane and engine development, p 303-8.

USS AKRON: p 37, 41.

ALASKA: see entries under USS TEAL.

ALEUTIANS: p 54-5; the first survey party, p 69; weather problems, p 69-71.

ASLITO AIRFIELD - Saipan: p 118-119.

ASTRONAUTS: The choosing of a contingent of fifty test pilots, p 321-3.

A/S WARFARE: Pirie's ship, USS SICILY, employed in exercises, p 175 ff.

ATOMIC TESTS - Bikini: p 145-6.

AURAND, VADM Evan Peter: Aide to President Eisnehower, (1957), p 263; p 265.

USS BAFFIN: Commissioned (Apr. 1943) in Tacoma, p 102; turned over to the Royal Navy, p 102-3.

BANFF, Scotland: Pirie's visit to his father's birthplace, p 174.

USS BARRY: Pirie assignment to her followed torpedo school in Newport, p 9-10.

BLANDY, ADM. Wm. H. P.: in command of Task Force for tests at Bikini, p 145.

BOGAN, VADM Gerald F.: Takes command of VF-3 on the USS LEXINGTON, p 19; becomes head of test section at Anacostia, p 42; commander NAS Miami (1940), p 42; becomes skipper of the SARATOGA, 1942, p 91; Pirie reports as Chief of Staff to Bogan on board FANSHAW BAY (May 8, 1944), p 111; Bogan in command of jeep carriers for invasion of Saipan, p 113; goes without permission on B-24 bombing mission against Truk, p 114-5; improves close air support for marines at Saipan, p 117-8; orders to command Carrier Task Group 38.2 in USS ESSEX, p 121; for invasion of Guam, p 122; not willing to recommend a surface attack force for San Bernadino Strait, p 137; his recommendations to Halsey on action to protect ships in Typhoon, p 139-141; p 240.

BRIDGET, LT. CDR Frank: Assistant N.A. in Japan - sent reports on capabilities of Japanese night fighters - information didn't get through to the fleet, p 79-80.

BROWN, ADM Charles (Cat): CincMed, p 205; p 254, p 257, p 279.

BURKE, ADM Arleigh: Had same reactions as Pirie - at Leyte Gulf - wanted to recommend surface attack force for San Bernadino Strait, p 137, gives Pirie two tasks when he takes office as DCNO, p 285; sends Dryden to Pirie to select test pilots for NATO, p 322.

CAB - Advisory Board to the CNO: primary concern with the Budget, p 288.

R. B. Pirie

CAGLE, VADM Malcolm W. (Chris): his training command, p 312.

CAR DIV 6: Pirie in command (March, 1956), p 235; his reorganization of watch officer system, p 238-9; combined exercise off the East Coast, p 250-1; Mediterranean duty, p 251-2; Pirie uses deception as a tool of command, p 252-4; night refueling, p 257 ff; joint plans with British for taking Suez Canal, p 258-60; Pirie relieved by RADM Frank Ward (fall of 1956), p 261.

CASSIDY, ADM John: relieves Adm. Wright as CincNelm, p 218.

C.I.C.: p 148-9; Pirie's experience with the fleet - evolvement of the modular CIC, p 149; as installed in the USS FORRESTAL, p 235-6; Pirie draws up rough plan for modern CIC, p 236; his efforts with the Ship's Characteristics Board, p 237; gradual germination of the modular idea based on Pirie's experience, p 240-1; the complicated modern command system, p 241-3.

CINC LANT: Pirie as Deputy Chief of Staff - duties, p 221-2; coordinator of nuclear warfare, p 221-2; his plan for an adequate Op Con Center for Cinc Lant, p 233-4; development of War Plan plot room, p 224-6; VIP educational cruises, p 228; new weapons coming on stream without adequate personnel to operate, p 228-9.

CINC NELM: Pirie as Chief of Staff to Admiral Wright, p 210 ff; the 6th fleet on mission of mercy to Greek Islands, p 213; visit to fleet unit in Persian Gulf, p 214-6; the Naval Review (Queen's Coronation) at Spithead, p 216-7.

CLIFTON, RADM Jos. C.: instructor at NAS, Miami, p 84.

COMINCH - Air Operations Officer: see entries under Admiral King. Also: p 134-5 ff; departure of uniformed staff elements with Japanese surrender, p 153-4; problems of reorganization with coming of ADM Nimitz as CNO, p 154; Pirie's post-war concern was largely with FATUS (fleet air electronics training units), p 155-6; problems with mothballing aircraft, etc. p 157.

COMMANDANT OF MIDSHIPMEN - Naval Academy: see entries under U. S. Naval Academy.

CONNOLLY, VADM Thomas F.: p 304-5; p 320.

CONTROL TOWER OPERATORS: p 335.

COOLIDGE, The Hon. Calvin: p 42-3.

USS CORAL SEA: Pirie relieves ADM Russell as skipper, (Feb. 1, 1952), p 204; duty in the Mediterranean, p 205-210; Pirie selected for Rear Admiral, assigned to ADM Wright in London - detached from the Coral Sea in November, p 208; Pirie, as commander of CarDiv 6, flys flag in CORAL SEA, p 235; p 235-6; p 250-1.

DATA LINK SYSTEM: modern communications system in fleet - derived from program of astronauts, p 243-4; p 274.

DAVIS, VADM Wm. V. Jr.: his place in the development of naval aircraft, p 304.

DCNO - Deputy Chief of Naval Operations: Pirie takes up duties in May, 1958, p 284 ff; ADM Burke gives him two tasks to accomplish during his tenure, p 285; the first task, to get an aircraft carrier authorized, p 285-6 ff; the second task to master the

Navy's budget, p 285 ff; the problem of closing bases in the interests of economy, p 288-90; the question of the P-6M - the SEAMASTER, p 290 ff; 1958 a transitional year in naval developments, p 294 ff; plane types and developments, p 294 ff the aircraft nuclear propulsion program, p 298-9; work with the deficiency appropriations committees in the Congress, p 301-2, plane types - development - a summary, p 303-8; training system for pilots and crews, p 310-313; provisioning teams for knowledge of replacement parts on planes, p 317; NASA, p 323 ff; lighter than air, p 326-8; the FAA and air control matters, p 329-333; supersonic drag waves, p 332; aircraft safety, p 333-4; control tower operators - use of women operators, p 335; the TFX story, p 336 ff.

DECEPTION - as a Tool of Command: Pirie employs deception in an exercise off Sardinia, p 252-6; uses deception again in Strike Back operations, p 270.

de FLORES, RADM Luis: p 89; p 233.

DENNISON, ADM Robert L.: Aide to President Truman - makes inquiry of the Naval Academy about the honor code in effect - for information of President Truman, p 194-5.

DIEHL, Walter, CAPT: leading aerodynamicist, p 42.

DIXON, RADM Robert E.: his interest in plane development for U. S. Navy, p 304.

USS DOBBIN: Pirie's first duty as assistant gunnery officer after graduation (1926), p 8-9.

DRYDEN, Dr. Hugh: Deputy Director of NASA, p 321-2.

DUTCH HARBOR: p 69, p 72.

EISENHOWER, The Hon. Dwight D. - President of the United States: on board the USS SARATOGA for demonstration of carrier power, p 263-5; signs commission of Pirie as Vice Admiral and gives him command of of 2nd fleet at breakfast on the SARATOGA, p 266; p 267.

ENIWETOK: p 113-114; fleet base in operations against Saipan, Guam, etc., p 121-3; p 127.

USS ENTERPRISE: p 286.

ENTHOVEN, Dr. Alain: systems analyst with Secretary McNamara, p 336; 347.

ERDELATZ, Eddie: p 168; becomes football coach at Naval Academy, p 179.

ESPIRITU SANTO: p 96-7.

F-4: p 294-5.

F-14 (Grumman), p 305-6; p 318.

FAA - Federal Aeronautics Agency: replaces the old CAA, p 239; the first administrator is Lt. Gen. Quesada, p 329; 2nd Administrator was Najeeb E. Halaby who had some air control ideas not acceptable to Navy, p 330-1; a confrontation between Halaby and the Service Representatives, p 331-2; the Navy and problems with the supersonic drag waves, p 332-3.

USS FANSHAW BAY: hit by Japanese bomb at invasion of Saipan, p 116-7; p 119.

FATU (Fleet Air Electronics Training Units): see COMINCH staff.

FELT, ADM H. D.: Commander, 6th Fleet at time Pirie arrived in Mediterranean as Commander, Car Div 6, p 252; p 254, p 257.

FITCH, ADM Aubrey W.: Pirie and Pennoyer consult with him on logistic problems in South Pacific, p 98-9; discussions on replacement of patrol planes and crews, p 100; Superintendent of Naval Academy, p 159; p 161.

FLIGHT TEST PILOT - Anacostia: p 20-21; duty as a transport flyer, p 23; plane types for testing, p 24-25; relations with aircraft manufacturers, p 25-26; the Pitcairn Autogyro, p 26-27; more plane types, p 26-30; the Lockheed ORION, p 29-31; catapult testing, p 32; the BM-1 bomber, p 35-36; the Martin BM-2 dive bomber, p 37; the F-11C Curtiss fighter, p 38; the Curtiss HAWK, p 39-40; defects in new plane types, p 40-1; care exercised in test flights over city of Washington, p 41.

USS FORRESTAL - CV: first of its class to be commissioned- p 235; Pirie compares operational features with those of the USS CORAL SEA, p 235-6; combined exercise, p 250-1; ability to operate in rough weather, p 250-1.

GATES, The Hon. Thomas S.: Secretary of the Navy (1958), p 288; asks Pirie for a judgement on the SEAMASTER, p 291; SecNav's compromise proposals to Martin Company rejected, p 293.

GENERAL DYNAMICS: Awarded the TFX contract against recommendations of the military, p 340.

GRUMMAN plane types: for testing at Anacostia, p 27; p 33, p 36.

GUADALCANAL: p 95, p 97, p 101.

USS GUADALCANAL: 6th of the Kaiser jeep class carriers, p 103; p 111.

GUAM - invasion: p 114-115; p 117; p 121-2.

Gust LOADING: problems with jet aircraft development, p 343.

HALABY, Najeeb: see entries under FAA.

HALSEY, Fl. ADM Wm.: p 131; p 136; p 139.

HELICOPTER: Sikorsky's early efforts in the area, p 27.

HILL, ADM Harry W.: Superintendent of the U. S. Naval Academy (1950), p 178; his interest in Athletic program, p 180, p 185-6; p 193, p 204.

HOLLOWAY, ADM James: Superintendent of Naval Academy, p 165; p 168; calls Pirie as Commandant of Midshipmen, p 177-8; p 182; his great interest in education, p 182; the Eisenhower committee and the proposals effecting the service academies, p 182; he establishes a teacher's forum at the Academy to raise standards, p 182-3.

HOOVER, ADM John: in Pirie's class at Pensacola, p 11; Executive to King on the LEXINGTON (1929), p 19, relieves Mitscher as Chief of Staff to ADM Alfie Johnson, p 57; his battle with a manta, p 58.

USS INDEPENDENCE: used effectively in fighting off Okinawa, p 124-5; 133.

INGALLS, David: p 42-3.

INGERSOLL, ADM Slim: Chief of Staff to Admiral Wright, p 223-4.

USS INTREPID: Becomes flagship of Bogan and Task Group when ESSEX returns to port for overhaul, p 127; hit by kamikazes in vicinity of Leyte, p 129-30; Bogan takes her back to Ulithi and transfers to the LEXINGTON, p 132.

ISRAELI-ARAB War: Statistics on losses, p 316.

JAPANESE AIRCRAFT TRAFFIC - Clark Field, p 150-1; U. S. interception of dawn traffic with devastating effect, p 151-2.

JAPANESE SHIPPING: U. S. carrier attacks on Japanese shipping in coastal areas of SE Asia, p 134.

JOHNSON, VADM Alfred W. (Alfie): Commander, Aircraft Scouting Force (1933) - Pirie becomes his aide and flag lieutenant, p 50-2; p 54-7; insists on flying from Midway to Pearl Harbor to pay call on widows of two pilots lost in Midway exercise, p 60.

JONES, H. McCoy: Organized the Naval Academy Foundation (1936), p 168, 171.

KAISER Class jeep carriers: see entries under USS MISSION BAY and USS GUADALCANAL: - general comments on usefulness of the jeep carrier, p 112.

KAMIKAZE ATTACKS: first attacks off the Philippines, p 129-32.

KING, Flt. ADM Ernest J.: p 11; skipper of the LEXINGTON, p 19; Pirie becomes air operations officer on King's COMINCH staff - March, 1945, p 141; job description, p 141-2; watch officer, p 142; conferences, p 144; comments on King, p 146-7; King's orders relative to RADM Rich Byrd, p 147-8; p 150.

KINKAID, ADM Thos. C.: At Leyte Gulf, p 137.

KODIAC: survey party to Kodiac, p 69; p 72.

LEE, VADM Fitzhugh: his training establishment in Memphis, p 313.

USS LEXINGTON (CV-2): Pirie joins VF-3 from Pensacola, p 13, p 17; first amphibious exercises off Monterey, p 18; notes on arresting gear, p 20; Pirie leaves squadron in 1931 for flight test section, p 20; public relations efforts, p 22-3; (CV-16) becomes flagship of ADM Bogan, p 132; carrier operation off Luzon and Camranh Bay, p 133; Mitscher calls conference at Eniwetok before attack on Palau, p 140-1.

LEYTE GULF: Pirie's account of the actions of TF 38, p 135-8.

LIGHTER-THAN-AIR CRAFT: Pirie, as DCNO for air instituted studies to evaluate lighter than air craft, p 326; decision made to discontinue program, p 326-8; present day views on lifting power of blimps, p 328.

LINTON, Ron: Representative of the Kennedy Administration in the Defense Department, p 340.

LOUGHLIN, RADM Elliott C.: Executive Director of the Naval Academy Foundation, p 171.

MacARTHUR, General Douglas: p 126, p 128.

MARINE MILITARY ACADEMY: Pirie is a member of the Board, p 350-1.

MARTIN, Glen: p 34.

McCAIN, ADM John Sydney: at Task Group Commanders meeting on LEXINGTON before Palau, p 140.

McFALL, CDR. Andy: p 50, p 63.

McGINNIS, CAPT. Kneffler: skipper of the first PB2Y flight to Hawaii, p 52-3.

McNAMARA, The Hon. Robert S. - Secretary of Defense: his role in the TFX controversy, p 336 ff.

MIDWAY - island of the Pacific: PB2Ys fly to island for first time p 53 (1934): beginning of its development for fleet operations p 53-4; p 59-60; fleet exercise in spring of 1935, p 61-62.

USS MISSION BAY: Fifth of the Kaiser Class Jeep Carriers - put into commission Oct. 1943, p 103; undergoes training at San Diego with 6th jeep carrier, GUADALCANAL, p 103; convoy duty in Atlantic, p 104-5; stormy passage back to U. S., p 105-8; passage to India with P-47s for Far Eastern Front, p 109-110; capacity for night flying, p 111; p 116.

MITSCHER, ADM Marc: Chief of Staff to ADM Alfie Johnson, Commander Aircraft Scouting Force, p 51; goes with CAPT. McGinnis on the PB2Y's flight to Hawaii, p 52-3; p 57; in command of Fast Carriers at invasion of Saipan, p 115; refuses to recommend to higher authorities formation of surface attack force at San Bernadino Strait, p 137; holds conference of his Task Group Commanders before battle for Pelau, p 140.

MOFFETT, RADM Wm. A.: Chief of Bureau of Aeronautics, p 31; killed in the AKRON disaster, p 31.

USS MONTEREY: hit by kamikaze off Leyte, p 129-131.

NACA - National Advisory Committee for Aeronautics: p 34; p 36; p 324; some of the members serving in 1958, p 324.

NASA: the formation of NASA, p 323 ff; initial navy fear that certain interests of the Navy would be submerged in the larger program, p 325.

NATO Operations: p 209, 218, 226; Pirie draws up plans (1957) for carrier Task Force operation in STRIKE BACK, p 231-2;

R. B. Pirie

a NATO unit Atlantic on a continuing basis since STRIKE BACK, p 275. Strike Fleet units in the NATO command - purpose, p 280-1; question of over-all NATO fleet command, p 281-2; U. S. attatude towards NATO operations, p 282-3.

NATS - Naval Air Transport: p 95.

U. S. NAVAL ACADEMY: Pirie's appointment to the Academy, p 2-3; years at the Academy, p 4-5; midshipman cruises, p 5-7; aviation summer, p 7-8; Pirie (June, 1936) becomes Chief engineer and material officer of the aviation detachment - also acts as P.I.O. to athletic department, p 63; interest in program to obtain athletes for the Academy team, p 64-5; the development of aviation indoctrination at the Academy, p 66; Pirie becomes first head of Aviation Dept. - Jan. 1946, p 159-161; problems of coordination with other departments, p 162-3; organization for aviation indoctrination (1946), p 163; Air Force takes volunteers from the Naval Academy for service (1947-8) duty with the newly independent Air Force, p 164-5; Pirie serves as member of athletic committee-selection of a civilian coach, p 167-8; efforts to get an airfield for the Naval Academy, p 165-6; Pirie becomes Commandant of Midshipmen - summer duties, p 195-6; Pirie entertains various members of Board of Visitors, p 196; fiscal responsibility of the Commandant p 197; the physical plant, p 198-9; the Naval Academy Dairy, p 200; the Tailor ship, p 201; Cooperation with other service academies, p 201; improvements gained by checking on aptitude of men for service, p 202-3.

R. B. Pirie

U. S. NAVAL ACADEMY - BOARD OF VISITORS: p 196-7.

NAVAL ACADEMY FOUNDATION: origin of the Foundation, p 64-5.
p 168-171; charter granted in 1944, p 168; formal meetings of Trustees, p 171-2.

NAVAL AIR BOARD: The navy board that deals with plane characteristics, p 309-10; the Naval Air Systems Command functions under the policy decisions of the Board, p 310.

NAVAL AIR MUSEUM: Pirie becomes Chairman, p 350.

NAVAL AIR STATION - Miami (Opa Locka): put into commission in 1940 to train carrier pilots, p 72; p 76-78; necessity at outbreak of war to assist in fighting SS attacks on shipping off the Florida coast, p 81-4; training relationships with Washington, p 86; knowledge of new type planes, p 86; logistic problems after Pearl Harbor, p 87-8; use of training simulators, p 88-9; flight training emotional casualties, p 90; the balance between carrier pilot training and building of new carriers, p 91.

NAVAL AVIATION: preliminary flight training at Norfolk (1927), p 9-10; Pirie goes to Pensacola in July, 1928, p 10; Pirie is senior ranking student, p 11-12; course of training, p 11-12; Pensacola facilities, p 13-16; student aptitude for training, p 14-15; period 1931-33 evaluated in development of naval aviation, p 44-47, p 59; Ford Trimotor transport plane, p 46; the Seaplane, p 44, p 46-48; personalities of the period 1931-33, p 48-50; joint exercises (1940) of carrier planes with surface ships in A/S warfare,

R. B. Pirie

NAVAL AVIATION - FAST CARRIERS: p 135-6; also see entries under:
ADM Bogan, Battle of Leyte Gulf, Okinawa, Philippines.

NAVAL TRAINING COMMAND: ADM Zumwalt puts emphasis on training - sets up training command for the entire Navy, p 232; present use of simulators that grew out of experience in WW II, p 233-4.

U. S. NAVY DEPARTMENT - Deficiency Appropriations: to cover expenditures on navy involvement with 'brush fires' throughout the world, p 300-302.

U. S. NAVY DEPARTMENT - RESEARCH AND DEVELOPMENT: p 299-300.

NIMITZ, Fl. ADM Chester W.: p 126; p 128, 154, 156.

O'DONNELL, General Emmett T. (Rosy): Deputy Chief of Air Force for Personnel, p 314, p 316.

OFSTIE, VADM Ralph: head of flight test section in Anacostia (1931) - invites Pirie to be Assistant Flight Test Pilot, p 20, p 24; p 37.

OKINAWA: Carrier attacks in preparation for invasion, p 123-6.

PALAU: invasion, p 122-3.

PEARL HARBOR: facilities in mid 1930s, p 56. facilities in 1942, p 101-2.

PENSACOLA: see entries under Naval Aviation.

PERRY, Captain John - C. E.: arrived at Naval Academy, post WW II, to take charge of the Civil Engineering Department. His inspection of buildings produced results - extensive repairs to Bancroft Hall, p 199.

PHILIPPINES: Carriers under Bogan turn to attacks on airfields after Okinawa, p 126; p 129; kamikaze attacks on fleet units.

p 129; further planning for Philippines, p 133.

PIRIE, VADM Robert Burns: Personal data, p 1-2; boyhood interest in the Naval Academy, p 2; family penchant for acquiring facts about history, literature, geography, p 3; father's enterprisi background, p 4; marriage in New York on Nov. 25, 1926; p 9; birth of son Robin, p 50; promotion to Captain, p 122; ordered back to States (Feb., 1945) - duty on staff of ADM King. p 134-5; promoted to Rear Admiral (June 1952), p 208; leave in Scotland after detachment from duties at CincNelm, p 220-1; retired, Nov. 1962 - a resume of his activities since that time, p 349-352.

POWER, VADM Loffy - Royal Navy: p 258-60.

PRINCESS FLYING BOATS: British seaplanes - U. S. Navy interested in experimenting with them - nuclear propulson plants, p 298-9.

PROVISIONING TEAMS: for knowledge of replacement requirements for modern warplanes, p 317.

PULLER, Col. Louis: on Guadalcanal, p 97-8.

RA-5: story of the Navy's reconnaissance plane, the RA-5C, p 296-7.

RABORN, VADM Wm. F.: p 223, p 225.

RADFORD, ADM Arthur: 146.

USS RANDLOPH: Pirie uses her as flagship in Mediterranean with Car Div 6, p 252; skipper has a heart attack - Pirie's Chief of Staff, Dan Smith, takes command, p 257.

REES, VADM Wm. L.: skipper of the jeep carrier, MISSION BAY, p 102 ff.

REEVES, ADM Joseph Mason: p 46.

REGULUS I: p 229-30; p 234.

RICKOVER, ADM Hyman: in opposition to the Navy's plan to develop a nuclear propulsion plant in a large seaplane, p 298-9.

RILEY, VADM Herbert D.: takes over USS CORAL SEA from Pirie, Nov. 1952, p 208.

ROTA: importance of this base to the U. S. Fleet, p 247; problems with Congressional appropriations, p 247-8; multiple usage, p 248-9.

ROTRIG, Cy: first Catholic Chaplain at the U. S. Naval Academy, p 190-1; p 204.

RUSSELL, ADM James: In Aleutians at beginning of WW II, p 55, his interest in development of aircraft for the U. S. Navy, p 304.

SA-3 (Lockheed): p 307-8.

SAIPAN invasion: p 113; p 121.

SALVAGE OPERATIONS: on damaged airplanes - Towers sends Pirie and Pennoyer to South Pacific to urge this practice -- supply was so short, p 93 ff.

SAN BERNADINO STRAIT: p 136-8.

SANDINI: Nicaraguan rebel general, p 21-22..

USS SARATOGA: unit of Car Div 6 (1956), p 250; ability to operate in rough weather, p 250-1; Pirie plans a two day operation from the USS SARATOGA to demonstrate for President Eisenhower the capacity of the aircraft carrier, 263.

SAUER, George: becomes first civilian football coach at the Naval Academy, p 167-8.

SCHOECH, VADM Wm. A.: his role in development of aircraft engines, p 305.

SEAMASTER: The P-6M - nuclear seaplane - story of it's development p 290 ff.

SECOND FLEET: Pirie takes command of 2nd fleet in July, 1957, p 26 commission handed him by President Eisenhower at breakfast ceremony on board the SARATOGA, p 265; takes strike force units to Scotland for NATO exercise in North Sea waters, p 269 p 279-80.

USS SEQUOIA: p 143.

USS SICILY: Pirie takes command of her in Boston, p 172, deplorabl state of ship, p 172-3; ferries fighter squadron from Panama to Europe, p 173-4; becomes an anti-submarine warfare unit in Atlantic, p 175-7; conducts extensive experiments with blimps off Vieques, p 327.

SIKORSKY, Igor: p 34.

SITKA: see entries under USS TEAL.

SMITH, RADM Daniel F. Jr.: (Dog): Chief of Staff to Pirie in Car Div 6, p 237; becomes skipper of the CV RANDOLPH, p 257.

SPANGENBERG, George: Civilian aerodynamicist who studied designs for the TFX, p 342.

STRIKE BACK: code name for NATO operation in North Sea (1957) - Pirie plans carrier Task Force operations and acts as Carrier

Task Force Commander, p 261-2; p 267-9; FORRESTAL, SARATOGA and one ESSEX Class CV in the striking force, p 269; method of operating various units, p 271; difficulties with communications because of aurora borealis, p 271-2; observers, p 273; air defense proves to be disappointment in the exercise, p 272; efforts at improvement on the way back, p 274; expense of an exercise of this nature, p 276; a critique at conclusion, 277; lessons learned, p 277-8.

STRIKE FLEET: p 280-1.

SUEZ CANAL: Pirie joins with VADM Manley (Lofty) Power of the Royal Navy in planning a Suez Canal operation, p 258-9.

SUPERSONIC DRAG WAVES: p 332; problems that have developed with high speed flyers, p 332.

TAYLOR, Whitey: p 168; director of athletics at U. S. Naval Academy, p 179.

USS TEAL: p 54; Pirie takes command in Alaska (1938), p 66-67; her base at Sitka, p 67-8.

TFX story (swept-wing fighter): p 336 ff; dual purpose plane for Navy and Air Force - significant differences in concept of fighter roles in two services, p 337-8; principal differences in two designs submitted originally by Boeing and General Dynamics, p 342; gust loading and the TFX, p 345.

TITO: Pirie has a carrier demonstration for Tito off SPLIT, p 206-7.

TOWERS, ADM John: Pirie named as Assistant Operations Officer on his staff - ComAirForPac, 1942, p 92; stresses the need for cannibalizing damaged planes to conserve numbers, p 94;

sends Pirie and Pennoyer to Solomons in the interests of salvaging spare parts from damaged planes, p 93-5; p 101.

TRAINING SYSTEM - Pilots and Crews: comments on the system, p 310- Pensacola, p 312; Memphis, p 313; Secretary of Defense efforts to cut program, p 314-5; test pilots training at Patuxent, p 320-1; the choosing of the astronauts, p 321-2.

TRAPNELL, VADM Frederick M.: 3rd ranking officer at Naval Test Center, 1930 - p 24; p 26; p 30; p 37; p 41; p 54; p 304; p 32

TULAGI: p 97.

TURNER, ADM R. Kelly: in command of amphibious operations for invasion of Saipan, p 113; displeased with ADM Bogan's bombing trip to Truk, p 114-5; his apology to DD skipper for damage sustained in too close action off Saipan, p 119-20.

TYDINGS, Senator Millard: his opposition to Naval Academy Air Field, p 166.

TYPHOONS - and the fleet: p 127-8; the great typhoon of Dec. 17-18, 1944, p 138; Pirie's representations to Bogan and Bogan recommendations to Halsey, p 139-140.

ULITHI: Becomes advance fleet anchorage after Saipan, p 127; hasty departure from inner lagoon to avoid typhoon, p 127-8; p 132; Christmas rest in Ulithi, p 132-133.

USS WASP: her sinking frees the skipper - Capt. Sherman, to the staff of Adm. Towers, p 92-3.

WEAPONRY: Pirie on the subject of new weapons coming on stream without trained personnel and logistics to make them operatio p 228-32; summary of new systems and their requirements, p 245-6; especial demands on the commanding officer, p 245-6.

WEATHER REPORTING: primitive state in time of early PBY operations in Pacific, p 54-5.

WELLBORN, VADM Charles: Commander, 2nd fleet (1957), p 262.

USS WHITE PLAINS: Bogan and staff transfer to WHITE PLAINS for invasion of Saipan, p 117.

WHIZZ KIDS: p 347-8.

WILSON, CDR Eugene E.: head of Chance-Vought (1930), p 26.

USS WRIGHT, p 52; p 56; p 60.

WRIGHT, ADM Jerauld: As CincNelm (1952) asks for Pirie as his Chief of Staff, p 208-9; p 213-14; relieved as CincNelm, becomes CincLant - calls Pirie to become his Deputy Chief of Staff, p 264, p 269.

WSEG: p 343.

YARNELL, RADM Harry E.: commandant of 14th Naval District (1934-5), p 56.

USS YORKTOWN: Pirie ordered to Bombing Squadron 5 in 1939, p 73 ff; experiences with first monoplane dive bombers (BT-1s), p 73; long range observation flights from Hawaii, p 74; A/S warfare exercises, p 74-5; joint exercises off Hawaii, p 74-5.

ZUMWALT, ADM Elmo: sets up training command in Pensacola, p 232.